WILDLIFE

of South Africa | A PHOTOGRAPHIC GUIDE

Duncan Butchart

for Julia Lily

Struik Nature (an imprint of Penguin Random House South Africa (Pty) Ltd)
The Estuaries No 4, Oxbow Crescent, Century Avenue, Century City, 7441

Company Reg. No. 1953/000441/07

Visit **www.penguinrandomhouse.co.za** and join the Struik Nature Club for updates, news, events, and special offers.

First published 2009

10 9 8 7 6

Publishing manager: Pippa Parker
Managing editor: Helen de Villiers
Editor: Colette Alves
Design director: Janice Evans
Designers: Martin Endemann, Louise Topping
Typesetter: Natalie Petersen
Proofreader: Glynne Newlands

Reproduction by Hirt & Carter Cape (Pty) Ltd
Printed and bound in China

ISBN 978 1 77007 632 7 (PRINT)
ISBN 978 1 43170 188 9 (EPUB)

Front cover: (top) African Elephant – Johan Swanepoel; (bottom, left to right) Spotted Bush Snake – Duncan Butchart; Greater Double-collared Sunbird – Margaret Westrop/Images of Africa; Arum Lily Reed Frog – Michael Langford; Quiver-Tree – Walter Knirr/Images of Africa; **Back cover:** (top to bottom) Leopard – Nigel Dennis/Images of Africa; Violet-backed Starling – Albert Froneman/Images of Africa; Flap-neck Chameleon – Ian Michler/Images of Africa; Bubbling Kassina – Duncan Butchart; Impala-Lily – Duncan Butchart; **Page 1:** Cape Dwarf Chameleon – Leonard Hoffmann/Images of Africa; **Page 3:** Plains Zebra – Duncan Butchart; Spectacled Weaver – Albert Froneman/Images of Africa; Spotted Bush Snake, Painted Reed Frog, Pride-of-De-Kaap – Duncan Butchart

ACKNOWLEDGEMENTS

The study and appreciation of nature is often a solitary pursuit, but the following people have either cultivated, inspired or simply shared my interest in nature. Over the years I have enjoyed spending time in the field with James Culverwell, John Freer, Pete Hancock, Peter Mundy, John Ledger, Keith Cooper, Paul Dutton, Steven Piper, Ken Newman, Bonnie and Russel Friedman, Ian Davidson, Vincent and Jane Carruthers, Colin Bell, James Marshall, Kevin Mansfield, Billy Doepel, John and Sandie Burrows, Hugh and Julie Marshall, Les Carlisle, Dee and Tony Adams, Drew Paterson, Lex Hes, Mark Tennant, Gary Lotter, Marie Holstenson, Freddie Shingange, Ingrid Meyer, Chris Roche, Menziwa Sibanda, Simon and Tina Naylor, Kevin Pretorius, Alastair Kilpin, Graham Vercueil, Shelagh and Cecil Peterson, Beth Peterson, Graeme Butchart and last, but certainly not least, my wife Tracey.

I am grateful to James Culverwell for his valuable comments on the introductory pages, to Braam van Wyk for clearing up some recent plant taxonomy issues, and to Ingrid Meyer for providing vital reference material on alien trees. I'd also like to thank Chris and Mathilde Stuart, Vincent Carruthers, Johan Marais and Graham Alexander for generously agreeing to let us feature distribution maps from their own field guides, and especially Graham Alexander for supplying additional maps. Thanks, too, to Braam van Wyk and Meg Coates-Palgrave for permitting usage of their tree distribution maps and to Random House Struik for use of the bird maps. Ann Cameron, Louise Grantham, John and Sandie Burrows, Jane and Vincent Carruthers, Chris and Mathilde Stuart, Braam van Wyk, Tony Rebelo, Paul Skelton, Wolf Haacke, Bob Scholes and James Culverwell all provided input into the three regional *Wild About* guide books from which this work has been expanded.

Finally, thanks to the team at Penguin Random House for their support and patience: Pippa Parker for proposing what began as an amalgamation of my three regional guides for the Lowveld, Highveld (Johannesburg) and Cape Peninsula but has evolved into something richer; and to Colette Alves, Louise Topping, Janice Evans and Martin Endemann for their editorial and production skills.

Duncan Butchart, Mbombela

CONTENTS

Yellow-billed Oxpecker and African Buffalo

INTRODUCTION

South Africa is a land of astonishing natural diversity. From the snow-capped peaks in the Drakensberg to the expansive subtropical beaches of Zululand, and from the flower-carpeted semi-deserts in Namaqualand to the moss-clad forests of Tsitsikamma, there is a variety of plants and animals that is unrivalled elsewhere on the continent. The warm, tree-dotted savanna – 'the bush' as it is known to locals – harbours Elephant, Giraffe, Lion, Cheetah and other large mammals, while the Cape fynbos, semi-arid Karoo, Wild Coast and high-altitude grasslands support their own distinct and equally precious wildlife communities.

This compact book is intended as a portable guide for visitors to national parks and other places rich in wildlife, as well as to landowners and those who enjoy nature from their own doorsteps. It is not a comprehensive field guide, for several such books are already available on the respective taxa, but rather an introduction to the more conspicuous and interesting mammals, birds, reptiles, frogs and trees of the country.

The opening pages provide a brief overview of the South African landscape, climate and wildlife habitats, with a map showing protected areas and localities mentioned in the species accounts. The book illustrates and describes a carefully selected range of species, providing details on their identification and habits. There are also notes on habitat, status and measurements, as well as the best viewing localities for each species.

Due to space limitations, some fairly common animals and plants have been excluded in order to provide wide coverage of as many families and groups as possible. Since the book is specific to South Africa, several uncommon yet endemic species such as Riverine Rabbit, Cape Parrot and Sungazer lizard are featured, even though they are rare and difficult to find. These and the many other endemics confined to South Africa are among the top priorities of local conservation groups, as their survival is dependent upon wise and sensitive land management in this country. Pages have been arranged so that similar or related species are placed together for easy comparison, but this has meant that the sequence more typical of comprehensive reference books has not always been followed.

Not included are representatives of the enormously diverse insect, spider or other invertebrate groups, or any of the region's freshwater or marine fish. The absence of these smaller creatures notwithstanding, this book is a celebration of the extraordinary biodiversity at this southern tip of the continent.

GEOGRAPHY AND CLIMATE

South Africa has a truly ancient geological history, with the granite-greenstone rocks of Barberton and other parts of the eastern Lowveld estimated to be over 3.5 billion years old. Once part of the Gondwana supercontinent, Africa's topography is a result of tectonic movements that have created mountains and tilted entire landscapes, as landmasses collided, were wrenched apart or fractured. During a succession of cyclical ice ages in which the climate has fluctuated from warm and wet to cool and dry, giant lakes have appeared and disappeared, carving out river valleys and leaving behind mineral deposits in the sedimentary rocks.

Today, the South African landscape might be compared to an inverted bowl, tilted to one side, with the high central plateau falling away to a coastal plain of variable width. The Drakensberg escarpment in the east is tilted upwards to an altitude of 3 400 metres, while the western escarpment is a more modest 900 metres above sea level. All of the country's important rivers originate in the grasslands of the high-rainfall eastern escarpment, with the Orange-Vaal system draining west into the Atlantic, and the Limpopo-Olifants, Tugela and other, shorter rivers flowing east into the Indian Ocean. In the south-western Cape, a series of parallel 'fold mountains' from the Cederberg to the Outeniqua create a dramatically rippled landscape that restricts the fynbos to the seaward slopes, forming longitudinal mosaics of differing vegetation in the northern 'rain shadows' of the mountains. Other important topographic features of the country are the tilted, quartzite-based mountain ranges of the Magaliesberg, Waterberg and Soutpansberg in the northern bushveld, the eroded koppies and 'tafels' of the Karoo, and the vast Kalahari Basin filled with deep deposits of wind-blown sand.

The country's climate is not only as diverse as its wildlife; it is responsible for that diversity. The cold Benguela Current moves up the Atlantic on the west coast, lowering inland temperatures when onshore winds blow, while the warm Agulhas Current sweeps down the Indian Ocean on the east coast, delivering tropical moisture. Elevation and aspect are key determinants of both temperature and rainfall, with the eastern half of the country being considerably wetter than the west. The south-western Cape experiences a short, cold, wet winter (May–Aug) and a long, dry, hot summer (Oct–Mar), while the rest of the country has a long, hot, wet summer (Oct–Mar) and a short, cold, dry winter (May–Aug). September and April, roughly corresponding to spring and autumn, are usually months of transition, but these are becoming increasingly unpredictable. Along the southern coast and parts of the Eastern Cape, rain may fall throughout the year.

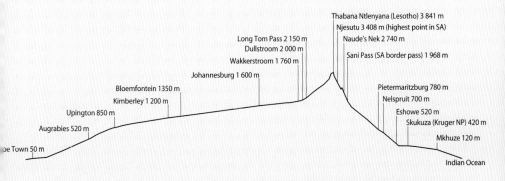

Diagrammatic representation of the elevation of various localities in South Africa; altitude above sea level is a key determinant of climate, vegetation zones and the distribution of plant and animal species.

IDENTIFYING AND WATCHING WILDLIFE

With the exception of city centres and industrial sites, you can see wildlife virtually anywhere in South Africa. Even the largely sterile monocultures of wheat, maize, sugar cane and timber plantations have wildlife at their fringes. Suburban gardens and parks may be home to a variety of wildlife, particularly if indigenous plants are cultivated, as they provide nesting sites, berries and nectar for birds, and also host invertebrates upon which larger animals feed.

However, it is in natural habitats that wildlife is richest and most easily discovered. In addition to a network of 20 national parks, South Africa is blessed with numerous provincial nature reserves and a coastline that is relatively intact for much of its length and still pristine in parts. In the past couple of decades, the number of privately managed wildlife and nature reserves has expanded as the country has attracted growing numbers of international tourists. Some of these reserves offer exclusive guided safaris, while others promote hiking, birdwatching and other ecotourism activities.

Before setting out to watch wildlife, it is a good idea to familiarize yourself with the species that might be encountered in a particular region or habitat. Identification is often a process of elimination, so the more species with which you are familiar, the easier it becomes to identify the others. For all plants and animals, the first step to identification is establishing the family to which a particular organism belongs.

Finding animals to watch and photograph is often a matter of luck, combined with an awareness of the preferred habitat and habits of a particular species. Although being in a vehicle prevents direct contact with nature, it holds advantages as most mammals and birds regard vehicles as unthreatening and often allow a close approach. This is especially true for well-used routes in national parks and other protected areas.

With the exception of Cheetah and African Wild Dog, all of the larger predatory mammals are primarily nocturnal. Leopard, Caracal and Lion frequently become active just before sunset and may still be on the prowl after dawn, making these prime times for finding cats.

Most national parks and private reserves offer guided night tours, driving slowly along vehicle tracks and searching for nocturnal wildlife with a spotlight. This requires great sensitivity on the part of the guide, and a red filter should ideally be placed on the beam when observing cats, genets, bushbabies or owls.

Consideration for wildlife should always take priority. Sensitivity is vital when watching animals, to ensure that they are not unduly disturbed, threatened, or forced to behave in an unnatural way. Nesting birds and mammals with dependent young should not be interfered with, as some sensitive species may abandon their offspring. Attacks on humans by Elephants, Lions, venomous snakes or other potentially dangerous animals are rare. The limited number of incidents that do occur can usually be ascribed to animals that are feeling threatened, particularly when they have not been given space to pass or retreat. Baboons and monkeys can become a nuisance around picnic sites, camps and lodges where they scavenge or steal fruit and other food; these primates should be treated with caution as they are capable of delivering a severe bite.

One of the most productive and exciting situations in which to watch wildlife is at a waterhole. It is here that various species often congregate and where predators frequently lie in wait to ambush their prey.

Making use of local guides can be highly beneficial, as well-trained individuals, who will get you into optimal situations for viewing particular mammals or birds. Most private safari lodges have resident trackers and guides, while BirdLife South Africa trains and supports many local guides at birding hotspots such as Wakkerstroom and in Zululand.

One of the most rewarding situations in which to learn about wildlife is in a 'home patch'. This could be a wild garden or, better still, a local nature reserve that you can access on a regular basis. Over time you will begin to notice the favoured microhabitats of particular species, the plants upon which they depend and the other species with which they interact. It is only by visiting such a site regularly that you will be able to observe the cycles of nature.

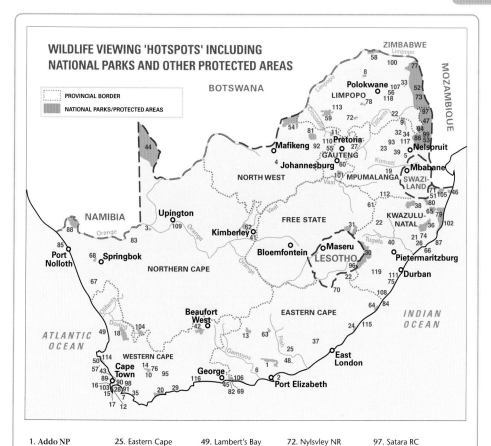

WILDLIFE VIEWING 'HOTSPOTS' INCLUDING NATIONAL PARKS AND OTHER PROTECTED AREAS

- PROVINCIAL BORDER
- NATIONAL PARKS/PROTECTED AREAS

1. Addo NP
2. Algoa Bay
3. Augrabies NP
4. Barberspan
5. Barberton
6. Baviaanskloof
7. Betty's Bay
8. Blouberg NR
9. Blyde River Canyon
10. Bontebok NP
11. Borakalalo GR
12. Boulders Beach
13. Camdeboo NP
14. Cape Mountains
15. Cape of Good Hope NR
16. Cape Peninsula
17. Cape Point
18. Cedarberg
19. Chrissiesmeer
20. De Hoop NR
21. Dlinza
22. Drakensberg
23. Dullstroom
24. Dwesa
25. Eastern Cape mountains
26. Eshowe
27. Ezemvelo
28. False Bay
29. Garden Route
30. Giant's Castle
31. Golden Gate NP
32. Graskop
33. Hans Merensky NR
34. Hazyview
35. Hermanus
36. Hluhluwe-iMfolozi
37. Hogsback
38. Ithala GR
39. Kaapsehoop
40. Karkloof
41. Kamfer's Dam
42. Karoo NP
43. Kirstenbosch
44. Kgalagadi TP
45. Knysna
46. Kosi Bay NR
47. Kruger NP
48. Kwandwe PNR
49. Lambert's Bay
50. Langebaan
51. Lebombo mountains
52. Letaba RC
53. Lower Sabie RC
54. Madikwe GR
55. Magaliesberg
56. Magoebaskloof
57. Malgas Island
58. Mapungubwe NP
59. Marakele NP
60. Marievale
61. Memel
62. Mokala NP
63. Mountain Zebra NP
64. Mkambati
65. Mkhuze
66. Mtunzini
67. Namaqualand
68. Namaqua NP
69. Nature's Valley
70. Naude's Nek
71. Ndumo GR
72. Nylsvley NR
73. Olifants RC
74. Ongoye Forest
75. Oribi Gorge
76. Overberg
77. Pafuri
78. Percy Fyfe NR
79. Phinda PGR
80. Phongola NR
81. Pilanesberg GR
82. Plettenberg Bay
83. Pofadder
84. Port Edward
85. Port Nolloth
86. Pretoriuskop RC
87. Richard's Bay
88. Richtersveld NP
89. Robben Island
90. Rondevlei
91. Rooiels
92. Rustenberg
93. Sabie
94. Sabi-Sand PNR
95. Sanbona
96. Sani Pass
97. Satara RC
98. Sir Lowry's Pass
99. Skukuza RC
100. Soutpansberg
101. Suikerbosrand
102. St Lucia (isiMangaliso)
103. Table Mountain
104. Tankwa-Karoo NP
105. Tembe Elephant Park
106. Tsitsikamma
107. Tzaneen
108. Umthamvuna
109. Upington
110. Vaalkop Dam
111. Vernon Crooks NR
112. Wakkerstroom
113. Waterberg
114. West Coast NP
115. Wild Coast
116. Wilderness
117. White River
118. Woodbush
119. Xumeni

VEGETATION ZONES FOR WILDLIFE

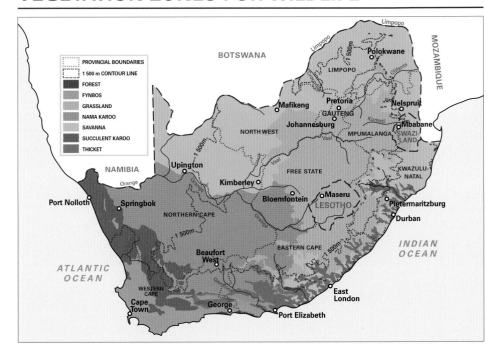

Plant species depend upon specific combinations of soils, rainfall and climate. Plant communities develop according to these conditions, and a variety of animals – from large mammals and birds to invertebrates and microbes – have evolved alongside them. Many species have become specialized and are able to thrive only within a restricted community, while others are 'generalists' and are able to flourish in a variety of habitats. In most cases, animals are adapted to the structure of vegetation, whether it is a closed-canopy forest, a tall grassland or a gravel plain dotted with small succulents. Each and every species operates within a niche and interacts with other species in a complex web of life known as an ecosystem.

Vegetation zones (also known as biomes) are sometimes referred to as habitats, although this term can also apply to the set of factors in which an individual organism lives, such as a marsh (vlei), termite mound or rocky outcrop (koppie). In South Africa there are eight distinct vegetation zones.

Pretoriuskop, Kruger National Park

SAVANNA is a combination of extensive grass cover with scattered trees and/or bush clumps. This habitat prevails in the Bushveld, Lowveld and Kalahari, where grass palatability and woody plant density vary in accordance with soil type, rainfall and aspect. Various *Acacia* and *Combretum* trees often dominate open, wooded savannas. This is a very productive habitat for large, herbivorous mammals and their attendant predators. All of South Africa's larger protected areas occur in this biome: Kruger, Kgalagadi, Hluhluwe-iMfolozi, Pilanesberg and Madikwe. There is high species diversity but low endemism, as this biome extends north to Kenya and Uganda.

GRASSLAND occurs in the wetter, north-eastern part of the Highveld and eastern escarpment where winter frosts and fires restrict woody plant growth. Grasses are dominant, but small flowering plants are prolific. Trees and woody shrubs are confined to seasonal watercourses, koppies and kloofs. Diversity of plants, birds and frogs is relatively high, with numerous endemic species. The grassland biome has been extensively cultivated and developed so that up to 80% of its former area has been irreversibly transformed. All of the country's major rivers rise in this biome, which is in urgent need of better protection.

Drakensberg escarpment, Graskop

THICKET consists of spiny, evergreen shrubs, succulent *Euphorbias* and *Aloes*, and small trees with some grass cover. This fragmented biome occurs mostly in the Eastern Cape, where moderate rainfall occurs throughout the year. Plant diversity and endemism are high, but few animals are confined to this region. Thickets of tangled, woody plants are present in most other habitats, but the term is used here in line with accepted classifications of South African biomes. Much of this biome has been severely degraded due to overgrazing by sheep and goats.

Greater Addo Elephant National Park, Eastern Cape

NAMA KAROO is a semi-arid biome on the south-central part of the Highveld plateau. The landscape is characterized by flat plains interrupted by low hills and rocky outcrops (koppies). The vegetation is a mix of grasses, succulents, bulbs and annual forbs, with hardy shrubs and small trees along seasonal watercourses and in sheltered ravines (kloofs). Rainfall is low and sporadic, falling mostly during summer. The diversity of plants, mammals, birds, reptiles and frogs is relatively low, but many species are endemic. Prior to the arrival of European settlers, vast herds of Springbok and Black Wildebeest roamed the Nama Karoo.

Karoo National Park, near Beaufort West

SUCCULENT KAROO is an arid biome characterized by low, succulent shrubland and annual grasses on flat, undulating or mountainous landscapes. Spectacular shows of annual forbs (especially daisies) and bulbous lilies transform parts of the Succulent Karoo into a spring wonderland. The diversity of plants, mammals, birds, reptiles and frogs in this winter-rainfall region is relatively low, but many species are endemic. Research suggests that the Succulent Karoo biome is shrinking due to global warming.

Richtersveld, far Northern Cape

Overberg, Western Cape

FYNBOS is characterized by fine-leaved bushes growing on the sandy, low-nutrient soils of mountains and flats. This heathland vegetation has species of *Erica* and *Protea* dominating alongside annual bulbs and reed-like restios. One of only six 'botanical kingdoms' on the planet, this winter-rainfall region has more than 8 000 plant species, most of which are endemic. Fire is a key element in the maintenance of fynbos, with numerous plant species dependent upon heat for seed germination. Mammal, bird and reptile diversity is low, but many species are restricted to fynbos. Research suggests that the fynbos biome is shrinking in the face of global warming.

Tsitsikamma, Garden Route of southern Cape

FOREST is a community of trees with canopies that touch or interlock, with little or no grass cover. Ferns, mosses and leaf-litter occur in the understorey. There are several distinct types of forest, including montane (cloud) forest, coastal dune forest, dry sandforest, mangrove forest, and the riverine (gallery) forest that occurs in ribbons along watercourses in savanna and grassland. South Africa's forests are small, fragmented and vulnerable to woodcutters. Plant diversity is high in this biome. Although birds are well represented, few species are endemic, as most types of forest extend further north into tropical Africa.

Wakkerstroom, Mpumalanga Highveld

FRESHWATER WETLANDS include rivers, streams, lakes, vleis, ephemeral pans (seasonal rain-filled depressions), floodplains and reedbeds, as well as man-made dams and waterholes. All of these habitats host communities of aquatic plants and animals, and provide moisture and refuge for a variety of terrestrial mammals and birds. Wetlands are invariably a focal point of animal activity and warrant close attention from wildlife observers. One of the most productive wetland types is the estuarine habitat, where rivers meet the sea; this blend of fresh and salt water creates conditions for salt marshes, mangroves (on the east coast) and important nursery grounds for marine fish and other life.

Cape Peninsula

SEASHORE is a turbulent, transitional habitat that is home to fishes and birds, as well as a host of specialized marine invertebrates such as crustaceans. Seashore plants consist of algae (seaweeds) and sea-grasses in the warmer north-east. In some places, most notably at Cape Point on the Cape Peninsula, sheer cliffs drop directly into the ocean. Beaches usually consist of fine sand, crushed shells or pebbles. Rocky shores include intertidal pools and reefs. Excluding offshore island territories, the South African coastline extends for 2 954 kilometres.

CONSERVATION OF WILDLIFE

Although South Africa is the most industrialized country on the continent, it is still a developing nation struggling to meet the diverse needs of its rapidly growing human population. Trying to stimulate economic growth while also taking care of scarce or sensitive natural resources is a balancing act that few, if any, countries have been able to manage.

Ideally, the objective of conservation is to protect sufficiently large parts of all representative habitats so that the complex variety of life forms (the biodiversity) can continue to interact and reproduce. The biological processes of natural ecosystems – which include the provision of fresh water and oxygen, as well as services such as pollination and the natural regulation of insects – are services upon which humankind is completely dependent, although many developers, industrialists and even some farmers frequently give the impression that nature is expendable.

The first natural step in conserving biodiversity is to establish protected areas, which may take the form of a national park or some other category of reserve. South Africa's network of protected areas includes 20 national parks and over 600 state-owned nature reserves, which together encompass just 8% of the land surface. Major successes have been achieved in recent times with regard to population recovery of threatened species such as Black and White rhinos, both of which were on the brink of extinction in the 20th century. Significant areas of most biomes are incorporated in the national protected area network, but temperate grasslands are in urgent need of formal protection.

Traditionally, protected areas excluded people, but there is now a realization that local communities should benefit from such areas – whether through ecotourism or ecological services. This is a potential win-win scenario that has already proved successful in 'contractual reserves' such as Madikwe and Phinda.

Conserving biodiversity within reserves does not, however, guarantee survival of all the species or all biological processes. Many bird species are migratory and depend on areas well beyond parks and reserves, while mammals confined to smaller areas must, over time, have outside genetic inputs to avoid potential inbreeding. Even the country's largest wildlife reserve, the Kruger National Park, is impacted upon by careless utilization of the Highveld rain-catchments feeding the Olifants, Sabie and other rivers that provide sustenance to so much of the reserve. For these and other reasons, protected areas cannot exist indefinitely as 'islands' in a sea of development.

WHAT YOU CAN DO

Individuals can contribute towards the conservation of biodiversity by supporting effective non-governmental organizations such as Endangered Wildlife Trust (*www.ewt.org.za*), Wildlife & Environment Society of South Africa (*www.wessaonline.co.za*), and BirdLife South Africa (*www.birdlife.org.za*). You can also limit your environmental footprint by using energy responsibly and recycling waste. Individuals can become aware of environmental transgressions and lend their voices and signatures to protest campaigns and petitions. Finally, gardeners and landowners can cultivate plants native to their region, thus creating micro-environments for insects and birds, as well as limiting the need to irrigate and fertilize.

Promoting the plight of endangered species, such as the Wattled Crane, can serve to gain public support for habitat conservation.

Martin Harvey/Images of Africa

MAMMALS

South Africa is richly endowed with mammal species, including virtually all of the continent's most impressive and charismatic species. Overall, there are approximately 230 species of land mammal in the country, but nearly half of these are bats, rodents or shrews, most of which are nocturnal and seldom seen. Over 40 of the country's mammal species are endemic or near-endemic.

On the following pages, 100 of the more eye-catching, widespread or interesting indigenous mammals are featured. These include almost all of the larger mammals (hare size and upwards), as well as the four most prominent marine mammals. In most cases, the accompanying photograph depicts an adult male of each species, but the text describes the appearance of the female where this differs.

Not included here are the fossorial golden-moles (12 of the 14 African species are endemic to South Africa), which spend their entire lives underground and are seldom seen. Of the few alien mammal species that have become naturalized, only the Grey Squirrel is featured; although abundant in towns and on farms, the House Mouse and House Rat are excluded.

Most larger mammals in South Africa are confined to wildlife reserves with fenced boundaries, and some of these are subject to population management. There has been a huge increase in the amount of land set aside for wildlife in recent years, with the establishment of private wildlife sanctuaries and the expansion of park and reserve networks. As a result, populations of African Elephant, Black Rhino, White Rhino, Giraffe, Lion, Cheetah, African Wild Dog, African Buffalo and several species of large antelope have all grown in the past ten years.

In most cases, viewing and photographing of mammals is most easily done from a vehicle, but some reserves have excellent hides located at favoured drinking spots that can offer rewarding sightings. The experience of tracking large mammals on foot with a knowledgeable guide is perhaps the best way to appreciate the acute senses and behaviour of mammals.

The names used here largely follow those in the 3rd edition of *The Mammals of the Southern African Subregion* revised by John D. Skinner and Christian T. Chimimba (Cambridge University Press, 2005) and *Field Guide to the Larger Mammals of Africa* by Chris and Tilde Stuart (Struik Publishers, 2006).

The measurements given in this section are height (foot to shoulder) and length (nose to tail tip).

AFRICAN ELEPHANT   *Loxodonta africana*

Habitat: woodland, succulent thickets
Height: 4 m   **Length:** 7–9 m   **Mass:** 6 000 kg (♂);
3 500 kg (♀)   **Status:** locally abundant; restricted to
fenced wildlife reserves

Huge, unmistakable herbivore. Male is larger than female, with a
rounded forehead and thicker tusks. Matriarchs lead family units;
males keep to themselves in smaller 'bachelor' groups. Feeds
on leaves, bark and grass for over 14 hours per day, modifying
woodlands in the process. A single calf is born after a 22-month
gestation period.
Best viewing: Addo, Kruger, Pilanesberg, Madikwe, Mapungubwe,
Marakele

Hein von Hörsten/Images of Africa

ROCK HYRAX   *Procavia capensis*

Habitat: koppies, hillsides and mountains
Height: 15 cm   **Length:** 40 cm   **Mass:** 3–5 kg
Status: common to abundant

Compact, short-eared mammal with no obvious tail. Frequently
basks in the sun, particularly in early mornings. Colonies comprise
several family units. Latrines are characterized by white and brown
urine streaks on rocks, and spherical pellets. Diet includes grass,
leaves and berries. Call is a sharp bark. Predators include large
eagles and Caracals.
Best viewing: widespread in suitable habitat

Erhardt Thiel/Images of Africa

AARDVARK   *Orycteropus afer*

Habitat: open areas with termite mounds
Height: 60 cm   **Length:** 140–180 cm   **Mass:** up to 70 kg
Status: rare to uncommon

A pig-like creature with truncated snout, donkey-like ears and
powerful, bear-like paws. Short coat is a pale, sandy colour.
Nocturnal and shy, therefore seldom encountered. Active burrows
have fresh spoor and flies present at entrance. Feeds almost
exclusively on ants and termites. A single baby is born in a burrow.
Leopards and Lions are the main predators.
Best viewing: Mapungubwe, Karoo, Tankwa-Karoo, Mountain
Zebra, Namaqua, Nylsvley

Nigel Dennis/Images of Africa

GROUND PANGOLIN   *Manis temminckii*

Habitat: open woodland   **Height:** 35 cm
Length: 70–110 cm   **Mass:** up to 15 kg
Status: rare; hunted for purported value of scales
in traditional medicine

Distinctive, low-slung mammal with large, overlapping scales.
Somewhat similar to the armadillos of the New World, to which
it is unrelated. Forages alone, with males and females occupying
overlapping ranges. Primarily nocturnal, shy and seldom seen.
Feeds entirely on ants and termites. A single baby is born in a
burrow. Lions are its only predators.
Best viewing: Kruger-Lowveld (Sabi-Sand), Madikwe, Pilanesberg,
Kgalagadi

Nigel Dennis/Images of Africa

Nigel Dennis/Images of Africa

LESSER BUSHBABY *Galago moholi*

Habitat: *Acacia* woodland **Height:** 8–10 cm
Length: 30 cm (incl. 20 cm tail) **Mass:** 150 g
Status: fairly common

Tiny primate with huge, bulging eyes and long, fluffy tail. Strictly nocturnal, it bounds through trees with great agility. Females and offspring occupy a home range; males have larger territories. Aerial pathways are scent-marked with urine. Feeds on insects and Acacia gum. Calls include a high-pitched wail. Genets and larger owls are the main predators.
Best viewing: Nylsvley, Kruger, Pilanesberg, Mapungubwe

Ariadne van Zandbergen/Images of Africa

THICK-TAILED GALAGO *Otelemur crassicaudatus*

Habitat: woodland and forested kloofs, coastal scrub
Height: 15 cm **Length:** 70 cm (incl. 30 cm tail)
Mass: up to 1.5 kg **Status:** fairly common

Cat-sized primate with large eyes and long, bushy tail; much larger than the Lesser Bushbaby. Strictly nocturnal, it bounds through trees with great agility. Pairs or groups occupy a home range. Calls include loud barks and eerie wails. Sleeps in a tree hole or thicket. Feeds mainly on fruit, Acacia gum and insects. Leopards and Verreaux's Eagle-Owls are the main predators.
Best viewing: Kruger-Lowveld, Hluhluwe-iMfolozi, Mkhuze, Phinda

Duncan Butchart

VERVET MONKEY *Cercopithecus pygerythrus*

Habitat: wooded watercourses, coastal scrub, forest fringe, orchards **Height:** 20–25 cm
Length: 100–130 cm **Mass:** 5–8 kg (♂); 4 kg (♀)
Status: abundant; persecuted by fruit farmers

Inquisitive, agile primate with pale grey coat. Lives in troops of up to 20, comprising adult females and offspring accompanied by one or more males. Readily comes to ground but retreats to trees, sleeping on branches at night. Feeds on a variety of fruit, flowers, insects and nestling birds; also raids orchards and lodges. Predators include eagles and Leopards.
Best viewing: widespread in suitable habitat

Ariadne van Zandbergen/Images of Africa

SAMANGO (SYKES'S) MONKEY *Cercopithecus albogularis*

Habitat: coastal and montane forest, orchards
Height: 20–25 cm **Length:** 120–140 cm
Mass: 8–10 kg (♂); 4–5 kg (♀) **Status:** locally common, but endemic; *C.a. labiatus* sub-species is endangered

Agile primate with variably coloured coat, dark forelimbs and white throat. Lives in troops of 10–40 individuals, with one or more dominant male. Forages mostly in trees, feeding on berries, fruit and flowers. Call is a loud bark. A single baby is born to mature females. African Crowned-Eagles are the main predators.
Best viewing: Woodbush, Soutpansberg, Karkloof, St Lucia, Kosi Bay, Dwesa

SAVANNA BABOON *Papio ursinus*

Habitat: almost all habitats, requires trees or rocky outcrops for night roost **Height:** 40–60 cm **Length:** 120–180 cm **Mass:** 35–45 kg (♂); 15–25 kg (♀) **Status:** common to abundant; persecuted by fruit and crop farmers

Large, dog-like primate with grey-brown coat and long, bare snout. Male is much larger than female, which has naked buttocks. Babies often ride on mother's back. Lives in troops of up to 100, with adult males in strict hierarchy. Feeds on a wide variety of plants and animals. Call is a hoarse bark. Leopards are the chief predators, but only of females and young.
Best viewing: widespread in suitable habitat

Nigel Dennis/Images of Africa

COMMON WARTHOG *Phacochoerus africanus*

Habitat: open woodland, mud wallows **Height:** 60–70 cm **Length:** 150 cm **Mass:** 105 kg (♂); 70 kg (♀) **Status:** common to locally abundant

Sparsely haired pig with curved tusks and wart-like swellings on the face. Male has longer tusks and 2 pairs of 'warts'. Tail is held upright when on the run. Strictly diurnal, retreating to burrow after dark. Sexes live apart, with females caring for piglets. Grazes on short grass or digs for tubers on folded knees. Preyed upon by all larger carnivores.
Best viewing: widespread in suitable habitat

Daryl Balfour/Images of Africa

BUSHPIG *Potamochoerus larvatus*

Habitat: dense woodland, montane and coastal forest **Height:** 70–80 cm **Length:** 150 cm **Mass:** 80–100 kg (♂); 50–60 kg (♀) **Status:** common

Coarse-haired pig with rust-brown coat and pale mane. Tusks are short and hidden by facial hair. Tail is held down when on the run. Largely nocturnal. Lives in sounders of up to 15. Piglets have chestnut coats patterned with white stripes and spots. Feeds on bulbs, tubers, roots, fruit, and also scavenges refuse and carrion. Leopards are the main predators.
Best viewing: Soutpansberg, Mapungubwe, Tsitsikamma, Hluhluwe-iMfolozi

Nigel Dennis/Images of Africa

HIPPOPOTAMUS *Hippopotamus amphibius*

Habitat: rivers, lakes and dams **Height:** 150 cm **Length:** 4 m **Mass:** 2 000 kg (♂); 1 700 kg (♀) **Status:** locally common

Huge, aquatic herbivore with an almost hairless body. Broad mouth has tusk-like teeth. Usually remains in water during the day, with only its tiny ears, eyes and nostrils protruding above the surface. Typically found in small herds of 10–12 individuals. Noisy, aggressive and fearsome clashes ensue between rival males. Comes onto land after dark to feed on grass.
Best viewing: Ndumo, St Lucia, Kruger, Pilanesberg, Marakele, Hluhluwe-iMfolozi

Nigel Dennis/Images of Africa

Nigel Dennis/Images of Africa

BLACK RHINOCEROS *Diceros bicornis*

Habitat: dense woodland and thickets **Height:** 160 cm **Length:** 3.5–4 m **Mass:** 1 000 kg **Status:** sparse to uncommon, restricted to wildlife reserves; only the arid subspecies (*D. b. bicornis*) is endangered

Massive herbivore with short head held upright, and hooked upper lip. Colour does not differ from that of larger White Rhino. Occurs singly or in mother-and-young pairs. Poor eyesight and belligerent nature make this a dangerous animal. Exterminated from most of its range by the 1930s, but strong population recovery. Browses on foliage of Tamboti and other plants.
Best viewing: Hluhluwe-iMfolozi, Pilanesberg, Karoo, Marakele, Mokala, Addo

Duncan Butchart

WHITE RHINOCEROS *Ceratotherium simum*

Habitat: grassland, open woodland **Height:** 180 cm **Length:** 4–6 m **Mass:** 2 500 kg (♂); 1 600 kg (♀) **Status:** locally common, restricted to wildlife reserves

Massive herbivore with long head carried low, and broad lips, ideal for grazing grass. Colour does not differ from that of smaller Black Rhino. Occurs singly or in family groups; most active during the day. Poor eyesight, but calm by nature. Exterminated from the Lowveld by the late 1800s but re-introduced from Zululand in the 1960s and now flourishing. Diet consists of a variety of short grasses.
Best viewing: Kruger-Lowveld, Marakele, Hluhluwe-iMfolozi, Phinda, Pilanesberg, Mokala

Duncan Butchart

PLAINS ZEBRA *Equus quagga*

Habitat: open woodland, grassland **Height:** 130 cm **Length:** 250–300 cm **Mass:** 340 kg (♂); 290 kg (♀) **Status:** locally common; restricted to wildlife reserves

Unmistakable, horse relative with pale brown 'shadow' stripes. Lives in family units (harems) of several mares and their single offspring, and a dominant stallion. Often in the company of Giraffe and antelope. Grazer of tall or short grass, and usually the first to feed at new growth after fire. Call is a bark-like 'gwa-ha'. Lion and Spotted Hyaenas are the chief predators.
Best viewing: widespread in suitable habitat

MOUNTAIN ZEBRA *Equus zebra zebra* (Cape) & *E.z.hartmannae* (Hartmann's)

Habitat: grassy hills and mountains **Height:** 125 cm **Length:** 260 cm **Mass:** 250 kg (♂); 230 kg (♀) **Status:** locally common in restricted range; Hartmann's subspecies is endangered

Zebra of mountainous regions. Lacks shadow stripes and has longer ears than Plains Zebra. There is a distinctive dewlap on the throat. Lives in small family units (harems) of several mares and their single offspring, and a dominant stallion. Grazes on tall or short grass. Fewer than 1 000 of this endemic species survive. Foals may be vulnerable to Leopard.
Best viewing: Mountain Zebra, Karoo, De Hoop, Camdeboo, Richtersveld, Augrabies

Nigel Dennis/Images of Africa

GIRAFFE *Giraffa camelopardalis*

Habitat: woodland **Height:** 3 m **Length:** 4–5 m
Mass: 1 200 kg (♂); 900 kg (♀) **Status:** locally
common; restricted to wildlife reserves

Unmistakable, long-necked herbivore. Small horns of male are bald at
the tips; those of female are tufted. Individuals become darker with
age. Feeds on leaves beyond the reach of other browsers. Favours
Acacia during summer, but switches to Mopane or evergreen trees in
the dry season. Ageing adults and calves are vulnerable to Lion
and Spotted Hyaena.
Best viewing: widespread in suitable habitat

Simon Butchart

AFRICAN BUFFALO *Syncerus caffer*

Habitat: floodplains, grasslands, open woodland and
thickets **Height:** 140 cm **Length:** 320–450 cm
Horns: 100 cm **Mass:** 800 kg (♂); 650 kg (♀)
Status: common to abundant in restricted range;
restricted to wildlife reserves

Massive relative of the domestic cow with short, sparse coat.
Gregarious but non-territorial. Family units may congregate in herds
of several hundred or more during the dry season, gathering to feed
on nutritious grass. Old bulls often form small bachelor groups.
Remains in shade for much of the day, feeding mostly at night. The
main predators are Lions.
Best viewing: widespread in suitable habitat

Duncan Butchart

BLUE WILDEBEEST *Connochaetes taurinus*

Habitat: open woodland **Height:** 150 cm
Length: 300 cm **Horns:** 60 cm **Mass:** 250 kg (♂);
180 kg (♀) **Status:** fairly common but declining in
Kalahari; restricted to wildlife reserves

Large, gregarious antelope with low hindquarters and high, muscular
forequarters. Adult is grey with a black face and mane, and darker
creases on the flanks. Both sexes have horns. Young is tawny
coated. Bulls are territorial during the breeding season, establishing
and defending a well-worn display and latrine site. Bulk grazer of
short grass. Lions and Spotted Hyaenas are the main predators.
Best viewing: Kruger-Lowveld, Kgalagadi, Pilanesberg, Mkhuze

Nigel Dennis/Images of Africa

BLACK WILDEBEEST *Connochaetes gnou*

Habitat: montane grassland, Karoo scrubland
Height:120 cm **Length:** 250 cm **Horns:** 52 cm
Mass: 180 kg (♂); 100 kg (♀) **Status:** fairly common in
small range; restricted to wildlife reserves; endemic

Smaller and darker, Highveld counterpart of the Blue Wildebeest.
Face and throat are adorned with long, brush-like tufts. Long tail and
base of the stiff mane are white. Forward-facing horns resemble the
handlebars of a racing bicycle. Feeds exclusively on grass in open
areas. Formerly abundant in grassland and Karoo scrub, but decimated
by European settlers. Calves may be vulnerable to Leopard.
Best viewing: Camdeboo, Mokala, Suikerbosrand, Golden
Gate, Karoo

Nigel Dennis/Images of Africa

Nigel Dennis/Images of Africa

RED HARTEBEEST *Alcelaphus buselaphus*

Habitat: grassy plains **Height:** 125 cm
Length: 230 cm **Horns:** 35 cm **Mass:** 150 kg (♂);
120 kg (♀) **Status:** locally common; restricted to
wildlife reserves; near-endemic

Large, long-headed antelope with sloping back. Short, shiny coat is chestnut-red with pale hindquarters; the upper legs and muzzle are black. Small herds of females occupy a home range that overlaps the territory of a male. Selective grazer of short grass. Small number of related Lichtenstein's Hartebeest A. lichtensteini occur in Kruger. Predators include Lions and Spotted Hyaenas.
Best viewing: Kgalagadi, Pilanesberg, Addo, Bontebok, Golden Gate, Karoo, Mokala

Nigel Dennis/Images of Africa

TSESSEBE *Damaliscus lunatus*

Habitat: open woodland **Height:** 120 cm
Length: 200 cm **Horns:** 34 cm **Mass:** 140 kg (♂);
110 kg (♀) **Status:** rare to sparse, restricted to wildlife
reserves, endangered

Large antelope with a distinctive sloping back. Short coat is reddish-brown with a maroon sheen; head and upper legs are darker. Both sexes carry short, ringed horns. Small herds of females occupy a home range that overlaps the territory of a male. Selective grazer of short grass. Lions and Spotted Hyaenas are the main predators. East African race is known as Topi.
Best viewing: Pilanesberg, Kruger (north), Nylsvley, Marakele

Lanz von Hörsten/Images of Africa

BONTEBOK/BLESBOK *Damaliscus pygargus dorcas/phillipsi*

Habitat: grassland and scrubland **Height:** 90 cm
Length: 170–200 cm **Horns:** 35 cm **Mass:** 62 kg (♂);
55 kg (♀) **Status:** Bontebok scarce in restricted range/
Blesbok common on game farms; endemic

Medium-sized antelope with purple-brown coat contrasting with white lower legs and underbelly. Bontebok can be distinguished by its white rump. Bontebok and Blesbok will interbreed, but their ranges are distinct. Occur in herds of up to 25 accompanied by dominant male. Grazes on various grasses. Cheetahs and Leopards are the main predators.
Best viewing: Bontebok, Cape of Good Hope, De Hoop/Golden Gate, Camdeboo

Duncan Butchart

SPRINGBOK *Antidorcas marsupialis*

Habitat: open grassy plains, Karoo scrubland
Height: 75 cm **Length:** 120 cm **Horns:** 35 cm
Mass: 40 kg (♂); 25–30 kg (♀) **Status:** common to
abundant; near-endemic

Distinctive gazelle with a broad, dark brown band on each flank. Both sexes have horns, but those of the male are more robust. Occurs in small herds, but larger groups undertake seasonal movements. Grazes on grass in summer and browses shrub foliage in winter; also relishes Acacia seedpods. Cheetahs and Leopards are the main predators. South Africa's national mammal.
Best viewing: Kgalagadi, Augrabies, Camdeboo, Karoo, Mokala, Golden Gate

GREATER KUDU *Tragelaphus strepsiceros*

Habitat: wooded hillsides and watercourses, succulent thickets **Height:** 150 cm **Length:** 250 cm
Horns: 120 cm **Mass:** 250 kg (♂); 180 kg (♀)
Status: common to abundant

Large antelope with grey-brown coat with six or more narrow, white stripes. Only the male carries magnificent spiral horns that attain full length after three years. Females gather in small herds, with males in tow during midwinter rut. Non-breeding males form bachelor herds. Browses on a wide variety of plants. Lions are the main predators.
Best viewing: widespread in suitable habitat

Nigel Dennis/Images of Africa

BUSHBUCK *Tragelaphus scriptus*

Habitat: wooded watercourses and thickets, coastal forest and scrub **Height:** 75 cm **Length:** 150 cm
Horns: 26 cm **Mass:** 45 kg (♂); 30 kg (♀)
Status: common to abundant

Medium-sized antelope with fawn-coloured coat with variable-patterned spots and stripes. Only the male carries spiral horns. Mainly nocturnal, but also active at dusk and dawn. Browses on leaves but also feeds on grass, fruit and flowers. May feed in the company of baboons. Leopards are the main predators.
Best viewing: Kruger-Lowveld, Pilanesberg, Tsitsikamma, Knysna-Wilderness

Ariadne van Zandbergen/Images of Africa

NYALA *Tragelaphus angasii*

Habitat: thickets and wooded watercourses, sandforest **Height:** 110 cm **Length:** 190 cm
Horns: 60 cm **Mass:** 110 kg (♂); 62 kg (♀)
Status: common to abundant; restricted to wildlife reserves; near-endemic

Medium-sized antelope with sexes very distinct. Male has a dark brown coat with a shaggy mane and fawn legs; female has a shorter chestnut coat. Occurs in small herds or bachelor groups. Chiefly a browser of shrub foliage but also grazes on grass. Leopards are the main predators. Introduced to many private reserves where not known historically.
Best viewing: Mkhuze, Hluhluwe-iMfolozi, Ndumo, Kruger (north), St Lucia, Phinda

Duncan Butchart

COMMON ELAND *Tragelaphus oryx*

Habitat: montane and coastal grassland, open woodland **Height:** 160 cm **Length:** 300–400 cm
Horns: 60 cm **Mass:** 900 kg (♂); 450 kg (♀)
Status: sparse to fairly common; confined to reserves

Massive, thick-set antelope with an ox-like appearance. Coat varies in colour from sandy-grey to ashy-grey. Male is much larger than female and has a pronounced dewlap and robust corkscrew horns. Usually in small groups, but larger herds undertake seasonal movements. Browses from shrubs but also eats fruits and grass. Lions are the only predators.
Best viewing: Drakensberg, Dwesa, Golden Gate, West Coast, De Hoop, Karoo, Addo

Nigel Dennis/Images of Africa

Duncan Butchart

GEMSBOK *Oryx gazella*

Habitat: grassy plains and dunes **Height:** 120 cm **Length:** 200 cm **Horns:** 85 cm **Mass:** 240 kg (♂); 210 kg (♀) **Status:** fairly common; restricted to wildlife reserves; near-endemic

Large antelope with lance-like horns and striking facial pattern. Sexes are alike, but females more lightly built with slender horns. Typically forms herds of up to 30 individuals, comprising adult females and their young, as well as sub-adult males. Mature males occupy fixed territories. Grazes on a variety of grasses but also eats tubers. Lions are the main predators.
Best viewing: Kgalagadi, Augrabies, Madikwe, Karoo, Mokala

Nigel Dennis/Images of Africa

SABLE ANTELOPE *Hippotragus niger*

Habitat: grassy clearings and vlei fringes **Height:** 130 cm **Length:** 230–250 cm **Horns:** 102 cm **Mass:** 270 kg (♂); 180 kg (♀) **Status:** rare and declining, successful captive breeding; restricted to wildlife reserves

Large, horse-like antelope with long mane and swept-back horns. Male is jet-black with contrasting white facial pattern and underbelly. Female is chestnut with shorter, thinner horns. Female herds of 10–25 individuals range over an area incorporating territory of a dominant bull. Selective grazer, but will also browse from shrubs. Lions are the main predators.
Best viewing: Pilanesberg, Rustenberg, Kruger (north), Marakele

Nigel Dennis/Images of Africa

ROAN ANTELOPE *Hippotragus equinus*

Habitat: savanna clearings with tall grass **Height:** 140 cm **Length:** 200 cm **Horns:** 75 cm **Mass:** 300 kg (♂); 220 kg (♀) **Status:** rare to uncommon in reduced range; restricted to wildlife reserves

Large, horse-like antelope with distinctive black-and-white facial pattern. The long ears are tufted. Sexes are alike with a grizzled grey to rufous coat; the swept-back horns are thicker and longer in the male. Small female herds often accompanied by a bull. A selective grazer, it favours medium or long grass; rarely occurring far from water. Lions are the main predators.
Best viewing: Nylsvley, Pilanesberg, Percy Fyfe

Duncan Butchart

WATERBUCK *Kobus ellipsiprymnus*

Habitat: savanna clearings, open woodland and reedbeds; near rivers **Height:** 130 cm **Length:** 180 cm **Horns:** 75 cm **Mass:** 260 kg (♂); 230 kg (♀) **Status:** fairly common; restricted to wildlife reserves

Large, robust antelope with coarse, shaggy coat. The rump is distinctively marked with a broad, white ring. Only male has the heavily ringed, arc-shaped horns. Territorial bulls dominate groups of females and their young. Rarely found far from water, it grazes on alluvial flats or in open areas. Preyed upon by all larger carnivores, particularly Lion.
Best viewing; Kruger, Hluhluwe-iMfolozi, Pilanesberg, Mapungubwe, Marakele

IMPALA   *Aepyceros melampus*

Habitat: open woodland and thickets   **Height:** 90 cm
Length: 170 cm   **Horns:** 50 cm   **Mass:** 50 kg (♂);
40 kg (♀)   **Status:** abundant

Graceful, reddish-brown antelope. Only males have impressive lyre-shaped horns. Herds of females occupy a home range, and males establish territories during the rut (Apr–May) with much roaring, snorting and chasing of rivals. Non-breeding males form bachelor herds. Adaptable grazer-browser of a wide variety of grasses and hrubs. Leopards, Wild Dogs and Cheetahs are the main predators.
Best viewing: widespread in suitable habitat

Ariadne van Zandbergen/Images of Africa

COMMON REEDBUCK   *Redunca arundinum*

Habitat: marshes and reedbeds   **Height:** 85 cm
Length: 140–180 cm   **Horns:** 30 cm   **Mass:** 50 kg (♂);
40 kg (♀)   **Status:** fairly common

Medium-sized, reddish-brown antelope. Only the male has the long, out-swept horns. A sharp whistle is the contact and alarm call. Bushy tail and dark band down the forelegs. Occurs singly or in loose groups. Largely nocturnal, but when active during the day it keeps to rank growth near water. Feeds on grass and herb foliage. Cheetahs are the main predators.
Best viewing: St Lucia, Nylsvley, Karkloof, Hluhluwe-iMfolozi, Kruger (south)

Daryl Balfour/Images of Africa

MOUNTAIN REEDBUCK   *Redunca fulvorufula*

Habitat: rocky hillsides and mountains
Height: 72 cm   **Length:** 140 cm   **Horns:** 14 cm
Mass: 30 kg   **Status:** locally common

Medium-sized, greyish-brown antelope with shaggy coat. Male has short, out-swept horns. Rams hold territories but females are nomadic. May share habitat with Grey Rhebok, which has longer neck and straight horns. Active during day and night. Selective grazer of grasses. Preyed upon by Leopard and Caracal.
Best viewing: Drakensberg, Karoo, Mokala, Suikerbosrand, Pilanesberg, Mountain Zebra

Clem Haagner/Gallo Images/Afripics

GREY RHEBOK   *Pelea capreolus*

Habitat: rocky hillsides   **Height:** 75 cm
Length: 135 cm   **Horns:** 20 cm   **Mass:** 20 kg
Status: fairly common; endemic

Medium-sized antelope with long neck, woolly coat and mule-like ears. The thin, pointed horns of the male are diagnostic. Occurs in family groups on grassy hillsides, where it grazes on a variety of grasses. Utters a sharp snort if disturbed and runs off with a rocking gait. Leopards and Caracals are the main predators; young are vulnerable to eagles.
Best viewing: Bontebok, De Hoop, Karoo, Drakensberg, Richtersveld, Mountain Zebra

Albert Froneman/Afripics

Albert Froneman/Afripics

GREY DUIKER   *Sylvicapra grimmia*

Habitat: thickets, woodland, plantations, grassland
Height: 50 cm   **Length:** 90 cm   **Horns:** 10 cm
Mass: 18 kg   **Status:** common to abundant

Small, grey-brown antelope with stocky build. The black blaze on the forehead and snout is diagnostic. Pre-orbital glands are conspicuous. Only the male has horns. Most active at dusk and dawn, and into the night. Occurs singly or in pairs in a fixed home range. Browses on a variety of shrubs and herbs. Leopards, Caracals and Martial Eagles are the main predators.
Best viewing: widespread in suitable habitat

Duncan Butchart

RED DUIKER   *Cephalophus natalensis*

Habitat: forest fringe, coastal thickets, bush clumps
Height: 45 cm   **Length:** 80 cm   **Horns:** 6 cm
Mass: 10–15 kg   **Status:** sparse to locally common

Small, stocky antelope, with bright chestnut-red coat. The short, backward-pointing horns are mostly hidden by a crest of long hair. Pre-orbital glands are conspicuous. Pairs occupy a home range but forage alone. Feeds primarily on fallen leaves of selected trees, as well as fruits and berries. Leopards, Caracals and African Crowned Eagles are main predators.
Best viewing: Phinda, Mkhuze, Ndumo, Thembe, Hluluwe-iMfolozi, St Lucia, Nelspruit

HPH Photography/Digital Source

BLUE DUIKER   *Cephalophus monticola*

Habitat: coastal forest and scrub
Height: 35 cm   **Length:** 60 cm   **Horns:** 3 cm
Mass: 4 kg   **Status:** locally common

Tiny, delicate antelope, with variable coat colour. Some individuals are charcoal-grey and appear bluish, others are pale or dark brown. Pre-orbital glands are conspicuous. Pairs occupy a home range but forage alone. Feeds on fallen fruit, figs, seeds, leaves and flowers. African Crowned Eagles are the main predators. Commonly snared by subsistence hunters.
Best viewing: Dwesa, Tsitsikamma, St Lucia, Karkloof

HPH Photography/Digital Source

SUNI   *Neotragus moschatus*

Habitat: sandforest and coastal thickets
Height: 35 cm   **Length:** 70 cm   **Horns:** 8 cm
Mass: 5 kg   **Status:** sparse to uncommon

Tiny, rufous-brown antelope. Differs from similar-sized Blue Duiker by more slender build, paler coloration and pointed ears. The longish tail is constantly flicked. Male has heavily ringed horns. Pairs occupy a territory demarcated by glandular deposits and dung heaps. Browses on foliage and berries. African Crowned Eagles are the main predators.
Best viewing: Phinda, Ndumo, Thembe, St Lucia, Kruger (far north)

STEENBOK *Raphicerus campestris*

Habitat: grassy clearings, Karoo scrubland and fynbos
Height: 50 cm **Length:** 75–90 cm
Horns: 12–15 cm **Mass:** 11 kg **Status:** common

Small, brick-red antelope with large, rounded ears. Only the male has horns. Monogamous and usually seen in pairs. Active at all hours, but rests in shade at midday. Young are born at any time of the year. Mixed diet of grass, leaves, seedpods and berries. Able to survive in areas devoid of surface water. Cheetahs and Martial Eagles are among the main predators.
Best viewing: widespread in suitable habitat

Duncan Butchart

ORIBI *Ourebia ourebi*

Habitat: montane grassland **Height:** 60 cm
Length: 100 cm **Horns:** 10 cm **Mass:** 18 kg
Status: scarce to rare, endangered

Small, brick-red antelope with short black tail. The black spots below the ear and pre-orbital gland are distinctive. Only the male has the slender upright horns. Occurs in pairs or small groups. Selective grazer of grass, often maintaining short 'lawns' in home range. Has a fragmented range with much habitat lost to timber plantations. Leopards are the main predators.
Best viewing: Golden Gate, Giant's Castle, Karkloof

Nigel Dennis/Images of Africa

CAPE GRYSBOK *Raphicerus melanotis*

Habitat: fynbos heathland, wooded dunes and gorges, orchards and vineyards **Height:** 50 cm
Length: 75 cm **Horns:** 6 cm **Mass:** 7 kg
Status: fairly common; endemic

Small, stocky antelope with reddish coat finely streaked with white. Male has short, pointed horns. Occurs in pairs, active mostly at night, but also in early morning or late afternoon. Feeds on leaves, berries and grass. Caracals and Martial Eagles are the main predators. Closely related Sharpe's Grysbok R. sharpei occurs in mopane woodland of northern Kruger.
Best viewing: Agulhas, Bontebok, Knysna, Cape of Good Hope, West Coast

Chris & Mathilde Stuart

KLIPSPRINGER *Oreotragus oreotragus*

Habitat: koppies, boulder outcrops, mountains
Height: 60 cm **Length:** 85 cm **Horns:** 8–10 cm
Mass: 13 kg **Status:** common

Small, stocky antelope with grizzled, grey-brown coat. This species' prominent orbital glands and habit of walking and jumping on hoof tips are diagnostic. Male has a pair of short, pointed horns. Occurs in pairs or family groups on rocky outcrops or cliffs, where it feeds on the leaves of small shrubs and herbs. Leopards and large eagles are main predators.
Best viewing: Augrabies, Pilanesberg, Karoo, Camdeboo, Namaqua, Richtersveld

Tony Camacho/Images of Africa

Duncan Butchart

Nigel Dennis/Images of Africa

Nigel Dennis/Images of Africa

LEOPARD *Panthera pardus*

Habitat: most habitats; favours wooded watercourses, mountains and forest **Height:** 70–80 cm **Length:** 160–200 cm **Mass:** up to 90 kg (♂); 60 kg (♀) **Status:** sparse to locally common; persecuted on farms

Large cat with relatively short legs and rosettes of black spots on tawny coat. Sexes only come together to mate. One or two cubs may remain with mother for up to two years. Females have overlapping home ranges; males have larger territories. Extremely diverse diet, but small and medium-sized antelope dominate. Larger kills are stored in trees, out of reach of hyaenas. **Best viewing:** Kruger-Lowveld (esp. Sabi-Sand), Phinda, Kgalagadi, Pilanesberg

CARACAL *Caracal caracal*

Habitat: most habitats; favours thickets and rocky outcrops **Height:** 45 cm **Length:** 100 cm **Mass:** up to 18 kg **Status:** sparse to common; persecuted by small stock farmers

Medium-sized cat with reddish coat and distinctive long black tufts on its ears. The tail is short and thick. Occurs singly except when female has kittens; up to three being born at any time of the year. Primarily nocturnal but may be active during the day in protected areas. Preys on birds up to the size of bustards and small mammals. **Best viewing:** widespread in suitable habitat

AFRICAN WILD CAT *Felis sylvestris lybica*

Habitat: thickets, open woodland, grassland and fynbos **Height:** 25–30 cm **Length:** 60–75 cm **Mass:** 3–5 kg **Status:** uncommon; threatened by hybridization with domestic and feral cats

Small to medium-sized cat, hardly distinguishable from a domestic tabby. The comparatively long legs and rust-red hair on the backs of the ears are diagnostic. Solitary and primarily nocturnal. Rodents, hares and ground birds make up the bulk of its prey. The Small-spotted Cat F. nigripes shares much of its range but is much smaller with short legs. **Best viewing:** Kgalagadi, Karoo, Augrabies, Pilanesberg

LION *Panthera leo*

Habitat: open woodland **Height:** 120 cm **Length:** 2–3 m **Mass:** 220 kg (♂); 150 kg (♀) **Status:** locally common; restricted to wildlife reserves

Very large, sociable cat living in prides of several adult females (often related) and their offspring, and up to three adult males. All defend a territory against rivals. Most active at night. Preys on anything from young elephant to hares, but favours larger herbivores. Also scavenges and pirates kills from other carnivores. The 'roar' may carry for several kilometres. **Best viewing:** Kgalagadi, Kruger-Lowveld, Phinda, Pilanesberg, Hluhluwe-iMfolozi, Addo

Duncan Butchart

CHEETAH *Acinonyx jubatus*

Habitat: open areas, clearings in woodland
Height: 80 cm **Length:** up to 200 cm **Mass:** 50–60 kg
Status: sparse to locally common; restricted to
wildlife reserves

Large, elegant cat with long legs, greyhound-like frame, solid black spots and black 'tear-marks' between eyes and mouth. Adult females often accompanied by two to five cubs for up to two years. Male frequently forms coalition (often brothers) of two or three. Hunts by day (mostly Impala and Springbok), thereby largely avoiding competition with other predators.
Best viewing: Kgalagadi, Phinda, Kruger-Lowveld, Pilanesberg, Marakele, Mountain Zebra

Duncan Butchart

SERVAL *Leptailurus serval*

Habitat: tall grassland, vleis, forest fringe
Height: 60 cm **Length:** 95–120 cm **Mass:** 8–15 kg
Status: sparse to uncommon

Medium-sized, slender cat with long limbs and short tail. Black spots merge into bands, and there are white bars on the back of its large ears. Males and females live apart in overlapping ranges. Up to three kittens are born in summer. Primarily nocturnal, elusive and shy. Preys on Vlei Rats (Otomys species) and other rodents, as well as birds, frogs and fish.
Best viewing: Karkloof, Drakensberg, St Lucia, Hluhluwe-iMfolozi, Pilanesberg

Nigel Dennis/Images of Africa

HONEY BADGER *Mellivora capensis*

Habitat: all habitats except high mountains
Height: 25 cm **Length:** 80–100 cm **Mass:** 8–14 kg
Status: sparse to uncommon; persecuted by
bee farmers

Stout, short-legged carnivore boldly marked in black and silvery-white. Usually seen alone, but lives in monogamous pairs. A powerful digger, it unearths mole-rats, reptiles and other prey. Climbs trees for honey and bee larvae, but its relationship with the Greater Honeyguide is disputed. Strips bark in search of reptiles. May scavenge around lodges and homesteads.
Best viewing: Kgalagadi, Kruger, Mapungubwe, Pilanesberg, Nylsvley

Tony Camacho/Images of Africa

CAPE CLAWLESS OTTER *Aonyx capensis*

Habitat: rivers, lakes, dams, rocky shores
Height: 20 cm **Length:** 100–150 cm **Mass:** 10–18 kg
Status: sparse to uncommon; persecuted by trout
farmers and fishermen

Medium-sized, low-slung carnivore with a short coat of brown fur. Underbelly and throat are creamy-white. Streamlined tail acts as a rudder and paddle. Feet are unwebbed and spoor shows five pads with no claw marks. Smaller Spotted-necked Otter Lutra maculicollis has webbed toes and long claws. Pups are reared in a burrow. Feeds on crabs, fishes and frogs.
Best viewing: Tsitsikamma, Drakensberg, Augrabies, St Lucia

Roger de la Harpe/Images of Africa

Nigel Dennis/Images of Africa

MEERKAT (SURICATE) *Suricata suricatta*

Habitat: open areas in arid Kalahari and Karoo
Height: 12 cm **Length:** 45–55 cm **Mass:** 650–950 g
Status: common; near-endemic

Small carnivore with black 'bandit' face mask and boldly striped back. Regularly stands up on its hind legs, using tail as a support. Active by day, in troops of 20 or so individuals led by an alpha pair. Two to five babies are born in a burrow. Forages for scorpions, beetles and other invertebrates. Eagles and jackals are the main predators.
Best viewing: Kgalagadi, Camdeboo, Karoo, Namaqua, Mountain Zebra, Richtersveld

Duncan Butchart

BANDED MONGOOSE *Mungos mungo*

Habitat: open woodland, coastal scrub
Height: 12 cm **Length:** 50–65 cm **Mass:** 800–1 500 g
Status: common

Small, stocky carnivore with distinctive vertical bands on the back. Diurnal and gregarious, in troops of up to 30, with as many as four breeding pairs. Packs forage together within a home range, teaming up against rivals or potential predators. Two to six babies are born in a termite mound den, or hole among rocks. Invertebrates and reptiles are the favoured food.
Best viewing: Kruger, Hluhluwe-iMfolozi, St Lucia, Pilanesberg, Nylsvley, Mapungubwe

Phil Perry/Images of Africa

WHITE-TAILED MONGOOSE *Ichneumia albicauda*

Habitat: grassy clearings and thickets
Height: 25 cm **Length:** 100–150 cm **Mass:** up to 5 kg
Status: sparse to fairly common

Medium-sized carnivore with dark legs and long, bushy, white tail. The overall body colour is grey. Nocturnal, it occurs singly or in small family groups within a fixed home range. Often forages along vehicle tracks or in open areas. Diet includes large insects, scorpions, rodents, birds' eggs, frogs and fallen fruit. Preyed upon by Leopard.
Best viewing: Kruger-Lowveld, St Lucia, Hluhluwe-iMfolozi, Mapungubwe, Nylsvley

Rita Meyer/Images of Africa

WATER MONGOOSE *Atilax paludinosus*

Habitat: fringe of all aquatic habitats, including river pools and estuaries **Height:** 18–20 cm
Length: 80–100 cm **Mass:** 3–5 kg **Status:** uncommon

Small, shaggy-coated carnivore with almost hairless toes adapted for a semi-aquatic lifestyle. Nocturnal, it occurs singly or in pairs, using regular pathways and latrine sites within its territory. Dark coloration and aquatic habits may lead to confusion with otters, but spoor shows four elongated toe pads and distinct claw marks. Feeds on frogs, crabs and fish caught in shallow water. May be preyed upon by Nile Crocodile.
Best viewing: Knysna-Wilderness, Wild Coast, Orange River, Drakensberg, Nylsvley

DWARF MONGOOSE *Helogale parvula*

Habitat: open woodland with termite mounds
Height: 7 cm **Length:** 35 cm **Mass:** 220–350 g
Status: common

Tiny carnivore with glossy, reddish-brown coat and distinctive, pink nose. Diurnal and highly gregarious, living in troops of up to 30, with a dominant alpha pair. Pack moves together within home range. Den is usually in an exposed termite mound with several entrance holes. Beetles, insects and berries feature in the diet. Preyed upon by eagles and other raptors.
Best viewing: Kruger, Pilanesberg, Mapungubwe

Nigel Dennis/Images of Africa

SLENDER MONGOOSE *Galerella sanguinea*

Habitat: rocky outcrops, grassland and thickets
Height: 10 cm **Length:** 60 cm (incl. 25 cm tail)
Mass: 650 g **Status:** common

Small, slim carnivore with long, black-tipped tail. Reddish coat in north and east of South African range; grizzled grey in south-west. Diurnal, often seen crossing roads with its tail held aloft. Most of its time is spent on the ground, but also an adept tree climber. One or two young are born in a rock cavity or burrow. Feeds on insects, lizards and birds' eggs. Preyed upon by eagles.
Best viewing: widespread in suitable habitat

HPH Photography/Digital Source

YELLOW MONGOOSE *Cynictis penicillata*

Habitat: open areas, bare pans, grassland
Height: 12 cm **Length:** 40–60 cm **Mass:** 850 g
Status: common; near-endemic

Small, slim carnivore with long, white-tipped tail. The coat is honey-yellow or greyish-ochre. Family groups of up to ten members excavate burrow systems in open areas, sometimes alongside Ground Squirrels. Two to five babies are born. Diet includes beetles, lizards and birds' eggs. Preyed upon by eagles.
Best viewing: Kgalagadi, Namaqua, Augrabies, Karoo, Mountain Zebra

Nigel Dennis/Images of Africa

SMALL GREY MONGOOSE *Galerella pulverulenta*

Habitat: Karoo scrubland, fynbos, cultivated lands
Height: 10 cm **Length:** 55–70 cm **Mass:** 850–950 g
Status: fairly common; near-endemic

Small, slim carnivore with grizzled, grey coat and long, bushy tail. Active by day and night. Occurs singly or in small family groups in a home range. May scavenge in parks and campsites. Diet includes insects, small rodents and carrion. Up to three babies are born in a burrow or among rocks. Preyed upon by eagles and other raptors.
Best viewing: Kirstenbosch, De Hoop, Bontebok, Mountain Zebra, Namaqua, Tsitsikamma

Rita Meyer/Images of Africa

Nigel Dennis/Images of Africa

Ariadne van Zandbergen/Images of Africa

Nigel Dennis/Images of Africa

Chris & Mathilde Stuart

AFRICAN CIVET *Civettictis civetta*

Habitat: wooded watercourses and thickets
Height: 40 cm **Length:** 120–140 cm **Mass:** 9–15 kg
Status: fairly common

Robust, raccoon-like carnivore with black mask and ringed tail. Long spinal crest is raised when alarmed. Nocturnal, it may be seen prowling sand roads and open areas after dark. Scent-marks territory and uses specific latrine sites. Diet includes millipedes, snakes and the fruit of the Wild Date Palm, Jackalberry and Marula. Preyed upon by Leopard.
Best viewing: Kruger-Lowveld (esp. Sabi-Sand), Mapungubwe, Pilanesberg

LARGE-SPOTTED GENET *Genetta tigrina*

Habitat: thickets, wooded watercourses, forest, coastal scrub **Height:** 12–15 cm **Length:** 100 cm
Mass: 2–3 kg **Status:** common

Slim, short-legged carnivore with spotted coat and long, ringed tail, usually black-tipped. Spots vary in colour from black to rusty. Nocturnal, it forages mostly within trees. Solitary and territorial. Up to five kittens are raised in a tree hole or rocky crevice. Diverse prey includes rodents, geckos, insects and nestling birds. Verreaux's Eagle-Owls are the main predators.
Best viewing: Kruger-Lowveld, Hluhluwe-iMfolozi, Garden Route, Cape of Good Hope

SMALL-SPOTTED GENET *Genetta genetta*

Habitat: open areas with scattered trees and rocky outcrops **Height:** 12–15 cm **Length:** 100 cm
Mass: 2–3 kg **Status:** common

Slim, short-legged carnivore with spotted coat and long, ringed tail, usually white-tipped. Nocturnal, it forages mostly within trees. Solitary and territorial. Up to five kittens are raised in a tree hole or rocky crevice. Diverse prey includes rodents, geckos, insects and nestling birds. Verreaux's Eagle-Owls are the main predators.
Best viewing: Kgalagadi, Augrabies, Namaqua, Madikwe, Karoo, Richtersveld

STRIPED POLECAT *Ictonyx striatus*

Habitat: most habitats **Height:** 10–12 cm
Length: 50–65 cm **Mass:** 800–1 400 g
Status: common; frequent road casualty

Small, carnivore with bold, horizontal striping; head and underparts are black. Nocturnal, solitary and secretive. Like the Skunk of the northern hemisphere (to which it is related), the polecat sprays a foul fluid from its anal glands in defence. The similar Striped Weasel *Poecilogale albinucha* is much smaller (300 g). Feeds mostly on rodents. Larger owls are the main predators.
Best viewing: Karoo, Kwandwe, Kgalagadi, Drakensberg, Tankwa-Karoo, Namaqua

BAT-EARED FOX *Otocyon megalotis*

Habitat: open areas in scrubland and fynbos
Height: 35 m **Length:** 80 cm **Mass:** 3–5 kg
Status: locally common; frequent road casualty

Small, bushy-tailed canid with enormous, rounded ears, face masked in black, grizzled grey coat and short, black legs. Most active at twilight and after dark, but active by day during winter. Lives in groups of three to seven consisting of a pair and their pups. Lizards, rodents, termites and other invertebrates are the main prey.
Best viewing: Kgalagadi, Namaqua, West Coast, Karoo, Bontebok, Camdeboo

Nigel Dennis/Images of Africa

CAPE FOX *Vulpes chama*

Habitat: open areas in scrubland and fynbos
Height: 35 cm **Length:** 85–95 cm **Mass:** 3–4 kg
Status: fairly common; frequent road casualty; near-endemic

Small, bushy-tailed canid with pointed ears and sandy-grey coat. The legs and face are tawny coloured. Usually forages alone, but pairs are territorial. One to five pups are born in a burrow or den. Primarily nocturnal, but may be seen in the early morning or at dusk in protected areas. Small rodents, reptiles and invertebrates are the main prey.
Best viewing: Kgalagadi, Namaqua, Mountain Zebra, Tankwa-Karoo, Richtersveld

Nigel Dennis/Images of Africa

BLACK-BACKED JACKAL *Canis mesomelas*

Habitat: most habitats, including farmlands
Height: 35–45 cm **Length:** 100–130 cm **Mass:** 6–12 kg
Status: common to abundant; persecuted by small stock farmers

Medium-sized canid with reddish-yellow coat and distinctive black and silver 'saddle'. Active by day or night. A pair defends a territory and raises three to four pups which remain with parents to help feed the next litter. May congregate to scavenge from larger carcasses. Call is a plaintive, drawn-out wail. Prey ranges from insects to young Impala.
Best viewing: widespread in suitable habitat

Duncan Butchart

SIDE-STRIPED JACKAL *Canis adustus*

Habitat: tall grassland, vlei fringes, coastal scrub
Height: 40 cm **Length:** 100 cm **Mass:** 8–12 kg
Status: fairly common

Medium-sized canid with greyish coat with pale stripe on flanks and a white-tipped tail. The snout is rather blunt and the ears are shorter than those of the Black-backed Jackal. Usually nocturnal. Occurs in pairs or family groups of up to six. An opportunistic predator of a wide variety of smaller animals and also scavenges. Call is a repetitive 'yap'.
Best viewing: Mkhuze, Phinda, Kruger-Lowveld, Nylsvley

Martin Harvey/Images of Africa

Nigel Dennis/Images of Africa

AFRICAN WILD DOG *Lycaon pictus*

Habitat: open woodland **Height:** 75 cm
Length: 120 cm **Mass:** 20–36 kg **Status:** rare and
endangered; restricted to wildlife reserves

Slender, long-legged carnivore with large, round ears. Coat is blotched in dark brown, fawn and white. Highly sociable, living in packs of between 6 and 15 adults (plus youngsters) with one dominant 'alpha' pair. Pack occupies den in old termite mound; pups born in winter. Active by day, running down prey (mostly Impala and young of larger antelope) after a chase.
Best viewing: Kruger, Madikwe, Pilanesberg, Mapungubwe

Duncan Butchart

AARDWOLF *Proteles cristatus*

Habitat: open areas with termite mounds
Height: 50 cm **Length:** 85–100 cm **Mass:** 6–10 kg
Status: fairly common; frequent road casualty

Smallest member of the hyaena family. The sandy-grey coat is striped with dark brown bands. The muzzle and lower legs are dark brown. Nocturnal, but may be active by day in winter. A pair and their offspring occupy a home range, but individuals forage alone. Dung middens and anal pastings demarcate territories. Feeds almost exclusively on harvester termites.
Best viewing: Karoo, Madikwe, Namaqua, Mountain Zebra, Bontebok, Pilanesberg

Martin Harvey/Images of Africa

SPOTTED HYAENA *Crocuta crocuta*

Habitat: open woodland **Height:** 85 cm
Length: 120–180 cm **Mass:** 60 kg (♂); 80 kg (♀)
Status: locally common; restricted to wildlife reserves

Large, heavily built carnivore with sloping back. Young pups are charcoal. Mostly nocturnal. Lives in female-dominated clans of varying size, which defend home range against rivals. Territories are marked with distinctive white droppings and anal pastings. Habitual scavenger, but also capable of preying on large antelope. Call is a drawn-out 'whoooop'.
Best viewing: Kruger, Madikwe, Hluhluwe-iMfolozi, Addo, Kgalagadi

BROWN HYAENA *Parahyaena brunnea*

Habitat: arid scrubland, rocky outcrops and
mountains, coastal dunes **Height:** 80 cm
Length: 130–160 cm **Mass:** 45 kg **Status:** sparse
to uncommon

Large, shaggy-coated carnivore with sloping back. Strictly nocturnal and usually secretive. Clans comprise an extended family unit that occupies a home range, but individuals forage alone. Territories are marked with white droppings and anal pastings. Males are often nomadic. Habitual scavenger, but also feeds on invertebrates and fruit. Rarely vocalizes.
Best viewing: Madikwe, Kgalagadi, Marakele, Pilanesberg, Richtersveld

Nigel Dennis/Images of Africa

EASTERN ROCK ELEPHANT-SHREW *Elephantulus myurus*

Habitat: koppies and boulder outcrops
Height: 6 cm **Length:** 22 cm **Mass:** 38–56 g
Status: fairly common

Very small insectivore with long tube-like snout, large rounded
ears and sandy coat. Occurs singly or in pairs. Active during daylight
hours, particularly in late afternoon and early morning. Termites,
ants and beetles are the main prey. Vulnerable to snakes and small
raptors. Several closely related species occur throughout South
Africa.
Best viewing: Suikerbosrand, Magaliesberg, Pilanesberg, Karoo,
Namaqua, Richtersveld

Chris & Mathilde Stuart

REDDISH-GREY MUSK SHREW *Crocidura cyanea*

Habitat: most habitats with sufficient cover
Height: 2 cm **Length:** 13 cm **Mass:** 6–9 g
Status: common

Tiny, nocturnal insectivore with pointed snout and small, rounded
ears. Males engage in fierce fights, squealing loudly in the process.
Young clasp mother's tail when on the move. A voracious predator
of small insects and worms, it often eats the equivalent of its own
body weight each night. Preyed upon by owls, genets and snakes.
Several other very similar musk-shrews occur in South Africa.
Best viewing: widespread in suitable habitat

Chris & Mathilde Stuart

SOUTHERN AFRICAN HEDGEHOG *Atelerix frontalis*

Habitat: clearings in grassland and scrubland
Height: 7 cm **Length:** 20 cm **Mass:** 400 g
Status: uncommon; near-endemic

Small insectivore with short black-and-white spines, and a pointed
snout. Nocturnal, spending days in a burrow or among leaf-litter.
If disturbed it rolls itself into a ball; hibernates during midwinter.
Feeds on termites, earthworms, snails, crickets and other
invertebrates. Verreaux's Eagle-Owls are the chief predators.
Best viewing: Golden Gate, Kgalagadi, Mountain Zebra, Nylsvley,
Addo, Suikerbosrand

Roger de la Harpe/Images of Africa

CAPE FUR SEAL *Arctocephalus pusillus*

Habitat: inshore waters, rocky coasts and islets
Height: 35–45 cm **Length:** 1.2–2.3 m **Mass:** 240 kg (♂);
60–75 kg (♀) **Status:** common to abundant;
population increase in recent years; near-endemic

The only seal commonly encountered on the South African coast.
Male has a thick, powerful neck and is considerably larger than
female. Often comes ashore to rest of rocky shores. Gregarious, but
feeds singly or in small groups, favouring shoaling fish. Breeds in
large, noisy colonies on islands along the West Coast.
Best viewing: Mossel Bay, Algoa Bay, False Bay (Cape Peninsula),
Robben Island

Peter Pickford/Images of Africa

Tony Camacho/Images of Africa

TREE SQUIRREL *Paraxerus cepapi*

Habitat: open woodland Height: 6–7 cm
Length: 35 cm Mass: 190 g
Status: common to abundant

Small, bushy-tailed rodent with grey to yellow-brown coat. Keeps mostly to trees but runs nimbly on the ground with raised tail. Usually seen singly or in small family groups. Male is territorial. Feeds on nuts, berries, flower buds and lichen. Makes a chattering, bird-like call when alarmed. Preyed upon by raptors, snakes and small carnivores.
Best viewing: widespread in suitable habitat

Nigel Dennis/Images of Africa

SOUTHERN AFRICAN GROUND SQUIRREL *Xerus inauris*

Habitat: open areas in Kalahari and Karoo scrubland
Height: 8–9 cm Length: 30–50 cm Mass: 500–300 g
Status: common to abundant; near-endemic

Large, terrestrial rodent with sandy-grey coat and a distinctive white stripe on each flank. The large, bushy tail is often raised behind the back in hot weather to create a sun-shield. Lives in family groups of up to 30 in a burrow system, which they excavate within a fixed erritory. Feeds mostly on bulbs, roots, seeds and termites. Preyed upon by eagles and hawks.
Best viewing: Kgalagadi, Augrabies, Mountain Zebra, Richtersveld

Peter Steyn/Digital Source

RED BUSH SQUIRREL *Paraxerus palliatus*

Habitat: coastal forest, sandforest Height: 6 cm
Length: 20–50 cm Mass: 200–300 g
Status: *P. p. tongensis* endangered; *P. p. ornatus* critically endangered; endemic

Small, chestnut-red rodent with bushy tail. There are two races in South Africa: one inhabiting closed-canopy sandforest P. p. tongensis and the other restricted to Ongoye Forest P. p. ornatus. Males and females occupy overlapping home ranges, and usually forage alone. Feeds on berries, nuts, seedpods, flower buds and lichen. Preyed upon by raptors and genets.
Best viewing: Thembe, Phinda, St Lucia, Kosi Bay/Ongoye Forest

Duncan Butchart

GREY SQUIRREL *Sciurus carolinensis*

Habitat: gardens and parks of south-western Cape
Height: 10 cm Length: 50 cm Mass: 600 g
Status: locally common; alien species

Medium-sized rodent with grizzled grey coat, pale underbelly and long, bushy tail. Occurs singly or in family groups among alien pine and oak trees. Feeds mostly on pine seeds and acorns. Young are raised in a ball-shaped 'drey' of twigs and leaves. Typically gives birth to two litters of two to four babies, each year. Larger raptors are the main predators.
Origin: native to North America, introduced to Cape Town from feral population in Britain

WOODLAND DORMOUSE *Graphiurus murinus*

Habitat: open woodland, coastal thickets, thatched huts, beehives, pump houses **Height:** 10 cm
Length: 16 cm **Mass:** 30 g **Status:** common

Small, silvery-grey rodent with white underparts and bushy, squirrel-like tail. Occurs singly or in pairs. It lives in trees (especially Acacia) but may frequent man-made structures. Nocturnal, its diet includes insects and grass seeds. A nest of fine grass, lichen and leaves is constructed within a tree hole or similar cavity. Preyed upon by snakes, genets and owls.
Best viewing: widespread in suitable habitat

Peter Steyn/Digital Source

FOUR-STRIPED GRASS MOUSE *Rhabdomys pumilio*

Habitat: most habitats **Height:** 3–4 cm
Length: 20 cm **Mass:** 50 g
Status: abundant

Small rodent with upperparts varying in colour from grey to fawn. The stripes running down the back are diagnostic. Diurnal, therefore the most frequently seen of South African mice. Grass seeds are the main food. Populations may 'explode' in seasons of high rainfall, which increase grass seed production. Black-shouldered Kites and kestrels are the main predators.
Best viewing: virtually anywhere

Duncan Butchart

SOUTHERN MULTIMAMMATE MOUSE *Mastomys coucha*

Habitat: most habitats **Height:** 3–4 cm
Length: 20 cm **Mass:** 50 g
Status: abundant

Small, long-tailed rodent with rounded ears and grey-brown coat. Nocturnal, often found in kraals and houses. Female has 12 pairs of teats, allowing it to reproduce faster than any other African mammal. Feeds mainly on grass seeds. Populations may 'explode' in seasons of high rainfall, which increase grass seed production. Owls and snakes are the main predators.
Best viewing: virtually anywhere

Chris & Mathilde Stuart

BUSHVELD GERBIL *Tatera leucogaster*

Habitat: open areas with sandy soils
Height: 3–4 cm **Length:** 26 cm **Mass:** 70 g
Status: common

Reddish-brown rodent with huge eyes, large ears and diagnostic dark stripe running down the length of its sparsely haired tail. Nocturnal, living in pairs within small colonies. Moves in short hops. Excavates burrows in sandy soil. Feeds on seeds and insects. Between three and seven babies are born in summer. Preyed upon by snakes, owls and genets.
Best viewing: Kgalagadi, Augrabies, Nylsvley, Madikwe, Pilanesberg

AJ Stevens/Digital Source

Martin Harvey/Images of Africa

CAPE PORCUPINE *Hystrix africaeaustralis*

Habitat: most habitats; favours rocky areas and kloofs
Height: 25–30 cm **Length:** 75–100 cm
Mass: 10–25 kg **Status:** common

Large rodent with long, black-and-white quills. Nocturnal; spends daylight hours in an underground burrow or cave. It is an avid digger, feeding primarily on roots and tubers, but the bark of certain trees is relished. Also scavenges carrion and bones. The quills are raised in alarm, and are used in defence against predators such as Leopards and Lions.
Best viewing: Kgalagadi, Karoo, Drakensberg, Addo, Mapungubwe, Tankwa-Karoo

AJ Stevens/Digital Source

GREATER CANE-RAT *Thryonomys swinderianus*

Habitat: reedbeds, marshlands and sugarcane plantations **Height:** 15–20 cm **Length:** 65–80 cm
Mass: 3–5 kg **Status:** common to abundant

Large rodent with coarse, grizzled coat. The head is small in relation to the body, and the ears are small. Nocturnal, but sometimes active at dusk. Lives in small colonies in reedbeds. Regular pathways are used within the home range. Feeds on stems and roots of sedges, reeds and grasses. Predators include African Pythons, Leopards and Verreaux's Eagle-Owls.
Best viewing: KwaZulu-Natal canefields, Hluhluwe-iMfolozi, Kruger, Nylsvley, Drakensberg

Jan Teede/Gallo/Afripics

ANGONI VLEI-RAT *Otomys angoniensis*

Habitat: vleis, swampy fringes of rivers
Height: 6–8 cm **Length:** 30 cm **Mass:** 100–200 g
Status: common to abundant

Short-tailed rodent with a blunt nose, shaggy fur and round ears. Although only visible when the skull of a corpse is examined, the upper incisor teeth are deeply grooved. Occurs in dense vegetation near water. Active during both night and day, feeding on grass roots, reeds and sedges. Predators include Servals and Long-crested Eagles.
Best viewing: Wakkerstroom, St Lucia, Drakensberg, Nylsvley

COMMON MOLE-RAT *Cryptomys hottentotus*

Habitat: most soils except heavy clay
Height: 6–8 cm **Length:** 15–18 cm **Mass:** 150 g
Status: common to abundant

Small, short-legged rodent with large protruding teeth. This is the creature responsible for the mounds of soil that appear on lawns and sports fields. Burrows underground in search of roots and bulbs. Lives in colonies of up to fourteen. Particularly active after rain when soil is softer. There are several closely related species in South Africa. Preyed upon by snakes.
Best viewing: widespread in suitable habitat

Peter Steyn/Digital Source

SPRINGHARE *Pedetes capensis*

Habitat: clearings on deep sand and pan fringes
Height: 10 cm **Length:** 80 cm **Mass:** 2.5–3.8 kg
Status: common to abundant

Kangaroo-like rodent with large eyes and square snout; not related to hares or rabbits. The coat is fawn-coloured, and the long, bushy tail tipped in black. Nocturnal, occurs in colonies in open areas of compressed sandy soil. Hops on powerful hind legs, using front limbs for digging up roots and bulbs. Predators include Caracals and Verreaux's Eagle-Owls.
Best viewing: Kgalagadi, Nylsvley, Madikwe, Mountain Zebra

JQV0691

SCRUB HARE *Lepus saxatilis*

Habitat: scrubland, grassland, woodland clearings, cultivated lands **Height:** 12 cm **Length:** 45–70 cm
Mass: 2–4 kg **Status:** common to abundant

Long-eared hare with white undertail and grizzled grey coat. Nocturnal, if flushed from its resting place will run in typical zigzag pattern. Feeds primarily on grass. Raises litters of one to three. Predators include Verreaux's Eagle-Owls, Caracals and Leopards. The practically identical Cape Hare L. capensis differs in having a rusty-red nape; it shares the western part of its range.
Best viewing: widespread in suitable habitat

Duncan Butchart

SMITH'S RED ROCK RABBIT *Pronolagus rupestris*

Habitat: rocky outcrops, koppies, mountains
Height: 12 cm **Length:** 40–60 cm **Mass:** 2–3 kg
Status: fairly common

Short-eared rabbit with compact build and rusty-red coat. Nocturnal, it usually bolts from cover within inches of being stepped upon, giving a startled observer a fleeting glimpse. Feeds on grasses and leaves. Lozenge-shaped pellets are deposited in urine-free latrines. Preyed upon by Cape Eagle-Owl and Caracal.
Best viewing: Golden Gate, Karoo, Pilanesberg, Richtersveld, Cape Mountains

Chris & Mathilde Stuart

RIVERINE RABBIT *Bunolagus monticularis*

Habitat: fringe of dry watercourses in Nama Karoo, Cape winelands, Klein Karoo **Height:** 12 cm
Length: 40–60 cm **Mass:** 2–3 kg **Status:** rare, critically endangered, endemic

Long-eared rabbit with grizzled grey coat and tail. Solitary and nocturnal. Females dig burrows in which one offspring is raised per year. Rests up during the day in shade of shrubs. Browses mostly on succulent shrubs and also eats fresh grass. Much of its natural range has been destroyed by agriculture and erosion. Preyed upon by cats and genets.
Best viewing: Karoo, Sanbona

Tony Camacho/Images of Africa

Duncan Butchart

WAHLBERG'S EPAULETTED FRUIT-BAT *Epomophorus wahlbergi*

Habitat: open woodland, fringe of coastal forest
Length: 15 cm **Wingspan:** 56 cm
Mass: 80–140 g (♀ larger) **Status:** common

Large, fruit-eating bat. Male has tufts of white hair on the shoulders that are erected into 'epaulettes'. Roosts under canopy of trees or under thatched buildings. Figs are the favoured food, snatched from the tree and eaten at a favoured perch. Call is a resounding 'ping'. Peter's Epauletted Fruit-Bat E. crypturus is hard to distinguish. Preyed upon at roost by snakes.
Best viewing: Kruger-Lowveld, St Lucia-Kosi Bay, Hluhluwe-iMfolozi, Wild Coast

EGYPTIAN SLIT-FACED BAT *Nycteris thebaica*

Habitat: most habitats; roosts in caves, hollow trees, under bridges and buildings **Length:** 10 cm
Wingspan: 24 cm **Mass:** 11 g **Status:** common

Small bat with enormous ears. Face is characterized by paired nose 'leaves' divided by a longitudinal slit. The tail is fully enclosed within a membrane, ending in Y-joint. Rarely emerges until well after dark. Catches moths and other insect prey in flight. Roosts in large colonies. Single young is born in early summer. Preyed upon by Bat Hawk and other raptors.
Best viewing: virtually anywhere

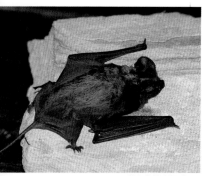

Jon Hall/www.mammalwatching.com

EGYPTIAN FREE-TAILED BAT *Tadarida aegyptiaca*

Habitat: most habitats except forest; often near water
Length: 11 cm **Wingspan:** 30 cm **Mass:** 14–18 g
Status: common to abundant

Small bat with more than half of the tail protruding beyond the membrane between hind legs. Ears are as broad as long, the face is mastiff-like with wrinkled lips. Captures moths and other insects on the wing. Colonies in caves, tree holes or buildings consist of dozens or hundreds. Single young is born in summer. Preyed upon by Bat Hawk and other raptors.
Best viewing: virtually anywhere

Chris & Mathilde Stuart

CAPE SEROTINE BAT *Neoromicia capensis*

Habitat: most habitats **Length:** 7 cm
Wingspan: 20 cm **Mass:** 4–9 g
Status: common to abundant

Tiny bat with no outstanding features. The tail is fully enclosed by a membrane between the hind legs. Emerges just before dark in slow, fluttering flight, to hunt moths and other small flying insects. Roosts in small numbers under tree bark, base of aloe leaves and roof structures. Preyed upon by Bat Hawk and other raptors. The even smaller Banana Bat Pipistrellus rueppellii is restricted to the warmer eastern parts of South Africa.
Best viewing: virtually anywhere

Chris & Mathilde Stuart

SOUTHERN RIGHT WHALE *Eubalaena australis*

Habitat: open sea: migrates from Antarctic to southern oceans **Length:** up to 15 m **Mass:** up to 60 000 kg (♂)
Status: seasonal visitor (May–Dec); population has recovered in recent years

The whale most often seen off the South African coast. The absence of a back fin and lack of grooves on the throat are diagnostic. Female gives birth to a single calf in shallow bays in late winter and spring. Feeds mostly on krill (tiny crustaceans). As it floats when harpooned, this whale was most sought after by whalers and was dubbed the 'right' whale to hunt.
Best viewing: Hermanus, Agulhas, Plettenberg Bay, Tsitsikamma

John Phielix/Images of Africa

HUMPBACK WHALE *Megaptera novaeangliae*

Habitat: open sea; migrates from Antarctica to east and west coasts of Africa **Length:** up to 18 m
Mass: up to 40 000 kg **Status:** seasonal visitor (Jul–Sep); population has recovered in recent years

Similar in size to the Southern Right Whale, but a much less common visitor to the coast in midwinter and spring. Its small dorsal fin, long, white flippers and grooved throat are diagnostic. Feeds on krill in Antarctic waters, hardly eating on migration. Highly vocal when breeding, their underwater sounds are the subject of 'whale song' recordings.
Best viewing: off KwaZulu-Natal coast

Rod Haestier/Images of Africa

SHORT-BEAKED COMMON DOLPHIN *Delphinus delphis*

Habitat: deeper pelagic waters **Length:** 260 cm (♂); 230 cm (♀) **Mass:** up to 150 kg
Status: fairly common

Indigo blue with white underbelly and peach-coloured criss-cross stripes on the flanks. The snout is long. May gather in large hunting pods of hundreds, or even thousands. Playful individuals often launch themselves out of the water. Frequently swims in the bow wave of boats. Feeds on smaller shoaling fish such as sardines, as well as squid.
Best viewing: False Bay, Plettenberg Bay, Tsitsikamma

Rod Haestier/Images of Africa

BOTTLENOSE DOLPHIN *Tursiops truncatus*

Habitat: coastal waters up to 20 m deep
Length: 260 cm **Mass:** up to 180 kg
Status: fairly common but migratory subspecies
T. t. aduncus endangered

Uniform light grey coloration with paler underparts. The snout is shorter than that of the Common Dolphin. Lives in small family groups (pods) but frequently gathers in larger schools of up to 100 individuals. Males form small bands, moving between female ranges. Feeds primarily on shoaling fish as well as squid and cuttlefish. Pods follow 'sardine run' up east coast in winter.
Best viewing: Tsitsikamma, Wild Coast, Plettenberg Bay, KwaZulu-Natal south coast

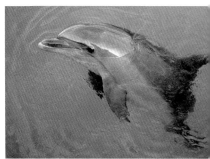

Andrew Woodburn/Images of Africa

BIRDS

Birds are the most visible, colourful and vociferous of all animals. They occur all around us, in gardens, parks and towns, but especially in wild places. For many beginners, the sheer diversity of birds can be overwhelming. In South Africa there are over 600 species that breed here, with another 150 or more species that are non-breeding migrants from the northern hemisphere or seasonal visitors to the southern ocean. There are 62 species that are endemic or near-endemic (found only in South Africa, or in one of the neighbouring countries) and these are of most significance to conservationists and travelling birders.

This is not a comprehensive guide to the country's birds, but presents 260 of the more eye-catching, widespread or endemic species. This includes representatives from almost all of the region's bird famiIes. In most cases, the photograph depicts an adult male; the accompanying text describes the female and immature bird when they differ. Brief notes on behaviour, diet and breeding are given, along with reference to species with which they might be confused.

When you encounter a bird you cannot identify, it is essential to note approximate size (in relation to a bird with which you are familiar), bill shape, overall plumage colour and distinctive field marks (such as pale eyebrow, brightly coloured rump, or wing bars), as well as the colour and length of legs. What the bird is doing, and whether it is alone or in a group, provides further clues to its identity.

It is essential to have a good pair of binoculars when out birding. Everyone has their own preference, but 8 × 30 mm or 10 × 40 mm roof-prism binoculars are most popular. Some people prefer small, lightweight binoculars, but these do not function very well in low light conditions. Spotting scopes are invaluable when birding in wetlands, or on shorelines and other open areas, and can also be used effectively in woodland and even forests; a scope must be mounted on a tripod at all times. The recognition of bird calls and songs is second nature to experienced birders, and this is a skill that all beginners should aim to acquire. There are several commercial bird call recordings available, but there is no substitute for investigating a call yourself and tracking down the bird responsible.

The names used here follow those in the 7th edition of Roberts' *Birds of Southern Africa* (Hockey et al, 2007), with two exceptions: Yellow-billed Kite is regarded as a full species (not a race of Black Kite), and the name White-faced Whistling-Duck is preferred to White-faced Duck.

Watching birds has become a hugely popular outdoor activity, and South Africa is high on the list of destinations for international birders. There are a number of regional bird clubs and birding routes that operate under the auspices of BirdLife South Africa, itself part of the global body BirdLife International. The measurements given here are length (bill tip to tail tip) and wingspan (from the tip of one outstretched wing to the other) on larger birds.

AFRICAN PENGUIN *Spheniscus demersus*

Habitat: feeds in inshore marine waters; roosts and breeds on rocky shores **Length:** 55–65 cm
Status: locally common resident; vulnerable; endemic

Unmistakable, black-and-white penguin with pale pink skin around the eyes. Immature is duller with a completely dark head. Feeds on shoaling fish and squid by day, returning to shore at dusk. Gregarious at roosts and breeding colonies. Call is a nasal, donkey-like bray, hence the former name Jackass Penguin. Lays 1 or 2 eggs in a rock crevice or burrow, usually on an island. The only penguin resident on the South African coast.
Best viewing: Boulder's Beach (Simon's Town), Robben Island, Betty's Bay, Algoa Bay

Erhardt Thiel/Images of Africa

GREAT WHITE PELICAN *Pelecanus onocrotalus*

Habitat: shallow lakes, pans, dams, lagoons and bays
Length: 160–180 cm **Wingspan:** 300–360 cm
Status: fairly common resident or nomad

Massive, white bird with huge bill, long neck and short legs. Bare skin around the eyes and upper bill is pink; lower bill and pouch are bright yellow. In flight, black wing feathers are distinctive. Immature has brownish upperwings. Feeds primarily on fish, but Western Cape population preys extensively on nestlings of cormorants and gannets. Lays 1–3 eggs in a ground scrape lined with feathers. Pink-backed Pelican *P. rufescens* has pinkish-grey wings.
Best viewing: St Lucia, Berg River Estuary, Rondevlei

Peter Pickford/Images of Africa

GREATER FLAMINGO *Phoenicopterus ruber*

Habitat: shallow water, saltpans, coastal mudflats
Length: 145–165 cm **Wingspan:** 150 cm
Status: locally common nomad; breeds in neighbouring Botswana and Namibia

Slender, predominantly white bird with extremely long legs and neck. Bill is pale pink with a dark tip, whereas smaller Lesser Flamingo has an all-dark bill. Outspread wings are pink and black, making this a spectacular bird in flight. Immature has a 'washed-out' look, being dusky white with pale bill and grey legs. Occurs in small flocks, filtering tiny invertebrates from mud. Single egg is laid in a bowl of mud and guano.
Best viewing: Highveld pans, Lake St Lucia, Barberspan, Port Nolloth

Nigel Dennis/Images of Africa

LESSER FLAMINGO *Phoenicopterus minor*

Habitat: shallow saline pans **Length:** 115–120 cm
Wingspan: 100 cm **Status:** locally abundant nomad; man-made breeding island near Kimberley

Slender, predominantly pink bird with extremely long legs and neck. Smaller than the Greater Flamingo, from which it differs by having a dark maroon bill. Immature has a muddy, 'washed-out' appearance, with dark grey bill. Filters microscopic algae and tiny organisms from mud. Flocks are nomadic, arriving and disappearing suddenly at inland waters. Single egg is laid in a bowl of mud and guano.
Best viewing: Kamfer's Dam (Kimberley), Chrissiesmeer, Barberspan

Nigel Dennis/Images of Africa

Albert Froneman/Images of Africa

REED CORMORANT *Phalacrocorax africanus*

Habitat: still or slow-moving fresh water, rarely at coast **Length:** 50–60 cm **Wingspan:** 85 cm **Status:** common resident

Medium-sized, all black cormorant with long tail and red eyes. Immature has an off-white breast. In common with other cormorants, feathers are not waterproof, so regularly perches with wings outstretched to dry. Forages singly or in loose groups, catching fish underwater. Lays up to 6 eggs in a stick nest. Breeds colonially in large trees or in reedbeds, often in the company of herons or storks. Crowned Cormorant *P. coronatus* is a strictly marine species of southern and Western Cape.
Best viewing: widespread in suitable habitat

Ryan Ebedes

CAPE CORMORANT *Phalacrocorax capensis*

Habitat: inshore marine habitat, including estuaries and lagoons **Length:** 64 cm **Wingspan:** 100 cm **Status:** common to abundant resident; near-endemic

Medium-sized marine cormorant with glossy black plumage, short tail, blue-green eyes. Adult has yellow-orange bare skin at the base of the bill. Immature is brownish. Highly gregarious, in flocks of up to thousands, which fly in long, single-file 'chains' just above the sea surface. Feeds on shoaling fish, often in the company of Cape Gannet. Lays 1–4 eggs in nest of sticks and seaweed. Bank Cormorant *P. neglectus* lacks yellow-orange skin on face.
Best viewing: Lambert's Bay, Cape Point, Robben Island, West Coast

Nigel Dennis/Images of Africa

WHITE-BREASTED CORMORANT *Phalacrocorax lucidus*

Habitat: marine and freshwater **Length:** 90 cm **Wingspan:** 140 cm **Status:** common resident

Large, black cormorant with snow-white throat and chest. Tail is short, eyes are green, base of bill has patch of bare yellow skin. Immature is dark brown with buffy-white underparts. Forages singly or in small groups, diving to seize fish underwater. Breeds colonially. Lays 3–5 eggs in bulky stick nest, built on man-made structures, offshore islands, cliffs or skeletal trees in dams.
Best viewing: widespread in suitable habitat

Nigel Dennis/Images of Africa

AFRICAN DARTER *Anhinga rufa*

Habitat: still and slow-moving fresh water **Length:** 85–95 cm **Wingspan:** 120 cm **Status:** fairly common resident

Large, dark brown, cormorant-like bird with long neck, often held in an S-shape, and dagger-like bill. Breeding adult has a rufous throat edged in white. Wings are held outstretched to dry. Forages singly, diving up to 6 m for fish, which are speared with the bill and brought to the surface. Often swims with only the neck and head above water, leading to its former name Snakebird. Lays 3–4 eggs in a stick nest.
Best viewing: widespread in suitable habitat

CAPE GANNET *Morus capensis*

Habitat: inshore marine water; breeds on rocky islands **Length:** 85–95 cm **Wingspan:** 180 cm **Status:** locally common resident; vulnerable; near-endemic

Large, white seabird with black flight feathers and tail. Head is pale yellow, with a thin, black line running down the throat. Sexes are alike, but male is somewhat larger. Immature is mottled, grey-brown. Large flocks assemble at fish shoals, plunging headfirst in spectacular dives to catch prey. Breeds in dense colonies on offshore islands; a single egg is laid in a mound of guano.
Best viewing: Lambert'-s Bay, Algoa Bay, Malgas Island, Cape Point

Hein von Hörsten/Images of Africa

KELP GULL *Larus dominicanus*

Habitat: beaches and rocky shores, shallow coastal waters **Length:** 60–65 cm (♂ larger) **Wingspan:** 135 cm **Status:** abundant resident; near-endemic

Large gull with black back and wings. Yellow bill has a red spot on lower mandible. Head, tail and underparts are white. Immature is mottled in brown, grey and white. Opportunistic feeder, scavenging and pirating from humans and other birds; also preys on eggs and nestlings. Gregarious, roosts and breeds in colonies. Lays 2–3 eggs in a ground scrape on a cliff, offshore rock stack, sandy beach or man-made structure.
Best viewing: Cape Peninsula, Garden Route, West Coast, Algoa Bay

Albert Froneman/Images of Africa

GREY-HEADED GULL *Larus cirrocephalus*

Habitat: inland pans and dams, farms and industrial sites, coastlines **Length:** 42 cm **Wingspan:** 100 cm **Status:** abundant resident

Medium-sized, grey and white gull with red bill and legs. Distinctive grey head, brighter bill and legs when breeding. Distinguished from Hartlaub's Gull by its pale yellow eyes. Immature and non-breeding adults have a white head smudged with grey. The only gull species of the interior. Gregarious, opportunistic feeder, scavenging and pirating food from humans and other birds. Up to 3 eggs are laid in a shallow bowl at the base of a grass tuft or floating nest.
Best viewing: widespread in suitable habitat

Peter Pickford/Images of Africa

HARTLAUB'S GULL *Larus hartlaubii*

Habitat: coastal **Length:** 42 cm **Wingspan:** 100 cm **Status:** abundant resident; near-endemic

Medium-sized, grey and white gull with red bill and legs. When breeding, head is milky-grey, and legs and bill are brighter. Distinguished from the Grey-headed Gull by its dark red eyes. Immature and non-breeding adult have a white head and dark bill. Restricted to the West Coast and south-western Cape. Opportunistic feeder, gathers around fishing boats, docks and piers. Lays up to 3 eggs in an untidy bowl among rocks or on a man-made structure.
Best viewing: Cape Peninsula, Robben Island, West Coast

Duncan Butchart

Nigel Dennis/Images of Africa

CATTLE EGRET   *Bubulcus ibis*

Habitat: farmlands, fields, open grassy savanna; roosts and breeds near water   **Length:** 54 cm   **Wingspan:** 95 cm   **Status:** abundant resident

Small, all-white egret with relatively short neck and legs. When breeding, crown, mantle and chest are adorned in buffy plumes, bill and legs become coral-pink, toes black. Non-breeding bird has yellow bill, olive-brown legs and toes. Gregarious, feeding on dry land, often in the company of livestock and other mammals that disturb insect prey; often follows tractors. Breeds colonially in reedbeds or trees; lays 1–7 eggs in bowl nest. Squacco Heron *Ardeola railoides* has streaks on buffy head and neck; restricted to wetlands.
Best viewing: virtually anywhere

Nigel Dennis/Images of Africa

LITTLE EGRET   *Egretta garzetta*

Habitat: shallows of lakes, pans, rivers and estuaries; beaches and rocky shores   **Length:** 65 cm   **Wingspan:** 95 cm   **Status:** fairly common resident

Small, all-white egret with long neck. Yellow toes at the ends of dark legs are diagnostic. Fine, white plumes droop from back of the head and mantle during breeding season. Bill is dark grey at all times. Often the only member of its species among mixed feeding flocks of herons and storks. Feeds on small fish, frogs and aquatic insects. Nests colonially with other egrets and herons; 2–4 eggs are laid in a bowl nest.
Best viewing: widespread in suitable habitat

Sam J Basch/Images of Africa

GREAT EGRET   *Egretta alba*

Habitat: shallows of lakes, rivers, seasonal pans and estuaries   **Length:** 95 cm   **Wingspan:** 170 cm   **Status:** uncommon resident

Large, all-white egret with long neck. Legs and toes are black at all times. Prior to breeding, bill is black and the bare skin around eyes lime-green. During and after breeding, bill and bare skin are yellow. Favours marshes, where it usually occurs singly, or in the company of other species. Feeds on fish and frogs. Lays 2–5 eggs in a stick nest built within reedbeds or in a dead tree. Yellow-billed Egret *E. intermedia* is smaller, with yellow upper legs.
Best viewing: widespread in suitable habitat

Ariadne van Zandbergen/Images of Africa

AFRICAN SPOONBILL   *Platalea alba*

Habitat: shallows of seasonal pans, dams and lagoons   **Length:** 80–90 cm   **Wingspan:** 145 cm   **Status:** fairly common resident or nomad

Large, all-white waterbird with a distinctive, spoon-shaped bill. Adult has long, pink legs and bare pink face; immature is duller. Flies with neck outstretched. Bill is used in a sweeping motion in shallow water to capture small crustaceans and aquatic insects. Small fish and frogs may also be taken. Occurs singly or in flocks that fly in V-formation. Lays 2–4 eggs in bowl of reeds or sticks, often nests alongside other species, in reedbeds or on islands.
Best viewing: widespread in suitable habitat

GREY HERON *Ardea cinerea*

Habitat: shallows of dams, lakes, rivers and marshes; rarely on rocky shores **Length:** 90–100 cm **Wingspan:** 155–175 cm **Status:** common to abundant resident

Large, pale grey heron with white head and neck, and long, yellow bill. A bold black streak runs above and behind the eye to form a crest. In flight, underwing is uniform grey. Flies with neck tucked in. Usually seen alone on floodplains or verges of rivers and lagoons where it hunts for frogs and fish. Forages by day and night. Lays 1–4 eggs in a platform nest of reeds and sticks, built in a tree or reed bed; often in mixed heronry with other species.
Best viewing: widespread in suitable habitat

Peter Pickford/Images of Africa

BLACK-HEADED HERON *Ardea melanocephala*

Habitat: open grassland, pastures, flooded fields; rarely in wetlands **Length:** 92 cm **Wingspan:** 150–160 cm **Status:** common to abundant resident

Large, dark grey heron with black head and neck, long, grey bill and white throat. In flight, underwing is black and white. Flies with neck tucked in. Immature has a pale, 'washed-out' look. Attracted to fires and recently burned ground, where scorched insects and reptiles are eaten. Lays 2–4 eggs in stick nest, near water in overhanging trees or reedbeds. Black-crowned Night-Heron *Nycticorax nycticorax* is half the size, with black back and is nocturnal.
Best viewing: widespread in suitable habitat

Tony Camacho/Images of Africa

GOLIATH HERON *Ardea goliath*

Habitat: shallows of lakes, dams, rivers and estuaries **Length:** 150 cm **Wingspan:** 230 cm **Status:** sparse to uncommon resident

Massive, slate-grey heron with rufous head, neck and underparts. Immature is paler with white on the throat extending to the chest. Flies with slow, deep wing-beats. Occurs singly or in pairs, often standing motionless at water's edge. Large fish and crabs are the main food but young crocodiles may also be taken. Lays 2–5 eggs in nest of trampled vegetation among reeds, less often in a tall tree. Purple Heron *A. purpurea* is smaller with black top to head.
Best viewing: Ndumo, Richard's Bay, Kruger, Barberspan, Marievale

Nigel Dennis/Images of Africa

GREEN-BACKED HERON *Butorides striata*

Habitat: wooded margins of ponds, lakes, rivers and lagoons; mangroves **Length:** 40 cm **Wingspan:** 80 cm **Status:** common resident

Small, dark heron with short neck and yellow-green legs. Back is dark grey-green with buffy edges to wing feathers, crown is black, underside is blue-grey. Immature is streaked on the throat and face, and spotted with white on the wings. Call is a harsh croak, uttered in flight. Perches motionless for long periods before striking out rapidly at frogs, tadpoles and fish; may use 'bait' to lure prey. Lays 2–5 eggs stick nest, often over water.
Best viewing: Ndumo, Kruger-Lowveld, Nylsvley, St Lucia, Pilanesberg

Nigel Dennis/Images of Africa

Duncan Butchart

HAMERKOP *Scopus umbretta*

Habitat: shallows of freshwater lakes, pools, rivers, ponds and puddles **Length:** 55 cm **Wingspan:** 95 cm **Status:** fairly common resident

Unmistakable, plain brown bird with distinctive, backward-pointing crest and pointed bill, giving the head a hammer-like shape. Occurs singly or in pairs. Often spends long periods standing motionless at the water's edge, waiting for opportunities to catch frogs and other aquatic life; may scavenge roadkills. Call sounds like a squeaky gate being opened. Lays 3–9 eggs in huge, dome-shaped nest of twigs and mud placed in the fork of a large tree.
Best viewing: widespread in suitable habitat

Nigel Dennis/Images of Africa

HADEDA IBIS *Bostrychia hagedash*

Habitat: farmlands, fields and wooded suburbs; open grassland and savanna **Length:** 75 cm **Wingspan:** 110 cm **Status:** abundant resident

Heavy-bodied, short-legged ibis. Plumage is predominantly olive-green, shoulders have metallic sheen of purple and emerald. Forages most often beneath shady trees where insects and worms are extracted from the soil or among leaves. Groups fly to and from tree-top roosts at dawn and dusk. One of the noisiest birds. Up to 5 eggs are laid in a stick nest built within the canopy of a tree. Glossy Ibis *Plegadis falcinellus* is more slender with longer bill.
Best viewing: widespread in suitable habitat

Roger de la Harpe/Images of Africa

SOUTHERN BALD IBIS *Geronticus calvus*

Habitat: montane grassland, farmlands **Length:** 75–80 cm **Wingspan:** 110 cm **Status:** uncommon resident; vulnerable; endemic

Slender, dark greenish-blue ibis with bare, pink face and bald, scarlet crown. Scythe-shaped bill and legs are red. Occurs in pairs or small flocks that forage for insects and grubs in short grassland, ploughed or recently burned lands. Groups fly to and from tree-top roosts at dawn and dusk. Up to 3 eggs are laid in a platform of sticks placed in a cliff pothole or ledge.
Best viewing: Wakkerstroom, Dullstroom, Blyde Canyon, Giant's Castle, Golden Gate

Ariadne van Zandbergen/Images of Africa

AFRICAN SACRED IBIS *Threskiornis aethiopicus*

Habitat: shallows of freshwater wetlands, lagoons and coast; sewerage works and rubbish dumps **Length:** 85 cm **Wingspan:** 120 cm **Status:** common to locally abundant resident

Slender, white ibis with long legs and scythe-shaped bill. Naked black head and neck are distinctive. Breeding adult has tail adorned with black plumes. Flight feathers are tipped in black. Occurs in small flocks that forage in shallow water for insects and frogs, or scavenge. Flocks fly in V-formation to and from roosts. Name refers to its place in Egyptian mythology, where it featured prominently in hieroglyphics.
Best viewing: widespread in suitable habitat

WHITE STORK *Ciconia ciconia*

Habitat: cultivated lands, pastures, grassland and open savanna **Length:** 120 cm **Wingspan:** 165 cm **Status:** common, non-breeding migrant (Oct–Apr); some resident in south-western Cape

Large, white stork with black flight feathers, and red legs and bill. Like most storks, the legs may be washed white with excreta. Gregarious, gathering in flocks to feed on locusts and grasshoppers on dry land. Attracted to bush fires; snaps up fleeing insects and small, scorched animals. Flocks regularly soar in thermals and may stand in water to cool down. Black Stork *C. nigra* has glossy black head and neck; Abdim's Stork *C. abdimii* is dark with white belly.
Best viewing: widespread in suitable habitat

Nigel Dennis/Images of Africa

YELLOW-BILLED STORK *Mycteria ibis*

Habitat: pools in rivers, lakes, dams and marshes **Length:** 100 cm **Wingspan:** 160 cm **Status:** fairly common resident or nomad

Large, white stork with broad, down-curved, yellow bill, red facial skin and legs. When breeding, the mantle and wings are washed with pink. Immature is dull grey-white with pale bill. Individuals and groups feed in shallow water, typically wading with bill partly open and half-submerged, ready to snap up fish and frogs. Lays 2–4 eggs in stick bowl nest. Woolly-necked Stork *Ciconia episcopus* is glossy greenish-black with white neck, black face and red bill.
Best viewing: Ndumo, St Lucia, Kruger, Nylsvley

Nigel Dennis/Images of Africa

SADDLE-BILLED STORK *Ephippiorhynchus senegalensis*

Habitat: pools in large rivers, lakes and dams in Lowveld savanna **Length:** 150 cm **Wingspan:** 270 cm **Status:** sparse resident; endangered

Large stork with pied plumage, black legs with pink toes and 'knee' joints. Massive red bill is divided by a black bar and has a yellow, saddle-shaped shield on top. Male differs from female in having black (not yellow) eyes and a small, yellow wattle at base of bill. Immature lacks red on bill or legs. Occurs in pairs or family groups. Feeds on catfish and frogs in shallow water. Lays 2–4 eggs in stick platform nest on tree top, often far from water.
Best viewing: Kruger, Mapungubwe

Peter Pickford/Images of Africa

MARABOU STORK *Leptoptilos crumeniferus*

Habitat: open areas and wetlands in Lowveld savanna **Length:** 150 cm **Wingspan:** 280 cm **Status:** fairly common resident, largely restricted to wildlife reserves

Massive grey-backed stork with white underparts, enormous bill and naked head and neck. Pink face is sparsely covered with bristles. A sausage-shaped pouch hangs beneath the throat. Legs are grey, but often washed white with excreta. Feeds mostly on carrion and is attracted to fish stranded in shrinking pools. Lays 1–4 eggs in large stick bowl nest situated in tall tree.
Best viewing: Kruger, Mapungubwe

Nigel Dennis/Images of Africa

Hein von Hörsten/Images of Africa

COMMON OSTRICH *Struthio camelus*

Habitat: stony plains and short grassland
Length: 200 cm **Weight:** 100 kg **Status:** fairly common resident, abundant as domesticated livestock

Unmistakable, huge, flightless bird with long neck and legs. Male is predominantly black with ginger tail plumes; when breeding, pink scales on the shins become red. Female is dull grey-brown. Able to run at great speeds. Feeds on succulent plants, grasses, seed pods and flowers. Call is a deep boom. Several females lay their egg clutches in a single ground-scrape nest incubated by male (at night) and dominant female.
Best viewing: widespread in suitable habitat

Nigel Dennis/Images of Africa

SECRETARYBIRD *Sagittarius serpentarius*

Habitat: open grassland, savanna and scrubland
Length: 140 cm **Wingspan:** 215 cm
Status: uncommon resident

Large, terrestrial raptor with long legs and quill-like plumes protruding from back of head. Bare face is orange and legs are pink. Elongated tail feathers extend past the tail to provide a unique flight profile. Occurs in pairs in open country where snakes, lizards and rodents are chased, pounced upon and eaten. Two eggs are laid in a large platform nest on the canopy of a low *Acacia* or *Boscia* tree.
Best viewing: Kgalagadi, Golden Gate, Bontebok, Ithala, Mtn Zebra

Roger de la Harpe/Images of Africa

GREY CROWNED CRANE *Balearica regulorum*

Habitat: marshes, vleis, grassland, cultivated fields
Length: 110 cm **Wingspan:** 200 cm
Status: uncommon resident; vulnerable

Large, long-legged bird with distinctive crown of golden feathers. Sexes are alike. Immature is duller, with dark face and small crown. Occurs in pairs or small flocks when not breeding. Feeds primarily on seeds of grass and sedges as well as insects and frogs. Call is a trumpeted 'mahem' made in flight, or a booming duet. Two to four eggs are laid in a mound-like nest hidden near water. Wattled Crane *Bugeranus carunculatus* has white neck and head with grey cap.
Best viewing: Karkloof, Vernon Crooks, Wild Coast, Wakkerstroom

Albert Froneman/Images of Africa

BLUE CRANE *Anthropoides paradiseus*

Habitat: grassland, vleis, stony plains, cultivated lands
Length: 110 cm **Wingspan:** 200 cm **Status:** scarce to locally common resident; vulnerable; near-endemic

Large, long-legged bird with uniform, blue-grey plumage and trailing wing plumes. Head is a bulbous shape with a pale crown. Sexes alike. Immature is buffy, with a pale head. Occurs in pairs or flocks when not breeding; undertakes seasonal movements. Feeds on bulbs, tubers, seeds, insects and frogs. National Bird of South Africa but eastern population is in sharp decline. Call is a bugle-like 'kronk', often in duet. Lays 1 or 2 eggs in a ground scrape.
Best viewing: Overberg, Addo, Karkloof, Dullstroom, Wakkerstroom, Mountain Zebra

KORI BUSTARD *Ardeotis kori*

Habitat: stony plains and short grassland
Length: 120–150 cm **Wingspan:** 220–250 cm
Status: sparse to fairly common resident; vulnerable

Massive, grey-brown bird with white underparts and neck finely barred in grey. One of the world's heaviest flying birds, weighing up to 12 kg. A small, black crest protrudes from back of head. Pairs spend the day striding slowly in search of insects, lizards and seeds, or resting in shade. Elaborate courtship display includes puffing-out neck feathers. Lays 1 or 2 camouflaged eggs in a scrape near a grass tuft. Denham's Bustard *Neotis denhami* has rufous nape.
Best viewing: Kgalagadi, Kruger (Satara region), Mapungubwe

Peter Blackwell/Images of Africa

RED-CRESTED KORHAAN *Lophotis ruficrista*

Habitat: grassland and scrub **Length:** 50 cm
Status: common resident

Small, short-legged bustard with white, V-shaped markings on back. Chestnut-red crest is rarely visible. Male performs a dramatic aerial display by flying up then dropping groundwards as though shot, breaking its fall at the last moment. Call is a series of clicks followed by a drawn-out, piping whistle. Occurs in pairs. Relies on camouflage and stands motionless when detected. Feeds on insects, seeds and berries. Lays 1 or 2 eggs in a shallow ground scrape.
Best viewing: Kruger, Mapungubwe, Pilanesberg

Peter Pickford/Images of Africa

BLACK-BELLIED BUSTARD *Lissotis melanogaster*

Habitat: grassy clearings in savanna
Length: 64 cm **Status:** fairly common resident

Medium-sized, long-legged bustard with fawn back blotched in dark brown. Male has a black line extending from belly to chin, and white cheek patches. Female has a white belly. Occurs singly or in pairs. Territorial males frequently stand on top of termite mounds to utter their strange, frog-like call – a grunt followed by a pause and a pop. Feeds on insects, seeds and berries. Lays 1 or 2 eggs in a shallow ground scrape.
Best viewing: Kruger, Hluhluwe-iMfolozi, Mkhuze

Marietjie Oosthuizen

NORTHERN BLACK KORHAAN *Afrotis afraoides*

Habitat: dry grassland, Karoo scrubland
Length: 50 cm **Status:** common resident;
near-endemic

Small bustard with yellow legs. Male has a glossy black head, neck and underparts, with distinctive white 'ear' patches. Female is greyish-fawn all over. Occurs singly or in pairs. Territorial male calls with a harsh 'krraa-krraa-kra-kra-kra', from a termite mound or in flight; the display is a parachute with dangling legs. Feeds on insects, seeds and berries. Southern Black Korhaan *A. afra* has black wingtips visible in flight; occurs only in fynbos of south-western Cape.
Best viewing: Kgalagadi, Karoo, Golden Gate, Pilanesberg

Nigel Dennis/Images of Africa

Nigel Dennis/Images of Africa

EGYPTIAN GOOSE *Alopochen aegyptiaca*

Habitat: dams, rivers, estuaries, marshes, cultivated lands, fields **Length:** 60–75 cm
Status: abundant resident

Large, fawn and chestnut goose with a dark mask around the eyes. Occurs in pairs or small groups along rivers and at dams, but may congregate in sizeable flocks. Feeds mostly on grass, sedges and pondweed. Noisy and aggressive during the breeding season, chasing off rivals and other animals. Up to 20 eggs are laid in a large tree hole or Hamerkop nest. South African Shelduck *Tadorna cana* has head plain grey (male) or white (female).
Best viewing: widespread in suitable habitat

Nigel Dennis/Images of Africa

SPUR-WINGED GOOSE *Plectropterus gambensis*

Habitat: larger dams and wetlands in grassland; fynbos and Karoo **Length:** 95 cm (♂); 85 cm (♀)
Status: common resident

Massive, greenish-black goose with variable amount of white on face and belly. Bill and legs are pink. Male is much larger than female. Usually occurs in flocks that rest on mudflats or in shallows. Feeds on sedges, tubers and grass, moving nomadically in response to rain. Up to 14 eggs are laid in a nest among reeds. Comb Duck *Sarkidiornis melanotos* is smaller, with white underparts and grey bill that, in the male, develops a swollen, fleshy knob when breeding.
Best viewing: Marievale, Wakkerstroom, Nylsvley, Barberspan

Nigel Dennis/Images of Africa

WHITE-FACED WHISTLING-DUCK *Dendrocygna viduata*

Habitat: seasonal wetlands and pools in grassland and savanna **Length:** 48 cm **Status:** common to locally abundant resident

Long-necked duck with upright posture. Call is flute-like whistle. White face, chestnut neck and black-and-white, barred flanks are diagnostic. Gregarious, gathering in large flocks at water's edge. Feeds on aquatic tubers and pondweed, as well as grass seeds on dry land. Lays 7–13 eggs in nest bowl concealed in grass or sedge clumps, sometimes away from water. Fulvous Whistling-Duck *D. bicolor* has buffy head, face and underparts.
Best viewing: Ndumo, St Lucia, Nylsvley, Kruger-Lowveld

Nigel Dennis/Images of Africa

SOUTHERN POCHARD *Netta erythrophthalma*

Habitat: deeper water of dams, lakes and pans with emergent vegetation **Length:** 50 cm
Status: fairly common resident

Medium-sized duck with dark, cinnamon-brown head, pale grey-blue bill and scarlet eyes. Female is duller, with white facial markings and dark eyes. In flight, the white wing feathers are conspicuous. Occurs in pairs or small flocks. Dives or upends for seeds, rhizomes and snails. Up to 15 eggs are laid in a concealed nest at the waterside. Maccoa Duck *Oxyura maccoa* is smaller, with bright blue bill, dark eyes and stiff tail held upright or fanned on water surface.
Best viewing: widespread in suitable habitat

Nigel Dennis/Images of Africa

YELLOW-BILLED DUCK *Anas undulata*

Habitat: open water of lakes, pans, dams, rivers and estuaries **Length:** 56 cm
Status: common resident

Medium-sized duck with bright yellow bill with a black 'saddle' on top. Brown feathers are rimmed with buff, giving a spangled appearance. In flight, the turquoise-blue wing speculum is distinctive. Occurs in pairs or flocks on floodplains and in pans, less commonly on rivers. Feeds on aquatic plants by upending in water, also grazes and strips grass seeds. Up to 10 eggs are laid in grassy nest bowl, lined with down feathers, hidden among reeds.
Best viewing: widespread in suitable habitat

Duncan Butchart

RED-BILLED TEAL *Anas erythrorhyncha*

Habitat: shallow seasonal pans and dams with emergent vegetation; avoids rivers
Length: 48 cm **Status:** common resident or nomad

Small duck with diagnostic crimson-red bill and dark cap. Rather inconspicuous due to its habit of foraging among aquatic grasses and other vegetation. Feeds on aquatic plants, grass seeds and some invertebrates. Lays 5–12 eggs in a nest bowl lined with down feathers among sedges or grass. In winter, moulting birds gather in flocks on open water. Hottentot Teal *A. hottentota* has powder-blue bill.
Best viewing: widespread in suitable habitat

Nigel Dennis/Images of Africa

CAPE TEAL *Anas capensis*

Habitat: saltpans, estuaries, coastal lagoons, vleis, sewerage ponds **Length:** 46 cm
Status: common resident or nomad

Small duck with bright, scarlet eyes and pink bill; lacks the dark cap of the Red-billed Teal. In flight the white wing patch with green speculum is distinctive. Occurs in pairs or small flocks in open water or shallow bays. Feeds by filtering surface or submerging bill to obtain small invertebrates and pondweed. Often feeds with flamingos or other ducks. Lays 4–13 eggs in a feather-lined bowl hidden in aquatic vegetation.
Best viewing: West Coast, Barberspan, Rondevlei, Marievale

Nigel Dennis/Images of Africa

CAPE SHOVELER *Anas smithii*

Habitat: shallow seasonal pans, estuaries, saltpans, sewerage ponds **Length:** 53 cm
Status: fairly common resident; near-endemic

Medium-sized, speckled duck with long, compressed bill. Male has a pale greyish-brown head, with lemon-yellow eyes, orange-yellow legs. In flight, the turquoise-green wing speculum is distinctive. Occurs in pairs or large post-breeding flocks. Feeds on snails, invertebrates and plant matter, filtering the water surface with the shovel-shaped bill. Lays 5–13 eggs in a bowl lined with downy feathers. African Black Duck *A. sparsa* is uniform chocolate brown with dark eyes.
Best viewing: Barberspan, Rondevlei, West Coast, Karkloof, Marievale

Nigel Dennis/Images of Africa

Nigel Dennis/Images of Africa

BLACK CRAKE *Amaurornis flavirostris*

Habitat: sedges and reeds on fringe of still or slow-flowing water **Length:** 20–22 cm
Status: common resident

Small, jet-black bird with lime-yellow bill, bright red legs and red eyes. Inconspicuous and shy but much less so than other crakes. Very long toes allow it to run across floating vegetation. Often located by its harsh, throaty warble call, frequently a duet between a pair. Aquatic insects are the main food, also feeds on birds' eggs and plants. Lays 2–6 eggs in a well-hidden nest among reeds.
Best viewing: widespread in suitable habitat

Albert Froneman/Images of Africa

COMMON MOORHEN *Gallinula chloropus*

Habitat: all freshwater habitats with fringing vegetation **Length:** 30–38 cm
Status: common resident

Black, hen-like bird with red frontal shield and yellow-tipped bill. Legs and feet are lime-yellow and there is a white bar running down each flank. When out of the water, the short tail is repeatedly flicked up and down to reveal the snow-white vent. Smaller, with a lighter build than Red-knobbed Coot with which it often shares habitat. Feeds on aquatic plants and invertebrates. Lays 4–9 eggs in a well-concealed nest.
Best viewing: widespread in suitable habitat

Nigel DennisImages of Africa

RED-KNOBBED COOT *Fulica cristata*

Habitat: open water of dams, pans and seasonal wetlands **Length:** 36–42 cm
Status: common to locally abundant resident

Black, hen-like bird with white bill and frontal shield, red eyes and a pair of red knobs on the forehead. Pugnacious and aggressive; waterborne chases between rivals are commonplace. Congregates in great numbers when not breeding. Feeds mainly on aquatic plants but also grazes grass. Lays 2–6 eggs on a floating mound of sedges and reeds. African Purple Swamphen *Porphyrio madagascariensis* has scarlet bill and frontal shield and royal blue underparts.
Best viewing: widespread in suitable habitat

Albert Froneman

LITTLE GREBE *Tachybaptus ruficollis*

Habitat: lakes, dams, seasonal pans, pools in rivers and estuaries **Length:** 20 cm
Status: common resident

Small, duck-like waterbird. Chestnut neck and pale spot at the base of the bill are diagnostic. Dives repeatedly below the water surface when foraging for dragonfly larvae, small fish, tadpoles and frogs. Call is a loud trill, often uttered during courtship or chases with rivals. Lays 2–7 eggs in a floating nest of clumped water plants. Black-necked Grebe *Podiceps nigricollis* has red eyes; Great Crested Grebe *P. cristatus* is much larger with long bill.x
Best viewing: widespread in suitable habitat

AFRICAN JACANA *Actophilornis africanus*

Habitat: still and slow-moving water with water lilies and other aquatic vegetation
Length: 28 cm **Status:** common resident

Slender, chestnut-red bird with white face and neck, and pale blue shield of bare skin on the forehead. Immature has white eyes. Long toes enable it to walk on floating vegetation. Feeds mostly on aquatic insects, also snails, small fish and tadpoles. Occurs singly or in noisy groups, often near Hippo. Lays 4 superbly camouflaged eggs in floating nest of sedge stems. Lesser Jacana *Microparra capensis* is much smaller with short bill and rufous cap.
Best viewing: Ndumo, Kruger-Lowveld, Nylsvley, St Lucia, Kosi Bay

Nigel Dennis/Images of Africa

BLACK-WINGED STILT *Himantopus himantopus*

Habitat: shallows of freshwater wetlands, saltpans, coastal lagoons **Length:** 35–40 cm
Status: common resident

Slender, black-and-white wader with extraordinarily long red legs and thin, pointed bill. Immature has grey smudges on the head. Usually forages alone or in loose groups. Probes mud for worms and insect larvae. Prone to seasonal movement depending upon water levels. Lays 2–5 eggs in a saucer-shaped mound, hidden at the water's edge. Pied Avocet *Recurvirostra avosetta* has sharply upturned bill, black head and pale grey legs.
Best viewing: widespread in suitable habitat

Peter Pickford/Images of Africa

SWIFT TERN *Sterna bergii*

Habitat: shallow coastal waters, beaches, rocky shores **Length:** 48 cm **Wingspan:** 130 cm
Status: common resident

Large, grey-backed tern with white underparts and yellow bill. Breeding adult has black crown with white forehead patch. Non-breeding adult has smaller, dusky-black crown. Immature is blotched and barred. Gregarious, flocks roost on beaches and at estuaries. Small fish are caught after a plunge dive. A single egg is laid on a scrape in the sand. Lesser Crested Tern *S. bengalensis* has orange bill; Caspian Tern *S. caspia* has red bill.
Best viewing: Robben Island, Plettenberg Bay, Lambert's Bay, Algoa Bay

Albert Froneman/Images of Africa

COMMON TERN *Sterna hirundo*

Habitat: shallow coastal waters, beaches, rocky shores
Length: 34 cm **Wingspan:** 80 cm **Status:** abundant non-breeding summer visitor (Aug/Sep–May)

Small tern with grey wings, back and tail, and white underparts. Most birds seen in SA are in non-breeding plumage with black, ivory-tipped bill; breeding adult has a black crown with a black-tipped red bill. Flocks roost on beaches and at estuaries. Small fish are caught after a dive. The commonest of several confusingly similar marine terns: Arctic Tern *S. paradisaea* and Antarctic Tern *S. vittata* have no pale tip to bill, wings protrude beyond tail when sitting.
Best viewing: entire South African coastline

John Graham

Albert Froneman/Images of Africa

CROWNED LAPWING *Vanellus coronatus*

Habitat: short grass and clearings, fields
Length: 30 cm **Status:** common to abundant resident

Sandy-brown lapwing with a white underbelly, black-and-white crown. Long legs and base of bill are red. Occurs in pairs when breeding, or flocks during winter. Feeds on termites, beetles and other invertebrates. Lays 2 or 3 eggs in a ground scrape. In defence of eggs and young, adults will dive-bomb intruders, call loudly and feign injury to distract predators. Senegal Lapwing *V. lugubris* has grey bill and legs.
Best viewing: widespread in suitable habitat

Federico Veronesi

AFRICAN WATTLED LAPWING *Vanellus senegallus*

Habitat: waterlogged grasslands, floodplains, fringes of dams **Length:** 34 cm
Status: common resident

Greyish-brown lapwing with pendulous, yellow wattles at base of bill. Long legs are bright yellow. Occurs in pairs when breeding, or small flocks during winter. Feeds on termites, beetles and other invertebrates. Lays 2 or 3 eggs in a ground scrape. In defence of eggs and young, adults will dive-bomb intruders, call loudly and feign injury to distract predators. White-crowned Lapwing *V. albiceps* has white underparts and wing bars.
Best viewing: widespread in suitable habitat

Nigel Dennis/Images of Africa

BLACKSMITH LAPWING *Vanellus armatus*

Habitat: mudflats of dams and wetlands, short grassland and fields **Length:** 30 cm
Status: common to abundant resident

Conspicuous black, grey and white lapwing with dark red eyes. Bill and long legs are grey. Occurs in pairs or family groups in open habitats, often near water. Feeds on small terrestrial invertebrates. Lays up to 4 eggs in a ground scrape, relying on egg and nestling camouflage for protection. When nests are threatened, the parents rise into the air above the intruders, dive-bombing and chanting their metallic 'tink-tink' call.
Best viewing: widespread in suitable habitat

Shaen Adey/Images of Africa

AFRICAN BLACK OYSTERCATCHER *Haematopus moquini*

Habitat: rocky shores, beaches, estuarine mudflats
Length: 44 cm **Status:** common resident;
near-endemic

Pitch-black wading-bird with scarlet bill and legs. Eyes are red, surrounded by yellow eye-rings. Sexes alike but the female is slightly larger. Usually seen in pairs, but groups gather to forage on mudflats and at night roosts. Mussels and limpets are levered off rocks with the flattened bill. Lays 1 or 2 camouflaged eggs in a sand scrape. Ruddy Turnstone *Arenaria interpres* has mottled upperparts, black bill and orange legs.
Best viewing: Tsitsikamma, Robben Island, West Coast, De Hoop, Plettenberg Bay, Dwesa

SPOTTED THICK-KNEE *Burhinus capensis*

Habitat: stony plains and clearings with scattered shrubs **Length:** 43 cm
Status: common resident

Cryptically coloured, lapwing-like bird. The long legs and large eyes are glowing yellow. Back is blotched in fawn and brown. Nocturnal; feeds on beetles, termites and other invertebrates. A piercing, flute-like call is uttered after dark. Roosts in shade of shrubs by day. Up to 3 camouflaged eggs are laid in a ground scrape where they and the young are vigorously defended. Water Thick-knee *B. vermiculatus* has white wing bar and is always found near water.
Best viewing: widespread in suitable habitat

Duncan Butchart

DOUBLE-BANDED COURSER *Rhinoptilus africanus*

Habitat: open areas in dry scrubland and semi-arid savanna **Length:** 22 cm
Status: common resident

Cryptically coloured, lapwing-like bird with two narrow, black chest bars. In flight, chestnut wings are conspicuous. Usually in pairs; standing in shade during heat of the day. Feeds on termites and other insects. Call is a plaintive whistle. Single, camouflaged egg is laid on bare ground. Bronze-winged Courser *R. chalcopterus* has red legs and eye-rings; Temminck's Courser *Cursorius temminckii* and Burchell's Courser *C. rufus* are plain, buffy-rufous.
Best viewing: Kgalagadi, Augrabies, Karoo

Ariadne van Zandbergen/Images of Africa

THREE-BANDED PLOVER *Charadrius tricollaris*

Habitat: mudflats of dams, lakes, river pools and estuaries **Length:** 18 cm
Status: common resident

Tiny, brown-backed plover with white underparts, pink legs and broad, red eye-rings. Name refers to the chest bands: two black and one white. Usually occurs in pairs, searching for small insects and worms. Not too shy, often allows a close approach. Lays 2 camouflaged eggs in a ground scrape. Common Ringed Plover *C. hiaticula* is a summer migrant with yellow-orange legs; Kittlitz's Plover *C. pecuarius* has grey legs and bill.
Best viewing: widespread in suitable habitat

Nigel Dennis/Images of Africa

WHITE-FRONTED PLOVER *Charadrius marginatus*

Habitat: beaches and dunes, rocky shores, broad sandy rivers **Length:** 18 cm
Status: fairly common resident

Tiny, sandy-backed plover with white collar and underparts. A dark line runs between the bill and black eyes. Adults live in pairs on beaches, lake shores or sandy riverbeds. Immature birds may gather in small flocks. May remain still to avoid detection. Feeds on invertebrates by day and night. Up to 3 camouflaged eggs are laid in a shallow scrape on the sand. Chestnut-banded Plover *C. pallidus* has narrow, chestnut band on throat, prefers saline waterbodies.
Best viewing: widespread in suitable habitat

Albert Froneman/Images of Africa

Nigel Dennis/Images of Africa

COMMON SANDPIPER *Actitis hypoleucos*

Habitat: shallows of rivers, fringes of freshwater dams, flooded grassland **Length:** 20 cm **Status:** common non-breeding migrant (Sep–Apr), some over-winter

Small, grey-brown wader with fairly short, grey-green legs and thin bill. Plain brown back and white shoulder patch in the shape of an inverted C are diagnostic. Forages alone on mudflats, stony rivers or flooded grassland. When walking, the tail is bobbed up and down. White wing bars are conspicuous in flight. Probes mud for invertebrates. Ruff *Philomachus pugnax* has scaled pattern to back and wings, pale orange legs and chubby appearance; gregarious. **Best viewing:** widespread in suitable habitat

Duncan Butchart

WOOD SANDPIPER *Tringa glareola*

Habitat: shallows and shorelines of seasonal pans, dams, lagoons and estuaries **Length:** 20 cm **Status:** common non-breeding migrant (Sep–Apr); some over-winter

Small, grey-brown wader with fairly long, yellow legs and a thin bill. Dark back is boldly spotted in white, white eye-stripe extends to back of the head. Usually solitary, but often in the company of other wading birds. Individuals may forage around a single body of water, but tend to space themselves out. In flight, the white rump is conspicuous. Probes mud for invertebrates. Marsh Sandpiper *T. stagnatilis* is more slender with longer legs and bill **Best viewing:** widespread in suitable habitat

Nigel Dennis/Images of Africa

CURLEW SANDPIPER *Calidris ferruginea*

Habitat: shallows and mudflats of coastal lagoons and bays, freshwater wetlands **Length:** 20 cm **Status:** common non-breeding migrant (Sep–Apr); some over-winter

Small, grey-backed wader with diagnostic down-curved bill. Back feathers are pale rimmed, rump is white. The white eyebrows are usually conspicuous. Highly gregarious, gathering in flocks of up to several thousand at estuaries. Some assume rust-coloured breeding plumage in April, prior to their long journey north to Siberian breeding grounds. Probes mud for invertebrate prey. Sanderling *C. alba* is smaller with black shoulder patches. **Best viewing:** Langebaan, Richard's Bay, Plettenberg Bay

Nigel Dennis/Images of Africa

COMMON GREENSHANK *Tringa nebularia*

Habitat: shallows of freshwater wetlands, estuaries and shorelines **Length:** 32 cm **Status:** fairly common non-breeding migrant (Sep–Apr); some over-winter

Slender, medium-sized, pale grey wader with long, grey-green legs. Slightly upturned bill is grey-green at its base. Back feathers have a scaly appearance. In flight, the white rump is conspicuous. Usually seen singly or in the company of other waders. When disturbed it flies off with a sharp 'chew-chew-chew' call. Probes mud for worms and other invertebrate prey. Common Whimbrel *Numenius phaeopus* has sharply decurved bill and barred flanks. **Best viewing:** widespread in suitable habitat

CRESTED FRANCOLIN *Dendroperdix sephaena*

Habitat: thickets and woodland in savanna
Length: 33 cm **Status:** common resident

Fawn, hen-like bird with intricately patterned plumage and white eyebrows. Bill is grey and the legs orange-pink. Occurs in pairs or family parties; walks in hunched posture. Call is a harsh, rattling 'chee-chatla' repeated excitedly at dawn, less often at dusk. Termites and other insects are the chief food. Lays 2–5 eggs in a concealed ground nest. Coqui Francolin *Peliperdix coqui* has yellow legs; male has a bright buffy-orange head.
Best viewing: Pilanesberg, Kruger-Lowveld, Nylsvley

Nigel Dennis/Images of Africa

SWAINSON'S SPURFOWL *Pternistis swainsonii*

Habitat: open savanna, short grassland, farmland
Length: 33–38 cm **Status:** common resident

Dark brown, hen-like bird with streaked plumage and bare red skin around eyes. The upper bill and legs are black. Call is harsh crowing, often made from a termite mound or branch of a tree. Nervous and quick to retreat into cover. Feeds mostly on seeds, berries and insects. Lays 3–12 eggs in a ground scrape hidden among vegetation. Red-necked Spurfowl *P. afer* has red legs; prefers moist thickets and forest edge.
Best viewing: widespread in suitable habitat

Albert Froneman/Images of Africa

CAPE SPURFOWL *Pternistis capensis*

Habitat: coastal fynbos, scrub and farmland
Length: 35 cm **Status:** common to abundant resident; endemic

Dark brown hen-like bird with delicately patterned plumage. The bill is grey with some red on the lower mandible; legs are orange-red. Occurs in pairs or family parties that emerge from dense cover to feed on invertebrates, bulbs, seeds, grain and fallen fruit. Call is a loud, repetitive 'kak-keek'. Lays 4–8 eggs in a concealed nest scrape. Natal Spurfowl *P. natalensis* has orange bill and legs; occurs in eastern half of South Africa.
Best viewing: West Coast, Kirstenbosch, Betty's Bay

Ryan Ebedes

HELMETED GUINEAFOWL *Numida meleagris*

Habitat: short grassland and bare plains, farmlands
Length: 54–58 cm **Status:** abundant resident

Distinctive, charcoal-grey bird profusely spotted with white. Bare facial skin is predominantly blue, with a variable amount of red around the eyes. Horny, helmet-shaped casque on the crown. Occurs in flocks; drinks regularly. Feeds on termites, beetles and seeds. Lays 6–8 eggs on the ground among dense vegetation. Crested Guineafowl *Guttera edouardi* has black head plumes and white bill; occurs in coastal forest and Lowveld thickets.
Best viewing: widespread in suitable habitat

Nigel Dennis/Images of Africa

Roger de la Harpe/Images of Africa

CAPE VULTURE *Gyps coprotheres*

Habitat: open grasslands and savanna
Length: 110 cm **Wingspan:** 250 cm
Status: locally common but declining resident;
vulnerable; near-endemic

Large, cream-coloured vulture with a long, almost bare neck. Adult has dark blue neck skin and yellow eyes; immature has pink neck and dark eyes. Soars in thermals or mountain updraughts. Gregarious scavenger; dozens feed at a carcass. Nests colonially on steep cliff faces. A single egg is laid in a bulky nest on a ledge. Vulnerable to poisons, electrocution on powerlines and food shortages.
Best viewing: Marakele, Drakensberg, Magaliesberg, De Hoop, Umthamvuna, Blouberg

Nigel Dennis/Images of Africa

WHITE-BACKED VULTURE *Gyps africanus*

Habitat: open savanna **Length:** 95 cm
Wingspan: 220 cm **Status:** locally common but
declining resident; vulnerable and largely restricted to
wildlife reserves

Large, brown vulture with a long, almost bare neck. Adult becomes paler with age, ranging from tawny to cream. The snow-white back of the adult is visible only in flight. Immature is dark brown with pale streaks, lacks the white back. Gregarious scavenger, with hundreds gathering to feed at a large carcass. A single egg is laid in a stick nest situated on canopy of a tall tree; usually in loose colony along drainage line. Vulnerable to poisons.
Best viewing: Kruger, Kgalagadi, Kimberley, Mkhuze

Tony Camacho/Images of Africa

LAPPET-FACED VULTURE *Aegypius tracheliotus*

Habitat: open savanna and semi-desert
Length: 110 cm **Wingspan:** 260–290 cm
Status: sparse to uncommon resident; vulnerable and
largely restricted to wildlife reserves

Massive, dark brown vulture with a pink face and huge, horn-coloured bill. The adult has a white breast with dark streaks and white leggings. Immature has a pale face and little or no white on the body. Usually seen in pairs. Dominates other vulture species at carcasses. A single egg is laid in a large platform nest on the canopy of a spiny or thorny tree.
Best viewing: Kgalagadi, Kruger, Mapungubwe, Mkhuze

Duncan Butchart

WHITE-HEADED VULTURE *Aegypius occipitalis*

Habitat: open savanna **Length:** 85 cm
Wingspan: 220 cm **Status:** sparse resident; vulnerable
and largely restricted to wildlife reserves

Large, black vulture with orange bill and sky-blue cere. Adult has a white top to the head and white leggings; the face is flushed pink when excited. Female differs from male in having white secondary feathers on the wings. Immature has a brown head and leggings. Occurs singly or in pairs. May catch its own prey but feeds mostly on carrion. A single egg laid in stick nest on top of a tall tree. Hooded Vulture *Necrosyrtes monachus* is smaller, with thin grey bill.
Best viewing: Kruger, Kgalagadi, Mkhuze

BEARDED VULTURE *Gypaetus barbatus*

Habitat: high mountains **Length:** 110 cm
Wingspan: 270 cm **Status:** sparse resident;
vulnerable to poisons

Large vulture with slender, pointed wings and long, wedge-shaped tail. Head is fully feathered, with a strange tuft of feathers forming a 'beard' below the bill. Adult has pale face with red-rimmed eyes, and rusty-ochre underparts. Immature has dark head and face with streaky underparts. Soars on mountain updrafts. Feeds mostly on bones, but also takes carrion. Lays 2 eggs in stick nest within a pothole on a cliff, but only one chick is reared.
Best viewing: Giant's Castle, Golden Gate

Nigel Dennis/Images of Africa

AFRICAN FISH-EAGLE *Haliaeetus vocifer*

Habitat: still or flowing water in rivers, dams and lakes; estuaries and seashore **Length:** 73 cm (♀); 63 cm (♂)
Wingspan: 190–240 cm **Status:** locally common resident

Unmistakable, chestnut-brown eagle with snow-white head and chest. Sexes alike but female larger. Immature is mottled in brown and white. The evocative 'kyow-kow-kow' call is made in flight or from a tree. Pairs often perch within sight of each other, swooping down to grasp fish from the water, or to steal a meal from another bird. Lays 2 eggs in a stick nest, usually below the canopy of a tall tree. Osprey *Pandion haliaetus* has dark line through face.
Best viewing: widespread in suitable habitat

Nigel Dennis/Images of Africa

MARTIAL EAGLE *Polemaetus bellicosus*

Habitat: savanna, scrub, heathland and forest edge
Length: 83 cm (♀); 78 cm (♂) **Wingspan:** 195–260 cm
Status: uncommon resident; vulnerable

Large eagle with white breast finely spotted in brown, and brown back and head peaked with a small crest. The eyes are yellow. In flight, the dark underwings are diagnostic. Immature is white below and pale brown above. Preys on animals up to the size of Steenbok but favours monitor lizards and guineafowl. A single egg is laid in a stick nest below the canopy of a tall tree. Black-chested Snake-Eagle *Circaetus pectoralis* has unspotted white underparts.
Best viewing: Kgalagadi, Kruger, Bontebok, Namaqua, Addo, Ithala, Golden Gate

Peter Pickford/Images of Africa

AFRICAN CROWNED EAGLE *Stephanoaetus coronatus*

Habitat: montane and coastal forest
Length: 90 cm (♀); 80 cm (♂) **Wingspan:** 180–210 cm
Status: uncommon resident

Large eagle with barred and blotched, buffy underparts. Head is peaked with a small crest, the eyes are yellow. Immature is white below, pale grey above. Call is a repetitive whistle 'kewee-kewee-kewee', usually in aerial display flight. Preys mostly on hyrax and monkeys. Two eggs are laid in a large stick nest in the fork of a large, evergreen tree; only one nestling survives. African Hawk-Eagle *Aquila spilogaster* is smaller, with black-streaked white underparts.
Best viewing: Oribi Gorge, Umgeni, Nature's Valley, Woodbush, Soutpansberg, Mpumalanga escarpment

Duncan Butchart

Albert Froneman/Images of Africa

VERREAUX'S EAGLE *Aquila verreauxii*

Habitat: mountainous areas with cliffs
Length: 96 cm (♀); 80 cm (♂) **Wingspan:** 190–210 cm
Status: fairly common resident

Large, jet-black eagle that never strays far from mountainous habitat. Adult is unmistakable, with a distinctive white cross pattern visible on the back when the bird is in flight. Immature is mottled in brown and fawn. Persecuted by small stock farmers, but Rock Hyrax (a grazing competitor of sheep) is its favoured prey. Lays 2 eggs in a bulky stick nest on a cliff ledge, but only one nestling survives. Nest sites are typically used for decades.
Best viewing: widespread in suitable habitat

Federico Veronesi

LONG-CRESTED EAGLE *Lophaetus occipitalis*

Habitat: woodland adjacent to marshes, forest edge, plantations, roadsides **Length:** 56 cm
Wingspan: 115 cm **Status:** locally common resident

Small, dark-brown eagle with distinctive crest of floppy feathers. Feet, cere and eyes are yellow. Male differs from female in having unblotched white leggings. In flight the boldly barred tail and white wing 'windows' are distinctive. Immature has short crest. Spends much of day on a perch, ready to pounce on vlei rats and other prey. Lays 1 or 2 eggs in a stick nest under canopy of *Eucalyptus* or other tall tree.
Best viewing: Nelspruit, White River, Karkloof, Hogsback, Tzaneen, Magoebaskloof

Nigel Dennis/Images of Africa

TAWNY EAGLE *Aquila rapax*

Habitat: open savanna and scrubland
Length: 77 cm (♀); 65 cm (♂) **Wingspan:** 165–185 cm
Status: uncommon resident; vulnerable to poisons and largely restricted to wildlife reserves

Large eagle with variable plumage: may be rufous or blonde, but most are tawny-brown. Female is often darker. The feet and cere are yellow. Preys and scavenges on a variety of small animals and often steals kills of other birds. Lays 2 eggs in stick nest built on canopy of a tall tree; only one nestling survives. Steppe Eagle *A. nipalensis* has gape extending beyond eye; Brown Snake-Eagle *Circaetus cinereus* has glowing yellow eyes and bare legs.
Best viewing: Kgalagadi, Kruger, Mapungubwe, Hluhluwe-iMfolozi

Peter Pickford/Images of Africa

WAHLBERG'S EAGLE *Aquila wahlbergi*

Habitat: woodland **Length:** 60 cm (♀); 55 cm (♂)
Wingspan: 140 cm **Status:** common breeding migrant (Aug–Mar)

Small, brown eagle with plumage varying from dark chocolate to blonde, usually medium brown. When perched, the diagnostic small crest is visible at the back of the head. In flight, the comparatively long tail is usually held closed (rather than fanned). Preys on small animals, from gamebirds to flying termites. A single egg is laid in a stick nest below the canopy of a tall tree. Booted Eagle *A. pennatus* has white shoulder patches; flies with fanned tail.
Best viewing: Kruger-Lowveld, Nylsvley, Marakele, Pilanesberg, Mapungubwe

YELLOW-BILLED KITE *Milvus parasitus*

Habitat: savanna, farmlands, villages, roadsides, coastal scrub **Length:** 55 cm **Wingspan:** 145 cm **Status:** common breeding migrant (Jul–Apr)

Medium-sized, brown raptor with long, dexterous wings. Broad, triangular tail, often held in a V-shape, is used as a rudder in flight. Legs, cere and bill of the adult are yellow. Immature has a black bill. Obtains most food by scavenging, but agile and also catches prey in flight. Up to 3 eggs are laid in stick nest within foliage of a leafy tree. Black Kite *M. migrans* has pale grey head and pale yellow eyes; non-breeding summer migrant.
Best viewing: widespread in suitable habitat

Ariadne van Zandbergen/Images of Africa

STEPPE BUZZARD *Buteo vulpinus*

Habitat: open grassland, farmlands, plantation fringes, roadsides **Length:** 50 cm (♀); 44 cm (♂) **Wingspan:** 110–130 cm **Status:** common non-breeding migrant (Sep–Apr)

Medium-sized, brown raptor with a smudgy, pale bar on the breast. The cere and legs are yellow. Much variation in plumage occurs. In flight, the dark tips of the feathers and pale wing panels are noticeable. Perches for long periods on telephone poles and fence posts. Drops down to prey mostly on large insects and rodents. Loose flocks can be seen on migratory passage flight. Forest Buzzard *B. trizonatus* has heavily blotched underparts; resident and vocal.
Best viewing: widespread in suitable habitat

Peter Pickford/Images of Africa

JACKAL BUZZARD *Buteo rufofuscus*

Habitat: hills and mountains including sea cliffs, open Karoo scrubland **Length:** 55 cm (♀); 44 cm (♂) **Wingspan:** 110–130 cm **Status:** common resident; near-endemic

Medium-sized raptor with charcoal-grey back and wings. The tail and breast are chestnut. The underwings show white wing panels. Immature is mottled rufous on the back and front. Often 'hangs' in the air in a stiff breeze, or soars on updraughts. Perches for long periods, dropping down on rodents and lizards. Lays 2 eggs in a stick nest on a cliff ledge but only one nestling survives.
Best viewing: widespread in suitable habitat

Nigel Dennis/Images of Africa

BATELEUR *Terathopius ecaudatus*

Habitat: flat terrain in savanna **Length:** 55–70 cm **Wingspan:** 170–185 cm **Status:** locally common resident; vulnerable to poisons so restricted to wildlife reserves

Stocky, black and rufous eagle with scarlet face and legs. In low, rocking flight it appears almost tailless. Female has thinner black line on the trailing edge of the white wings. Immature is plain brown with dark eyes. Feeds on birds, reptiles, small mammals and carrion. Immature birds often join vultures at carcasses. A single egg is laid in a stick nest below the canopy of a tree, often along watercourses.
Best viewing: Kruger, Kgalagadi, Ndumo, Mkhuze, Hluhluwe-iMfolozi, Mapungubwe

Nigel Dennis/Images of Africa

Nigel Dennis/Images of Africa

BLACK-SHOULDERED KITE *Elanus caeruleus*

Habitat: grassland, Karoo scrubland, farmlands, fynbos, open savanna **Length:** 30 cm **Wingspan:** 80 cm **Status:** common to abundant resident

Small, pale grey raptor with snow-white head and underparts. Feet and cere are yellow, eyes are bright red. Immature is blotched in ash-brown and white. Flies with languid beats like a seagull. Often perches on the highest available perch, wags its tail while peering down. Regularly hovers above grassland before dropping onto prey; usually the diurnal Four-striped Grass Mouse. Lays 3 or 4 eggs in twig nest within a large, leafy shrub or tree.
Best viewing: widespread in suitable habitat

Nigel Dennis/Images of Africa

GABAR GOSHAWK *Melierax gabar*

Habitat: dry *Acacia* savanna, wooded watercourses in arid areas **Length:** 36 cm (♀); 28 cm (♂) **Wingspan:** 60 cm **Status:** fairly common resident

Small, pale grey raptor with red legs and cere, and red eyes. The throat and chest are grey, with fine barring on the belly. Immature is brown and blotched but, like the adults, displays a distinctive white rump in flight. All black melanistic form also occurs. Preys mostly on small birds. Lays 2–4 eggs in a nest disguised with web of social spiders, concealed in a bush. Lizard Buzzard *Kaupifalco monogrammicus* is stockier, with black streak on throat.
Best viewing: Kgalagadi, Pilanesberg, Madikwe, Kruger

Peter Pickford/Images of Africa

AFRICAN GOSHAWK *Accipiter tachiro*

Habitat: montane and coastal forest, wooded suburbs **Length:** 45 cm (♀); 38 cm (♂) **Wingspan:** 65–85 cm **Status:** common resident

Medium-sized hawk. Sexually dimorphic: female is much larger, with dark brown upperparts; male has pale grey head and back with finer rufous barring on chest. Legs and eyes are yellow, cere is grey. Keeps to dense cover, bursting out in pursuit of birds and arboreal lizards. Call is loud 'chip!' made in flight or at perch. Up to 3 eggs are laid in a stick nest concealed within foliage. Shikra *A. badius* has red eyes; Little Sparrowhawk *A. minullus* is dove-sized.
Best viewing: Kirstenbosch, Tsitsikamma, Woodbush, Nelspruit, KwaZulu-Natal coast and Midlands

Nigel Dennis/Images of Africa

SOUTHERN PALE CHANTING GOSHAWK *Melierax canorus*

Habitat: open Karoo scrub and Kalahari savanna **Length:** 54 cm (♀); 48 cm (♂) **Wingspan:** 95–110 cm **Status:** common resident; near-endemic

Large, pale grey hawk with long, red legs. Pale underbelly is finely barred. Perches in an erect posture on open branches or telephone poles. Brown immature can be told from other hawks by its long legs and erect posture. Captures lizards, snakes, large insects, birds and rodents after pounce or chase. Call is a flute-like wail. Lays 1 or 2 eggs in a stick nest within a thorn tree. Dark Chanting Goshawk *M. metabates* occurs in eastern Lowveld.
Best viewing: Kgalagadi, Namaqua, Karoo, Augrabies, Camdeboo

AFRICAN HARRIER-HAWK *Polyboroides typus*

Habitat: wooded gorges, drainage lines and suburbs, forest edge **Length:** 65 cm **Wingspan:** 160 cm **Status:** fairly common resident

Medium-sized, small-headed raptor with broad wings and long tail. Adult is pale grey with bare yellow face, flushing pink when excited. In flight, the black tail, with a single, broad white band, is distinctive. Immature is brown and buff. Flies with buoyant wingbeats. Feeds primarily on nestling birds. Up to 3 eggs are laid in a stick nest built within a tall tree. African Marsh-Harrier *Circus ranivorus* has pale eyes, long wings and long tail; flies low over marshes.
Best viewing: widespread in suitable habitat

Albert Froneman/Images of Africa

AMUR FALCON *Falco amurensis*

Habitat: cultivated lands, grassland, open savanna, roadsides **Length:** 30 cm **Wingspan:** 75 cm **Status:** locally common non-breeding migrant (Oct–Apr)

Small, slim raptor with pointed wings, bright red feet, cere and eye-rings. Sexually dimorphic: male is uniform grey with chestnut vent and white underwings; female has pale, streaked underparts. Highly gregarious; small to large flocks feed mostly on grasshoppers and locusts. Large numbers congregate to roost in tall *Eucalyptus* trees at sunset. Red-footed Falcon *F. vespertinus* favours drier west of SA; female has buffy underparts, male lacks white underwings.
Best viewing: widespread in suitable habitat

Chris van Rooyen

ROCK KESTREL *Falco rupicolus (tinnunculus)*

Habitat: open grassland, scrubland and Karoo; breeds in mountainous areas **Length:** 32 cm **Wingspan:** 75 cm **Status:** common resident

Small, slim raptor with pointed wings. Chestnut back is finely spotted in black, the pale grey head is finely streaked. Sexes are alike but male has a terminal band on the tail. Occurs singly or in pairs. Preys mostly on grasshoppers and rodents. Up to 6 eggs are laid in a pothole on a cliff or tall building. Lesser Kestrel *F. naumanni* has plain grey head and unspotted, rufous back; gregarious summer migrant. Greater Kestrel *F. rupicoloides* has pale eyes.
Best viewing: widespread in suitable habitat

Peter Pickford/Images of Africa

LANNER FALCON *Falco biarmicus*

Habitat: open flat or hilly country, mountains, farmlands **Length:** 42 cm (♀); 36 cm (♂) **Wingspan:** 90–115 cm **Status:** fairly common resident

Medium-sized, grey-backed raptor with pointed wings and buffy underparts. The rufous crown and dark hood extend as 'tear marks' below the eyes. Immature is boldly streaked below. Flies rapidly in pursuit of birds up to its own size. Lays up to 5 eggs in a stick nest built by crows or other birds, often on pylons or cliffs, but also on ledges of tall buildings. Peregrine Falcon *F. peregrinus* has black head; Eurasian Hobby *F. subbuteo* has black head and rufous vent.
Best viewing: Marakele, Richtersveld, Kgalagadi, Drakensberg

Roger de la Harpe/Images of Africa

Nigel Dennis/Images of Africa

NAMAQUA SANDGROUSE *Pterocles namaqua*

Habitat: gravel and sandy plains **Length:** 25 cm
Status: common resident; near-endemic

Sand-coloured, dove-like bird with short legs and pointed wings. Male has a plain cinnamon head and underparts with an indistinct double breast band. Female is cryptically coloured with streaks and bars. Flight is fast and direct. Forages on the ground for seeds. Usually in pairs, but flocks gather to drink in early morning and evening. Lays 2 or 3 camouflaged eggs in a ground scrape. Burchell's Sandgrouse *P. burchelli* has white spots on back and chest.
Best viewing: Kgalagadi, Augrabies, Tankwa-Karoo, Camdeboo

Rita Meyer/Images of Africa

DOUBLE-BANDED SANDGROUSE *Pterocles bicinctus*

Habitat: gravel plains, Mopane woodland
Length: 25 cm **Status:** common resident

Sand-coloured, dove-like bird with short legs and pointed wings. Male is speckled on the back with a fawn breast rimmed with two bold bars in black and white. Yellow eye-rings are distinctive; the forehead is banded in black and white. Female is cryptically coloured with blotches and bars. Flight is fast and direct. Feeds on seed. Usually in pairs, but flocks gather to drink daily after sunset. Lays 2 or 3 camouflaged eggs in a shallow ground scrape.
Best viewing: Kruger, Pilanesberg, Mapungubwe

Nigel Dennis/Images of Africa

SPECKLED PIGEON *Columba guinea*

Habitat: mountains, farmlands, urban areas
Length: 33 cm **Status:** common to abundant resident

Large, reddish-grey pigeon, speckled with white spots on the wings. Head and underparts are pale grey, eyes are surrounded by bare red skin. Occurs in pairs when breeding, but flocks often gather in farmlands to feed on grain. Lays 2 eggs in a frail platform of twigs placed on a rocky ledge, base of palm leaf, window box or offshore island. African Olive-Pigeon *C. arquatrix* has bright yellow bill, eye-rings and feet; it occurs in forest and wooded gardens.
Best viewing: widespread in suitable habitat

Nigel Dennis/Images of Africa

NAMAQUA DOVE *Oena capensis*

Habitat: dry savanna, arid scrublands, farmlands
Length: 28 cm **Status:** common to abundant resident; seasonal nomad

Small dove with extremely long tail. Male has a black mask and throat, and yellow bill with a red base; female has a uniform grey head and throat. Both sexes have small, indigo-blue wing-spots. In flight, the chestnut wings are distinctive. Occurs in pairs or small flocks. Forages on the ground for grass seeds. Lays 2 eggs in a frail saucer-shaped bowl of twigs hidden within a bush or exposed on a branch fork.
Best viewing: Augrabies, West Coast, Karoo, Kgalagadi, Pilanesberg, Camdeboo

CAPE TURTLE-DOVE *Streptopelia capicola*

Habitat: savanna, farmlands, parks and gardens
Length: 28 cm **Status:** abundant resident

Medium-sized, pale grey dove with black neck collar finely edged with white. Black eyes and pale grey breast distinguish it from Red-eyed Dove. Call is repetitive 'work harder, work harder'. Usually found in pairs, but may gather in large flocks at water during the dry season. Lays 2 eggs in a small twig nest within a shrub or tree. Forages on the ground for seeds and grain.
Best viewing: widespread in suitable habitat

Nigel Dennis/Images of Africa

RED-EYED DOVE *Streptopelia semitorquata*

Habitat: woodland, forest edge, wooded gardens
Length: 35 cm **Status:** common resident

Large, pink-headed dove with bold, black collar. Breast is rosy-pink, red eyes are surrounded by red skin. Keeps to dense vegetation but may venture onto lawns in gardens and parks. Typical call is a drawn-out 'coooo-rooo' but the nasal alarm 'njeeh' is distinctive. Feeds on seeds and small berries. Lays 2 eggs in a substantial twig nest concealed within a bushy tree. African Mourning Dove *S. decipens* has pale yellow eyes and grey head.
Best viewing: widespread in suitable habitat

Albert Froneman/Images of Africa

LAUGHING DOVE *Streptopelia senegalensis*

Habitat: woodland, parks, gardens, farmyards, villages and towns **Length:** 25 cm
Status: abundant resident

Small, brick-red and grey dove with pink head and breast speckled in black. Common and widespread in more open habitats and, like other doves, dependent upon drinking water. Most often found in pairs but may form flocks at waterholes. Call is a soft cooing, often uttered at midday. Forages on the ground for seeds and crumbs. Lays 2 eggs in frail platform of twigs. Lemon Dove *Aplopelia larvata* is darker with white face, olive back; evergreen forest resident.
Best viewing: widespread in suitable habitat

Albert Froneman/Images of Africa

EMERALD-SPOTTED WOOD-DOVE *Turtur chalcospilos*

Habitat: woodlands, thickets and orchards
Length: 20 cm **Status:** common resident

Small, cinnamon-brown dove with pale forehead. Four or five emerald-green spots are displayed on each closed wing. Chestnut flight feathers are distinctive. The descending call – 'doo-doo-du-du-dududu' – is one of the bushveld's most evocative sounds. Usually shy and nervous. Lays 2 eggs in a platform of twigs among creepers or in an exposed site. Tambourine Dove *T. tympanistria* has snow-white face and underparts.
Best viewing: Pilanesberg, Hluhluwe-iMfolozi, Mkhuze, Kruger-Lowveld, Mapungubwe

Peter Pickford/Images of Africa

Nigel Dennis/Images of Africa

AFRICAN GREEN-PIGEON *Treron calvus*

Habitat: riverine woodland, dune forest, wooded koppies and gardens **Length:** 30 cm
Status: common resident

Chubby, parrot-like dove with olive-green back, grey-green head and yellow leggings. Eye is pale mauve, base of the bill and feet red, leggings are bright yellow. Gregarious, small flocks are often seen flying in and out of large trees. Feeds primarily on figs, but also the fleshy berries of other trees. Call is a series of ratchetty notes followed by a jumble of fluty whistles. Lays 2 eggs in a frail saucer-shaped bowl of twigs concealed by foliage.
Best viewing: Kruger-Lowveld, Ndumo, Mkhuze, Hluhluwe-iMfolozi

Nigel Dennis/Images of Africa

BROWN-HEADED PARROT *Poicephalus cryptoxanthus*

Habitat: woodland in Lowveld savanna
Length: 24 cm **Status:** fairly common resident

Small, green parrot with pale brown head. Underwings and vent are luminous yellow. Occurs in pairs or small flocks that draw attention to themselves with their shrill, piercing calls. Feeds on figs, fruit and the seeds of trees such as *Acacia* and *Terminalia*. Drinks regularly and is often seen at waterholes. Lays 2–4 eggs in a disused woodpecker hole or natural tree cavity. Meyer's Parrot *P. meyeri* has dark brown back and head.
Best viewing: Kruger, Ndumo, Mkhuze, Nylsvley

Gallo Images

CAPE PARROT *Poicephalus robustus*

Habitat: montane forest **Length:** 30 cm
Status: rare resident; endangered; endemic

Large parrot with olive-brown head, dark green back and apple-green underparts. Pale bill and red shoulder patches are distinctive. Occurs only in evergreen forest with mature *Podocarpus* trees, but may stray into adjacent pecan orchards. Lays 2–4 eggs in a tree cavity. Flocks form in the winter months. Threatened endemic in decline due to habitat loss and illegal pet trade. Grey-headed Parrot *P. fuscicollis* is confined in SA to far northern Kruger.
Best viewing: Xumeni, Hogsback, Woodbush, Magoebaskloof

Nigel Dennis/Images of Africa

DIDERICK CUCKOO *Chrysococcyx caprius*

Habitat: woodland, coastal bush, parks, gardens
Length: 18–20 cm **Status:** common breeding migrant (Aug–Apr)

Small, metallic-green bird with white underparts, red eyes with red eye-rings. Sexually dimorphic; female is bronze above, barred and spotted in buff. Immature has an orange bill. Call is a repetitive 'di-di-deederik'. Feeds mostly on caterpillars. A brood parasite, the female lays her eggs in the nests of sparrow, weaver or bishop hosts. Klaas's Cuckoo *C. klaas* has black eyes and plain green back; African Emerald Cuckoo *C. cupreus* has bright yellow belly.
Best viewing: widespread in suitable habitat

RED-CHESTED CUCKOO *Cuculus solitarius*

Habitat: forest, woodland, riverine forest, wooded gardens **Length:** 30 cm **Status:** common breeding migrant (Oct–Mar)

Pale grey bird with long, pointed wings. Upper chest is rufous, underparts are buffy with grey bars. Young birds are charcoal-backed. The repetitive 'piet-my-vrou' call of the male is a familiar sound in early summer, sometimes carrying on into the night. A brood parasite, the female lays her eggs in the nests of robin-chat and wagtail hosts. African Cuckoo *C. gularis* and Common Cuckoo *C. canorus* lack rufous chest; Black Cuckoo *C. clamosus* is uniform black.
Best viewing: widespread in suitable habitat

Albert Froneman/Images of Africa

GREY GO-AWAY-BIRD *Corythaixoides concolor*

Habitat: savanna, wooded suburbs
Length: 48 cm **Status:** common to abundant resident

Large, ashy-grey bird with a distinctive crest of lacy feathers and long tail. Occurs in pairs during the breeding season, but flocks may gather around waterholes in the dry winter months. Has established a population in leafy Johannesburg suburbs in past two decades. Call is a nasal 'gweeeh' ('go away') – often uttered in alarm. Feeds mostly on berries and leaf buds. Drinks regularly. Lays 2 or 3 eggs in flimsy bowl of twigs within in a tree.
Best viewing: widespread in suitable habitat

Nigel Dennis/Images of Africa

PURPLE-CRESTED TURACO *Gallirex porphryeolophus*

Habitat: riverine woodland, wooded hills and suburbs, coastal forest **Length:** 42 cm
Status: fairly common resident

Multi-coloured bird with blue-green back and tail, iridescent purple crest and red eye-rings. In flight the spectacular crimson wings are conspicuous. Immature lacks red eye-rings. Occurs in pairs or gatherings of a dozen or so. Hops and bounds along branches of large trees, feeding on figs and berries. Call is a raucous 'kok-kok-kok-kok'. Lays 2–4 eggs in flimsy bowl of twigs within a leafy tree.
Best viewing: Nelspruit, Barberton, White River, Kruger, Mkhuze, KwaZulu-Natal coast

Duncan Butchart

KNYSNA TURACO *Tauraco corythaix*

Habitat: montane and coastal forest **Length:** 46 cm
Status: fairly common resident; endemic

Predominantly green bird with white tip to crested head. The bill is orange, with white streaks above and below the red-ringed eyes. In flight, spectacular crimson wings are conspicuous. Immature lacks red eye-rings. Occurs in pairs or gatherings of a dozen or so. Feeds on berries of *Harpephyllum*, *Podocarpus* and others, as well as figs. Call is a hoarse 'khorr-khorr-khorr' or a rasping 'krrrrrrr'. Lays 1 or 2 eggs in a small bowl of twigs.
Best viewing: Garden Route, Wild Coast, Woodbush, Dlinza, Karkloof, Mpumalanga escarpment

Gerhard Dreyer/Images of Africa

Nigel Dennis/Images of Africa

BURCHELL'S COUCAL *Centropus burchellii*

Habitat: rank growth near water, coastal bush, wooded gardens **Length:** 42 cm
Status: common resident; near-endemic

Robust, chestnut-backed bird with large, hooked bill, black head and creamy-white underparts. Flies on broad wings in a floppy, unbalanced manner. Bubbling call sounds like liquid poured from a bottle, 'bob-bob-bob-bob-bobobob', uttered early morning and evening. Often suns itself on exposed perches. Feeds on large invertebrates, frogs and nestling birds. Lays 2–5 eggs in a bulky grass cup within foliage.
Best viewing: widespread in suitable habitat

Albert Froneman/Images of Africa

RED-FACED MOUSEBIRD *Urocolius indicus*

Habitat: *Acacia* savanna, wooded watercourses in dry areas, fynbos, gardens, orchards **Length:** 32 cm
Status: common resident

Small, pale grey, mouse-like bird with a long tail. Bright red facial skin and upper bill are distinctive. Occurs in small flocks, usually flying speedily from place to place. Birds huddle together at their roost. Soft fruit and berries are the main food. Call is a clear, three-note whistle. Lays 2 or 3 eggs in a tidy cup nest built within a tangled bush or creeper.
Best viewing: widespread in suitable habitat

Duncan Butchart

SPECKLED MOUSEBIRD *Colius striatus*

Habitat: dense woodland, thickets, forest edge, gardens, orchards **Length:** 33 cm **Status:** common to abundant resident

Small, dark grey, mouse-like bird with a long tail and buffy underbelly. Face is black, the lower bill is white. Unlike Red-faced Mousebird, individuals in flocks usually fly singly, in a panicky fashion, from bush to bush. Birds huddle together when roosting. Berries and soft fruit make up the bulk of their diet. Call is a harsh chatter. Lays 2–4 eggs in a shallow bowl among tangled foliage. White-backed Mousebird *C. colius* has white bill and red feet.
Best viewing: widespread in suitable habitat

NARINA TROGON *Apaloderma narina*

Habitat: montane and coastal forest, riverine forest
Length: 30 cm **Status:** uncommon resident

Spectacular but elusive forest bird. Male is unmistakable, with emerald head, breast and mantle, blood-red underparts. Female is more muted with a brown face and breast. The large, notched bill is pale yellow. Deep, hooting call draws attention during early breeding season. Large insects and berries are the main food. Lays 2–4 eggs in a natural tree cavity.
Best viewing: Dwesa, Tsitsikamma, Dlinza, Woodbush, Karkloof, St Lucia, Ndumo, Mtunzini, Mpumalanga escarpment

Chris van Rooyen

LITTLE BEE-EATER   *Merops pusillus*

Habitat: grassy clearings in woodland, dry fringes of marshes and floodplains **Length:** 16 cm
Status: common resident

Small, green-backed bee-eater with yellow throat with black collar. Square tail is green and buff with a black tip. Occurs in pairs or family groups. Hawks bees, butterflies and other winged insects from a low vantage point, typically returning to one or more favoured perches. Call is a variety of sweet, high-pitched notes. Lays 2–6 eggs in a burrow excavated in an earth bank or termite mound. Swallow-tailed Bee-eater *M. hirundineus* has deeply forked, blue tail.
Best viewing: Kruger-Lowveld, Nylsvley, Pilanesberg, Marekele

Andrew Schoeman

WHITE-FRONTED BEE-EATER   *Merops bullockoides*

Habitat: riverbanks, dry watercourses and eroded gulleys in woodland and grassland **Length:** 24 cm
Status: common resident

Medium-sized, green-backed bee-eater. Throat is red, forehead white and vent bright blue. A white band runs below the black mask. Immature is duller. Bees, butterflies and other insects are caught in flight. Comes to ground to sun and sandbathe. Call is a nasal 'tshipp', like a zip being pulled. Cooperative breeder, with several nest helpers. Lays 2–5 eggs in a burrow excavated in riverbank or quarry; colonies consist of up to 20 pairs.
Best viewing: widespread in suitable habitat

Duncan Butchart

EUROPEAN BEE-EATER   *Merops apiaster*

Habitat: grassland, woodland, farmland and lake shores **Length:** 28 cm **Status:** common non-breeding migrant in north (Sep–Apr); localized resident in fynbos and Karoo

Large, golden-backed bee-eater with turquoise underparts and yellow throat. A pair of streamers protrudes beyond the tail of the adult. Immature is duller. Occurs in flocks of up to 100 individuals in open habitats. Feeds mostly on bees and grasshoppers. Call is a liquid 'prrrup'. Cooperative breeder with nest helpers. Lays 2–6 eggs in a burrow excavated in an embankment. Blue-cheeked Bee-eater *M. persicus* has green head, back and underparts.
Best viewing: widespread in suitable habitat

Albert Froneman/Images of Africa

SOUTHERN CARMINE BEE-EATER   *Merops nubicoides*

Habitat: open woodland, grassy plains, floodplains and lake shores **Length:** 36 cm **Status:** common non-breeding migrant (Dec–Mar); breeds in northern Botswana and Zambezi Valley

Large, rosy-pink bee-eater with turquoise cap, blue rump and vent. Has black mask running through the eye. Immature is dull pink and lacks the long tail streamers of adult. Gregarious, in large flocks, sometimes in the company of European Bee-eaters. Soars with pointed wings, snapping up bees, dragonflies and other insects in flight. Comes to ground to sun and sandbathe. Call is a rolling 'trrerrk-trrerrk'.
Best viewing: Kruger-Lowveld (central and north), Mapungubwe, Marekele

Peter Pickford/Images of Africa

Duncan Butchart

PIED KINGFISHER *Ceryle rudis*

Habitat: rivers, seasonal pans, dams, estuaries, rocky shores **Length:** 25 cm **Status:** common resident

Medium-sized, black-and-white kingfisher. White underparts are divided by a double chest bar in the male, and a single broken bar in the female. Hunts by hovering above water and plunging in after fish, or dropping onto prey from perch. Occurs in pairs or small family groups. Call is a series of sharp, urgent twitters. Cooperative breeder with up to four male nest helpers. Lays 4-6 eggs in a tunnel excavated in sandbank.
Best viewing: widespread in suitable habitat

Nigel Dennis/Images of Africa

GIANT KINGFISHER *Megaceryle maximus*

Habitat: streams, rivers, dams, estuaries, rocky shores **Length:** 42–46 cm **Status:** uncommon resident

Large, charcoal-grey kingfisher with a white-spotted back. Sexes differ in that male has only the breast rufous, while female is rufous on the underbelly and underwings. Feeds mostly on crabs, but also takes fish and frogs; plunging into water from perch. Fishes alone or in pairs. The rattling 'khak-khak-khak' call is often made in flight. Lays 3-5 eggs in a tunnel excavated in a riverbank or quarry.
Best viewing: widespread in suitable habitat

Nigel Dennis/Images of Africa

MALACHITE KINGFISHER *Alcedo cristata*

Habitat: well-vegetated streams, rivers, pans, dams, canals, lagoons and estuaries **Length:** 14 cm
Status: fairly common resident

Tiny, jewel-like kingfisher with bright blue back, buffy underparts and long scarlet bill. The crest is the colour of malachite stone, banded in black. Immature has a black bill. Perches motionless on reeds and sedges, plunging down to catch small fish, frogs, tadpoles and aquatic insects. Call is a high-pitched 'tseek', given in flight. Lays 3-6 eggs in a tunnel excavated in a sandbank. Half-collared Kingfisher *A. semitorquata* is larger, with black bill.
Best viewing: widespread in suitable habitat

Carmen van den Berg

AFRICAN PYGMY-KINGFISHER *Ispidina picta*

Habitat: clearings in woodland and coastal forest, riverine forest **Length:** 12 cm **Status:** fairly common breeding migrant (Sep–Apr)

Tiny, jewel-like kingfisher with bright blue back, pale orange underparts and long, scarlet bill. The cheeks and nape are violet-purple. Immature has a black bill. Perches motionless on branches, dropping down to catch small lizards, frogs and insects; may also snatch insects from water surface. Call is a high-pitched 'tseet', given in flight. Lays 3-6 eggs in a tunnel excavated in a sandbank.
Best viewing: Kruger-Lowveld, Dwesa, KwaZulu-Natal coast, Mkhuze, Ndumo

WOODLAND KINGFISHER *Halcyon senegalensis*

Habitat: woodland with sparse ground cover, riverine forest, parks and gardens **Length:** 23 cm
Status: common breeding migrant (Oct/Nov–Apr)

Medium-sized, turquoise-blue kingfisher with black shoulders, red and black bill. Immature is duller with shorter, reddish-brown bill. Does not fish, but captures large insects and lizards on dry ground. Highly territorial, pairs chase rivals aggressively. Calls throughout the day with a piercing, repetitive 'chi-trirrrrrrr' trill. Lays 2–4 eggs in a tree hole usurped from a woodpecker or barbet. Grey-headed Kingfisher *H. leucocephala* has chestnut belly.
Best viewing: Kruger-Lowveld, Nylsvley, Marekele, Ndumo, Mkhuze

Peter Pickford/Images of Africa

BROWN-HOODED KINGFISHER *Halcyon albiventris*

Habitat: wooded watercourses, gardens, coastal scrub **Length:** 24 cm **Status:** common resident

Medium-sized kingfisher with long, dusky-red bill and turquoise-blue wings. Male has black back; female has brown back. Occurs singly or in pairs away from water, preying on large insects and lizards. Perches conspicuously and calls with a sharp, descending whistle, or a harsh 'klee-klee-klee' alarm. Lays 2–5 eggs in a tunnel excavated in a sandbank, quarry or road cutting. Striped Kingfisher *H. chelicuti* is smaller, with black upper bill.
Best viewing: widespread in suitable habitat

Nigel Dennis/Images of Africa

LILAC-BREASTED ROLLER *Coracias caudatus*

Habitat: open woodland with sparse ground cover
Length: 36 cm **Status:** common resident

Brilliantly coloured bird with electric-blue wings and tail, most striking in flight. Breast and cheeks are lilac. Long streamers extend beyond the tail. Occurs in pairs, perching conspicuously on dead trees and termite mounds. Courtship display involves aerial rolls and swoops. Lays 2–4 eggs in a tree cavity. Prey includes large insects, scorpions and lizards. Purple Roller *C. naevius* is larger; lacks blue belly and turquoise on head.
Best viewing: Kruger-Lowveld, Kgalagadi, Pilanesberg, Nylsvley, Mkhuze

Nigel Dennis/Images of Africa

EUROPEAN ROLLER *Coracias garrulus*

Habitat: open woodland and scrubland
Length: 31 cm **Status:** common summer non-breeding migrant (Dec–Mar/Apr)

Pale blue bird with rufous back and royal-blue wings. Spends long periods on an exposed perch, dropping onto prey that includes large insects, scorpions and toads. Also hawks winged termites and is attracted to bush fires where scorched or fleeing prey is easily obtained. Flocks of several hundred may be seen on migratory passage flight. Broad-billed Roller *Eurystomus glaucurus* is cinnamon above with yellow bill.
Best viewing: widespread in suitable habitat

Albert Froneman/Images of Africa

Duncan Butchart

SOUTHERN YELLOW-BILLED HORNBILL   *Tockus leucomelas*

Habitat: open *Acacia* woodland with sparse ground cover **Length:** 55 cm
Status: common to abundant resident

Black-and-white hornbill with distinctive, banana-like bill. Bare, red skin around pale yellow eyes; red throat patch. Spends much time on the ground in search of beetles and other invertebrates; also eats berries and seeds. The hollow 'toka-toka-toka' call is made with the head lowered and wings raised. Lays 3 or 4 eggs in a tree cavity, with the female enclosing herself and being fed by the male as she incubates.
Best viewing: Kruger-Lowveld, Kgalagadi, Madikwe, Pilanesberg

RED-BILLED HORNBILL   *Tockus erythrorhynchus*

Habitat: woodland with sparse ground cover
Length: 46 cm   **Status:** common resident

Black-and-white hornbill with red bill. Lacks bare skin on the face. Often occurs alongside Yellow-billed Hornbill. Feeds on beetles and other invertebrates, as well as berries and seeds. The 'kokok-kokok-kokok' call is made in a head-bobbing display. Lays 3 or 4 eggs in a tree cavity, with the female enclosing herself and being fed by the male as she incubates. Crowned Hornbill *T. alboterminatus* has unspotted, charcoal upperparts and head.
Best viewing: Kruger-Lowveld (picnic sites and rest camps), Pilanesberg, Nylsvley

Duncan Butchart

AFRICAN GREY HORNBILL   *Tockus nasutus*

Habitat: woodlands, often on hillsides
Length: 46 cm   **Status:** common resident

Grey and white hornbill with bold, white eyebrows. Male has black bill with yellow panel and small casque; female has horn-coloured bill with maroon tip. Occurs in pairs when breeding but forms small flocks during dry season. Insects and berries make up the diet. Call is a plaintive whistle. Lays 3 or 4 eggs in a tree cavity, female encloses herself and is fed by male as she incubates.
Best viewing: Marekele, Pilanesberg, Nylsvley, Kruger-Lowveld

Duncan Butchart

TRUMPETER HORNBILL   *Bycanistes bucinator*

Habitat: coastal forest; isolated fig trees
Length: 58 cm   **Status:** uncommon to locally common resident

Large, black hornbill with white underbelly. The massive bill is topped by a hollow casque, much larger in the male. Occurs in pairs, or troops of 20 or more. Figs are the favoured food but other soft berries and nestling birds may be taken. Call is a drawn-out wail, not unlike the cry of a human baby. Lays 2–4 eggs in a natural tree cavity, female encloses herself and is fed by male as she incubates.
Best viewing: KwaZulu-Natal coast, Dwesa, Ndumo, Kruger

Albert Froneman/Images of Africa

SOUTHERN GROUND-HORNBILL *Bucorvus leadbeateri*

Habitat: clearings in woodland, coastal grasslands **Length:** 90–130 cm
Status: uncommon resident, vulnerable

Huge, black hornbill with massive bill. Bare skin around the eyes and throat of the adult is red; female has a blue patch on the throat. Immature has pale yellow facial skin. Lives in family groups of up to seven, which walk along in search of prey such as tortoises, snakes and beetles. Call is a deep 'oooom'. Lays 2 eggs in large tree cavity but only one nestling survives; pairs do not breed every year.
Best viewing: Kruger, Hluhluwe-iMfolozi, Wild Coast

Duncan Butchart

GREEN WOOD-HOOPOE *Phoeniculus purpureus*

Habitat: forest fringe, wooded watercourses and gardens, coastal bush, woodland
Length: 34 cm **Status:** common resident

Long-tailed, ink-blue bird with a metallic green sheen. Long, curved bill and short legs are coral-red. Lives in noisy family groups of five or more. Cackling call is made in unison and often culminates with all the birds rocking back and forth. Beetle larvae and geckos are extracted from tree bark. Cooperative breeder with several nest helpers. Lays 2–4 eggs in a tree cavity. Common Scimitarbill *Rhinopomastus cyanomelas* is smaller, with black bill.
Best viewing: widespread in suitable habitat

Albert Froneman

AFRICAN HOOPOE *Upupa africana*

Habitat: woodland with sparse ground cover, lawns and fields **Length:** 26 cm **Status:** common resident

Brick-red bird with black-and-white wings and distinctive, fan-shaped crest. Long, curved bill is used for probing the ground for worms and insects. Flies with slow beats like a giant butterfly. Usually seen singly or in pairs, less often in family groups. Call is a repetitive 'hoop-hoop-hoop'. Lays 4–7 eggs in a tree cavity, often quite close to the ground; conspicuous when delivering food to nestlings.
Best viewing: widespread in suitable habitat

Duncan Butchart

GREATER HONEYGUIDE *Indicator indicator*

Habitat: woodland, wooded watercourses and hills in grassland and fynbos, forest edge
Length: 20 cm **Status:** uncommon resident

Drab, brown and buff bird with distinctive, white outer tail feathers obvious in dipping flight. Male has a pale pink bill, black throat and white ear-patch. Immature has pale yellow underparts. Guides people to beehives, and feeds on bee larvae and wax. Male calls 'whit-purr' monotonously from favoured songpost. A brood parasite that lays eggs (up to 20 per season) in the hole-nest of bee-eater, starling or other host. Lesser Honeyguide *I. minor* has short, stubby bill.
Best viewing: Marakele, Pilanesberg, Ithala, KwaZulu-Natal Midlands, De Hoop

Nigel Dennis/Images of Africa

Nigel Dennis/Images of Africa

CRESTED BARBET *Trachyphonus vaillantii*

Habitat: open woodland, wooded watercourses in grassland, gardens and parks
Length: 23 cm **Status:** common resident

Multi-coloured barbet with yellow and red underparts and face, black back blotched with white. Stout bill is ivory-yellow. The ragged crest is raised when the trilling 'alarm clock' call is made. Occurs in pairs. Fruit and berries are the favoured food, but ground-dwelling insects are also eaten. Lays 3 or 4 eggs in a hole excavated in a tree branch; also makes use of artificial nesting logs or boxes.
Best viewing: widespread in suitable habitat

Albert Froneman/Images of Africa

BLACK-COLLARED BARBET *Lybius torquatus*

Habitat: woodland, wooded koppies and watercourses in grassland, coastal bush
Length: 20 cm **Status:** common resident

Stocky barbet with crimson-red face bordered by a black collar. Occurs in noisy family groups. Call is a repetitive 'duduloo-duduloo' in duet or chorus. Feeds mainly on figs and berries, but insects are also taken. Cooperative breeder with several nest helpers. Lays 3 or 4 eggs in a hole excavated in a tree branch; also makes use of artificial nesting logs or boxes. White-eared Barbet *Stactolaema leucotis* is chocolate brown with white ear stripes and belly.
Best viewing: widespread in suitable habitat

Albert Froneman/Images of Africa

ACACIA PIED BARBET *Tricholaema leucomelas*

Habitat: dry woodland, scrub with scattered trees in grassland and Karoo, alien tree groves in fynbos
Length: 18 cm **Status:** common resident; near-endemic

Small, black-and-white barbet with scarlet forehead patch. Draws attention with its nasal 'nehh-nehh' or 'hoop-hoop' calls. Feeds on berries, especially those of mistletoe, and figs. Recent range expansion into the south-western Cape due to the spread of invasive wattle, which provides nesting sites. Lays 2–4 eggs in hole excavated in a dead tree branch or stem of large aloe.
Best viewing: Karoo, Pilanesberg, Augrabies, West Coast

RPB Erasmus/Digital Source

YELLOW-FRONTED TINKERBIRD *Pogoniulus chrysoconus*

Habitat: woodland **Length:** 12 cm
Status: common resident

Tiny barbet with bright yellow (or, rarely, orange) spot on forehead. Upperparts are black, flecked with white; underparts are pale yellow. Rather inconspicuous, but the monotonous 'pop-pop-pop-pop-pop' call is made with hardly a pause on warm days. Feeds on small berries, especially those of tree parasites such as *Tapinanthus* and *Viscum*. Lays 2–4 eggs in a small hole excavated in a tree branch. Red-fronted Tinkerbird *P. pusillus* has red spot on forehead.
Best viewing: Kruger-Lowveld, Magaliesberg, Pilanesberg, Nylsvley

BEARDED WOODPECKER *Dendropicos namaquus*

Habitat: open woodland, wooded watercourses
Length: 25 cm **Status:** uncommon resident

Large, green-backed woodpecker with pale grey underparts barred in white. Male has a scarlet crown and finely spotted forehead; female has no red on the head. Broad, black streaks below the bill resemble a 'beard'. Usually seen in pairs working up and down the branches of taller trees or trunks, pecking and probing for beetle larvae. Call is a rapid 'wik-wik-wik' or a resonant drumming. Lays 2 or 3 eggs in a self-excavated tree hole.
Best viewing: Kruger-Lowveld, Marakele, Nylsvley, Pilanesberg

Albert Froneman

CARDINAL WOODPECKER *Dendropicos fuscescens*

Habitat: woodland, wooded watercourses and koppies in grassland, Karoo and fynbos
Length: 15 cm **Status:** common resident

Small, green-backed woodpecker with pale, streaked underparts. Male has a scarlet crown; female has brown and black crown. Occurs in pairs, moving up and down smaller branches or inspecting seed pods for insects and beetle larvae. Joins mixed bird parties in winter. Call is chittering rattle. Lays 2 or 3 eggs in self-excavated tree hole. Red-throated Wryneck *Jynx ruficollis* has speckled upperparts and rufous throat; lacks scarlet crown or moustache.
Best viewing: widespread in suitable habitat

Albert Froneman/Images of Africa

GOLDEN-TAILED WOODPECKER *Campethera abingoni*

Habitat: woodland, wooded watercourses and koppies in grassland, sandforest, coastal bush
Length: 22 cm **Status:** common resident

Medium-sized, green-backed woodpecker with white underparts streaked in brown. Male has red crown and moustachial streak; female has red hind-crown only. Forages singly or in pairs, pecking branches for ants, termites and larvae. Joins mixed bird parties in winter. Call is a nasal shriek 'weeeeaa'. Lays 2 or 3 eggs in a self-excavated tree hole. Bennett's Woodpecker *C. bennettii* has spotted underparts; often feeds on the ground.
Best viewing: widespread in suitable habitat

Albert Froneman/Images of Africa

GROUND WOODPECKER *Geocolaptes olivaceus*

Habitat: boulder-strewn hillsides in montane grassland and fynbos **Length:** 25 cm
Status: uncommon resident, endemic

Large, terrestrial woodpecker with grey head and pale yellow eyes. Olive-brown back and wings flecked with pale spots. Underparts are washed with pink; red rump is most noticeable in flight. Occurs in family groups that forage on the ground for ants. Perches conspicuously on boulders. Lays 2–4 eggs in in a burrow excavated in an earth bank, road cutting or gulley. Olive Woodpecker *Dendropicos griseocephalus* has red crown (male); inhabits forests.
Best viewing: Giant's Castle, Golden Gate, Cape of Good Hope, Wakkerstroom, Namaqua

Nigel Dennis/Images of Africa

Peter Pickford/Images of Africa

SPOTTED EAGLE-OWL *Bubo africanus*

Habitat: rocky hillsides, wooded drainage lines, towns and suburbs **Length:** 45 cm
Status: common resident

Large, grey-brown owl with ear tufts. Breast is finely barred, eyes are bright yellow. Strictly nocturnal, but often hunts under street lights and sits on roads, often with dire consequences as many killed by traffic. Feeds on a wide variety of prey from large rodents to winged termites. Call is a low-pitched 'whoooo'. Up to 6 eggs are laid in nest scrape on a sheltered ledge, tree stump or building. Cape Eagle-Owl *B. capensis* has orange eyes, larger blotches on chest.
Best viewing: widespread in suitable habitat

Nigel Dennis/Images of Africa

VERREAUX'S EAGLE-OWL *Bubo lacteus*

Habitat: wooded drainage lines and rivers in savanna
Length: 60–65 cm **Status:** fairly common resident

Huge, grey owl with ear tufts and distinctive, pink eyelids. Immature is paler with fine barring. Pairs roost in tall riverside trees by day. Prey includes smaller mammals and birds up to the size of Helmeted Guineafowl. Call is a deep 'ooomph' grunt. Lays 2 eggs on the top of a Red-billed Buffalo-Weaver or Hamerkop nest, or in a disused raptor nest. Pel's Fishing-Owl *Scotopelia peli* is ginger with darks bands and blotches, and lacks ear tufts.
Best viewing: Kgalagadi, Kruger-Lowveld, Nylsvley, Mapungubwe

Albert Froneman/Images of Africa

AFRICAN WOOD-OWL *Strix woodfordii*

Habitat: forest, wooded kloofs and gardens, coastal bush **Length:** 30–35 cm **Status:** fairly common resident

Medium-sized, rufous-brown owl without ear tufts. The eyes are dark brown and the bill is yellow. The underparts are creamy-white with bold rufous barring. Occurs in pairs that often roost in close proximity. The melodic hooting call is a duet, often described as 'who, who, who are you'. Prey includes large moths, frogs and rodents. Up to 3 eggs are laid in a natural tree cavity.
Best viewing: Dwesa, Woodbush, Nature's Valley, Dlinza, Cape Town, Kosi Bay, Nelspruit, Barberton

Albert Froneman/Afripics

MARSH OWL *Asio capensis*

Habitat: tall grassland, often near wetlands
Length: 35 cm **Status:** common resident

Dark brown owl with pale, buffy underparts and face. Eyes are black and the tiny ear-tufts barely noticeable. Nocturnal, but often active in the late afternoon and early morning, especially in winter. Often perches on fence posts along roads, vulnerable to traffic. Flies low above grassland, dropping silently onto rodent prey. Call is a harsh croak. Lays 2–4 eggs on the ground within a cluster of dense grass tufts.
Best viewing: Wakkerstroom, Memel, Marievale, Dullstroom, Nylsvley

PEARL-SPOTTED OWLET *Glaucidium perlatum*

Habitat: open woodland with sparse ground cover
Length: 18–20 cm **Status:** common resident

Tiny, rufous owl with white, pearl-like spots on the head and back.
The yellow eyes framed with broad, white brows. Longish tail is often
wagged up and down. Unusually, this owl is active by day as well as
night. Call is a whistle, rising to a crescendo and ending in drawn-out
notes. Insects are the main prey but also small birds and rodents. Lays
2–4 eggs in a tree cavity. African Barred Owlet *G. capense* has fine
barring on head and upper chest.
Best viewing: Nylsvley, Pilanesberg, Kruger-Lowveld, Kgalagadi,
Marakele, Mkhuze

Nigel Dennis/Images of Africa

AFRICAN SCOPS-OWL *Otus senegalensis*

Habitat: open woodland, favouring Knobthorn
and Mopane **Length:** 14–18 cm
Status: common resident

Tiny, cryptically plumaged owl with ear tufts.The eyes are yellow.
Roosts by day against the trunk of a tree where it is superbly
camouflaged. Repetitive 'pruuup' call is one of the bushveld's
characteristic night sounds. Strictly nocturnal, it feeds primarily on
moths and other insects but also geckos and small rodents. Lays
2–4 eggs in a tree cavity. Southern White-faced Scops-Owl *Ptilopsis
granti* has orange eyes in white face; considerably larger.
Best viewing: Kruger-Lowveld, Nylsvley, Mkhuze, Kgalagadi,
Marakele

Duncan Butchart

BARN OWL *Tyto alba*

Habitat: virtually all habitats including farmlands,
villages and towns **Length:** 32 cm
Status: fairly common resident

Pale owl with white, heart-shaped face and no ear tufts. Back and
wings are sandy-grey. Nocturnal, shy and seldom seen. Call is a high-
pitched screech. Rodents, shrews and smaller birds are the favoured
prey. Breeds in abandoned or open-sided buildings, tree cavities or
Hamerkop nest. Up to 13 eggs are laid in 'boom years' following
an explosion of rodent numbers. African Grass-Owl *T. capensis* has
darker back; inhabits marshes and wetlands.
Best viewing: widespread in suitable habitat

Martin Harvey/Images of Africa

FIERY-NECKED NIGHTJAR *Caprimulgus pectoralis*

Habitat: woodland with dense leaf litter,
fynbos heathland **Length:** 24 cm **Status:** fairly
common resident

Nocturnal bird with cryptic, brown and fawn plumage. Strictly
nocturnal, and seldom seen, but familiar due to its beautiful whistled
call, often described as 'Good Lord, deliver us'. Most vociferous
during the dry season. Roosts and perches on branches, seldom
alighting on the ground. Moths and other insects are captured on the
wing. Lays 2 eggs in a depression among leaf litter. Other nightjar
species are best distinguished by their call.
Best viewing: Kruger-Lowveld, Garden Route, Bontebok,
Hluhluwe-iMfolozi, Mkhuze

Marietjie Oosthuizen

Albert Froneman

AFRICAN PALM-SWIFT *Cypsiurus parvus*

Habitat: palm groves in savanna, towns and suburbs
Length: 15 cm **Status:** common resident

Ashy-brown swift with slender, sickle-shaped wings and deeply
forked tail. Flies at great speed, capturing tiny insects on the wing.
Often seen in the company of other aerial feeders, skimming
the surface of water at dusk. Occurs in small flocks around large
Hyphaene, Washingtonia and *Livistonia* palm trees that have a
'skirt' of dry leaves. The shallow cup nest of feathers and saliva is
affixed to dry leaves, the 2 eggs are secured with a sticky secretion.
Best viewing: widespread in suitable habitat

Albert Froneman

LITTLE SWIFT *Apus affinus*

Habitat: virtually all habitats **Length:** 13 cm
Status: abundant resident

Black swift with a short, square tail and large, white rump. Highly
gregarious, gathering in large flocks to forage and breed. Spends
almost all its time on the wing, hawking for tiny insects; small
feet not able to perch on branches. Skims water at dusk. Up to 3
eggs are laid in closed bowl of grass, feathers and saliva, placed in
man-made structure such as a bridge or high-rise building. White-
rumped Swift *A. caffer* has forked tail. Alpine Swift *A. melba* is
larger with white belly.
Best viewing: widespread in suitable habitat

Peter Ryan

ROCK MARTIN *Hirundo fuligula*

Habitat: mountains and hillsides in grassland, fynbos
or Karoo, sea cliffs, tall buildings in towns
Length: 13 cm **Status:** common resident

Uniformly brown, swallow-like bird with square tail. Occurs in pairs
or small family groups. Flight is rather slow, often glides back and
forth around cliffs. Feeds on small insects captured on the wing.
Perches on rocks, roofs or overhead wires. Nest of mud pellets is
built beneath an overhang, roof or bridge. Brown-throated Martin
Riparia paludicola is smaller; always near water; Banded Martin
Riparia cincta is white below with broad, brown collar.
Best viewing: widespread in suitable habitat

Albert Froneman/Images of Africa

BARN SWALLOW *Hirundo rustica*

Habitat: virtually all open habitats including parks,
farmlands, sports fields and golf courses
Length: 18–20 cm **Status:** common to abundant
non-breeding migrant (Sep–Apr)

Blue-backed swallow with chestnut forehead and throat, dark collar
and cream underparts. Immature is dusky. Highly gregarious, flocks
of several hundred hawk flying insects in open habitats. Night-time
roosts in reedbeds may host tens of thousands of birds. Prior to
heading north in Mar–Apr, large numbers assemble on trees and
overhead wires. South African Cliff-Swallow *H. spilodera* has square
tail and buffy rump.
Best viewing: widespread in suitable habitat

WIRE-TAILED SWALLOW *Hirundo smithii*

Habitat: rivers, dams and canals in Lowveld savanna
Length: 14 cm **Status:** common resident

Blue-backed swallow with orange cap and snow-white underparts.
The wire-like tail streamers are so thin as to be almost invisible.
Occurs in pairs or small groups, invariably near water. Feeds on the
wing, taking small insects such as gnats and flies. Call is an excited
'chisik-chisik'. Lays 2or 3 eggs in a mud-pellet nest built under a
bridge, veranda or beneath the branch of a tree overhanging water.
Best viewing: Kruger-Lowveld, Ndumo-Mkhuze, KwaZulu-
Natal coast

Peter Pickford/Images of Africa

WHITE-THROATED SWALLOW *Hirundo albigularis*

Habitat: rivers, dams and wetland in grassland,
fynbos and Karoo scrub **Length:** 15 cm
Status: common breeding migrant (Aug–Apr)

Blue-backed swallow with white throat and underparts divided by
narrow, blue breast band. Orange forehead patch is obvious only
from close range. Occurs in pairs or small family groups. Usually
forages above open water, skimming through the air for insect prey;
also low above open grassland and sports fields. Lays 3 eggs in a
mud-pellet nest built beneath a low bridge or drainage culvert. Pearl-
breasted Swallow *H. dimidiata* has no breast band.
Best viewing: widespread in suitable habitat

Nigel Dennis/Images of Africa

LESSER STRIPED SWALLOW *Hirundo abyssinica*

Habitat: open savanna, farmland, coastal scrub,
usually near water **Length:** 16 cm
Status: common breeding migrant (Aug–Apr)

Blue-backed swallow with bright orange head and face, pale
underparts lined with bold, dark streaks. Occurs in pairs or small
flocks. Flies low, taking small winged insects such as gnats and flies
on the wing. Call is a series of nasal mewing notes. Lays 2-4 eggs
in a mud-pellet nest built under a bridge, porch, eave or the branch
of a waterside tree. May become tame around houses.
Best viewing: widespread in suitable habitat

HPH Photography/Digital Source

GREATER STRIPED SWALLOW *Hirundo cucullata*

Habitat: open habitats, often near water
Length: 20 cm **Status:** common breeding
migrant (Jul–May)

Blue-backed swallow with pale underparts lined with indistinct, dark
streaks. Crown and forehead are dull orange. Can be confused with
Lesser Striped Swallow, but larger and lacks orange face. Feeds on
the wing, taking small insects such as gnats and flies. Call is a soft,
metallic tinkle. Lays 2-4 eggs in a mud-pellet nest built under a
bridge, porch, eave or branch of a waterside tree. Red-breasted
Swallow *H. semirufa* is uniform orange-rufous below.
Best viewing: widespread in suitable habitat

Nigel Dennis/Images of Africa

Marietjie Oosthuizen

RUFOUS-NAPED LARK *Mirafra africana*

Habitat: open grassland with bare patches and termitaria, grassy clearings in woodland **Length:** 18 cm **Status:** common resident

Sandy-fawn bird with a loose crest of rufous feathers, raised when calling or alarmed. Pale eyebrows and rufous wing panel are noticeable features. Solitary or in pairs. Utters a sweet, drawn-out 'tseeu-tseeuoo' call from a fence post, termite mound or low bush. Forages for insects on the ground. Lays 2 or 3 eggs in a domed cup of plant material at the base of a grass clump. Other lark species are best distinguished by call and habitat preference.
Best viewing: widespread in suitable habitat

Albert Froneman/Images of Africa

SABOTA LARK *Calendulauda sabota*

Habitat: grassy clearings in open woodland, Karoo scrubland **Length:** 15 cm **Status:** common resident

Small, rufous-brown lark with distinctive, white eyebrows and throat. Back is heavily patterned, and the upper breast has a broad 'necklace' of brown streaks. Eastern birds are darker than those in the west, with sharper bill. Occurs singly or in pairs, frequently perching in low bushes to deliver its melodic song. Feeds on seeds. Lays 2–4 eggs in a cup of dry grass. Other lark species are best distinguished by call and habitat preference.
Best viewing: Kruger (central), Pilanesberg

Ryan Ebedes

AFRICAN PIPIT *Anthus cinnamomeus*

Habitat: open areas in grassland, Karoo and bushveld, farmlands and fields **Length:** 16 cm **Status:** common resident

Small, nondescript brown bird with pale, fawn underparts and white outer-tail feathers. Breast is finely streaked. Pipits are generally slimmer than superficially similar larks. Call is a 'chri-chri-chri' whistle, uttered in an aerial display flight. Up to 4 eggs are laid in a shallow cup at the base of a grass tuft or shrub. Other pipit species are best distinguished by habitat preference, behaviour and call.
Best viewing: widespread in suitable habitat

Duncan Butchart

CAPE LONGCLAW *Macronyx capensis*

Habitat: moist grassland, fynbos and vlei margins **Length:** 20 cm **Status:** common resident, near-endemic

Small, pale-brown bird with upright stance. Seen from behind it appears drab, but the belly and breast are sulphur yellow, the throat is brilliant orange. The hind toe is exceptionally long. Call is a cat-like 'meauw'. Perches on grass clumps, low bushes or bare ground. Occurs in pairs or family groups. Feeds on insects. Up to 4 eggs are laid in a neat cup between two grass tufts. Yellow-throated Longclaw *M. croceus* has lemon-yellow throat.
Best viewing: widespread in suitable habitat

CAPE WAGTAIL *Motacilla capensis*

Habitat: fringes of fresh water, rocky shores, lawns, city streets, farm pastures **Length:** 19 cm
Status: common resident

Small, ashy-grey bird with a long tail. Underparts are off-white, throat has a thin, brown bar. True to its name, the tail is constantly bobbed up and down in a wagging motion. Confiding and adaptable to human activities. Feeds on insects and scraps. Lays 2–4 eggs in a bulky cup placed in a crevice on a bank, or within leafy vegetation. Mountain Wagtail *M. clara* is slate-grey above, with longer tail; inhabits fast-flowing streams.
Best viewing: widespread in suitable habitat

Nigel Dennis/Images of Africa

AFRICAN PIED WAGTAIL *Motacilla aguimp*

Habitat: fringes of fresh water, rocks in rivers, lawns
Length: 20 cm **Status:** common resident

Small, black-and-white bird with a long tail that is constantly bobbed up and down. Immature is a dull version of the adult. Occurs in pairs or family groups along rivers, often seen foraging on lawns. Small insects and worms are the main food. Call is a strident whistle. Lays 3 or 4 eggs in a deep, bulky cup nest placed in a crack in a rock or under a low bridge.
Best viewing: Kruger-Lowveld, KwaZulu-Natal coast, Wild Coast, Augrabies

Nigel Dennis/Images of Africa

ANT-EATING CHAT *Myrmecocichla formicivora*

Habitat: open grasslands, Karoo scrub, Kalahari savanna, roadsides **Length:** 18 cm
Status: common resident

Small, brown, thrush-like bird with white wing panels obvious only in flight. Perches in an erect posture on termite mounds or fence posts. Usually in pairs or family groups. Feeds on ants, termites and other insects. Lays 3 eggs in a bowl of dry grass in a chamber at the end of a self-excavated tunnel, in a road cutting, quarry or the roof of an Aardvark burrow. Arnot's Chat *M. arnoti* is black with white markings; inhabits Mopane woodland of northern Lowveld.
Best viewing: widespread in suitable habitat

Albert Froneman

CAPPED WHEATEAR *Oenanthe pileata*

Habitat: bare plains, dry grassland, recently burnt areas, Karoo scrublands **Length:** 17 cm
Status: common resident; movements of non-breeding birds complex

Small, buffy-brown, thrush-like bird with bold, black-and-white head and chest markings. Perches conspicuously on termite mounds, bush tops and fences. Usually seen singly, or in pairs. Song is a jumble of whistles, including imitations of other birds. Captures ants and other insects on the ground. Lays 2–4 eggs in a cup-shaped nest placed down a rodent burrow, or similar hole.
Best viewing: widespread in suitable habitat

Peter Pickford/Images of Africa

Nigel Dennis/Images of Africa

CAPE ROCK-THRUSH *Monticola rupestris*

Habitat: rocky hillsides and mountains with grasses and low bush **Length:** 20 cm **Status:** fairly common resident, endemic

Small, thrush-like bird. Male has a brown back, orange underparts and a blue-grey head. Female has a dusky-brown head and back. Occurs in pairs, often perching in an upright position on an exposed rock, fence post or a telephone wire. Insects make up the diet. Call is a clear, fluty whistle. Lays 2–4 eggs in a bulky, untidy cup nest placed against a rock. Sentinel Rock-Thrush *M. explorator* has blue-grey back; favours higher altitudes.
Best viewing: Marakele, Blyde Canyon, Table Mountain, Drakensberg, Magaliesberg, Mountain Zebra

CAPE ROCK-JUMPER *Chaetops frenatus*

Habitat: boulder-strewn hillsides in fynbos
Length: 20 cm **Status:** uncommon resident; endemic

Small, thrush-like bird. Male is boldly marked with grey and black head, white moustachial streaks. Female is duller, lacks the white facial markings. Pairs perch on boulders and forage together on the ground in search of insect prey, occasionally fanning tail to display white tips. Lays 2 eggs in an untidy bowl nest, concealed at the base of a rock. Drakensberg Rock-Jumper *C. aurantius* has paler buffy underparts; occurs in Eastern Cape and southern KwaZulu-Natal.
Best viewing: Rooiels, Betty's Bay, Sir Lowry's Pass, Cedarberg

Glenice Ebedes

BUFF-STREAKED CHAT *Oenanthe bifasciata*

Habitat: boulder-strewn montane grasslands
Length: 17 cm **Status:** fairly common resident; endemic

Small, thrush-like bird. Male has buffy underparts and broad, buffy eyebrows, with black head and wings. Female is nondescript, buffy-ochre above, paler below. Occurs singly or in pairs, perching for long periods on boulder tops. Insects are the main food. Song is a series of sharp trilled notes. Lays 2–4 eggs in a nest bowl in crevice or beneath a boulder. Mountain Wheatear *O. monticola* is completely black or pale grey with white shoulder patch.
Best viewing: Drakensberg, Wakkerstroom

Nigel Dennis/Images of Africa

MOCKING CLIFF-CHAT *Thamnolaea cinnamomeiventris*

Habitat: rocky outcrops, cliffs and boulder-strewn hillsides **Length:** 22 cm **Status:** common resident

Dark, thrush-like bird. Male has black head, back and wings, with a bright chestnut rump and belly; variable-sized white shoulder patch. Female is charcoal-grey on the back with rusty underparts. As the name suggests, it is an accomplished mimic of other birds' songs. Forages in pairs for insects. Lays 2–4 eggs in a bowl of hairs placed in the mud-cup nest of a swallow, after breaking away the entrance tunnel.
Best viewing: Pilanesberg, Marakele, Magaliesberg, Drakensberg, Kruger-Lowveld

Duncan Butchart

WHITE-BROWED ROBIN-CHAT *Cossypha heuglini*

Habitat: wooded watercourses and gardens
Length: 20 cm **Status:** common resident

Bright orange robin with brown-grey back. Black head is divided by a bold, white eye-stripe extending to the nape. Immature is heavily speckled. Occurs in pairs. May become tame in gardens, but is otherwise secretive. Extremely vociferous, the strident call is a series of clear, whistled notes. Feeds on worms and insects. Lays 2 or 3 eggs in an open cup within hollow tree trunk or among hanging roots. Chorister Robin-Chat *C. dichroa* lacks white eyebrows.
Best viewing: Kruger-Lowveld, Mkhuze, Ndumo, Mapungubwe

Ariadne van Zandbergen/Images of Africa

RED-CAPPED ROBIN-CHAT *Cossypha natalensis*

Habitat: riverine forest and thickets, coastal forest, wooded valleys and gardens **Length:** 18 cm
Status: common resident and migrant

Bright orange robin with silvery-grey back. Cap is ginger rather than red. Immature is heavily mottled. Occurs in pairs in dense habitats. May become tame in gardens, but is typically secretive. Usual call is a soft seesaw 'tree-troou – tree-troou', but has a wide repertoire of liquid songs, and is a wonderful mimic of other birds. Most active at dusk and dawn. Feeds on insects. Lays 2–4 eggs in cup placed in hollow tree stump or crevice.
Best viewing: KwaZulu-Natal coast, Wild Coast, Kruger-Lowveld, Mkhuze

Marietjie Oosthuizen

CAPE ROBIN-CHAT *Cossypha caffra*

Habitat: forest fringe, wooded watercourses in grassland, fynbos heathland
Length: 18 cm **Status:** common resident

Brown-backed robin with orange throat and tail and white eyebrows. Immature is heavily speckled. Occurs in pairs, spending most time on the ground. Most active at dawn and dusk. Worms and insects are captured on lawns and among leaf litter. Song is a melodious whistle, the alarm a series of rasping notes. Lays 2 or 3 eggs in open cup in a hollow or bush. White-throated Robin-Chat *C. humeralis* has bold, white wingbar and white throat.
Best viewing: widespread in suitable habitat

Sam J Basch/Images of Africa

STONECHAT *Saxicola torquatus*

Habitat: open grassland, fynbos heath, marshes, cultivated fields **Length:** 14 cm **Status:** common resident; moves to lower altitudes in winter

Small, robin-like bird with distinctive white rump in flight. Male is boldly marked with chocolate back, black head, white neck collar and chestnut breast. Female is mottled on the back with grey head, and fawn underparts. Perches conspicuously on fences, posts and rocks. Captures insect prey on the ground. Call is a grating 'tsik-tsik' like two stones being tapped together. Lays 2–5 eggs in a deep cup of grass on the ground.
Best viewing: widespread in suitable habitat

Albert Froneman/Images of Africa

Albert Froneman/Images of Africa

KAROO SCRUB-ROBIN *Cercotrichas coryphoeus*

Habitat: Karoo and fynbos shrub with sparse groundcover; dunes and seashore
Length: 18 cm **Status:** common resident, endemic

Small, dark-brown robin with thin, white eyebrow and throat, distinctive white tips to dark tail feathers. The immature is mottled with buff. Spends most of its time on the ground. Forages singly or in pairs, for insects. Often inquisitive, it makes its presence known by its chattering alarm call. Song is a jumble of whistles and harsh notes. Lays 2–4 eggs in a deep cup placed on the ground at the base of a shrub.
Best viewing: Karoo, West Coast, Camdeboo

Alan Wilson/Digital Source

WHITE-BROWED SCRUB-ROBIN *Cercotrichas leucophrys*

Habitat: thickets, dry woodland, coastal bush
Length: 15 cm **Status:** common resident

Small, brown robin with white underparts heavily streaked in dark brown. Bold, white eye-stripes and white wing bars are distinctive. Long tail is chestnut with white tip: it is raised up and down to reveal the white vent. Call is a variable, fluty whistle. Lays 2–4 eggs in a deep cup usually placed in a grass tussock at the base of a tree. Kalahari Scrub-Robin *C. paena* has unstreaked underparts; Bearded Scrub-Robin *C. quadrivirgata* is buffy orange below.
Best viewing: widespread in suitable habitat

Nigel Dennis/Images of Africa

ARROW-MARKED BABBLER *Turdoides jardineii*

Habitat: thickets and bush clumps in woodland, fringe of marshes and reedbeds
Length: 24 cm **Status:** common resident

Brown bird with bright orange eyes and bold, white, arrow-marked streaks on the chest, crown and throat. Immature lacks white streaks and is paler overall. Favours tangled vegetation and is more often heard than seen. Feeds mostly on insects. Gregarious and noisy, the call is a raucous cackle uttered in unison by groups of up to 12 birds. Cooperative breeder with several nest helpers. Lays 2–5 eggs in a bulky bowl concealed in vegetation.
Best viewing: Kruger-Lowveld, Pilanesberg, Nylsvley, Hluhluwe-iMfolozi

Albert Froneman/Images of Africa

SOUTHERN PIED BABBLER *Turdoides bicolor*

Habitat: open *Acacia* woodland with sparse ground cover **Length:** 25 cm
Status: common resident; near-endemic

Striking, white bird with black wings and tail. The eyes are bright scarlet. Sexes are alike. Immature is mottled brown with a pale grey head. Occurs in noisy family groups that forage on the ground, or in the lower branches of trees, where small insects are sought. Cooperative breeder with several nest helpers. Lays 2–5 eggs in an open bowl nest placed on an outer branch of a thorn tree.
Best viewing: Pilanesberg, Madikwe, Kgalagadi, Mapungubwe

KAROO THRUSH   *Turdus smithi*

Habitat: riverine thickets, wooded gardens
Length: 24 cm **Status:** common resident,
near-endemic

Olive-brown thrush with dark underparts, yellow bill and legs.
Distinguished from very similar Olive Thrush by having completely
yellow bill, yellow eye-rings and lacking orange on flanks. Immature
is paler and speckled below. Occurs in pairs and is most active at
dawn and dusk. Forages on the ground for worms and insects, but
also feeds on berries. Call is a fluty whistle. Up to 4 eggs are laid in
an untidy cup nest, within a leafy shrub.
Best viewing: Karoo, Augrabies, Johannesburg gardens

Sam J Basch/Images of Africa

OLIVE THRUSH   *Turdus olivaceus*

Habitat: montane forest, wooded gardens
Length: 24 cm **Status:** common resident,
near-endemic

Olive-brown thrush with buffy-orange belly, and yellow bill and legs.
Distinguished from very similar Karoo Thrush by having bill dark at
the base, no yellow eye-rings, and orange flanks. Immature is paler
and speckled below. Occurs in pairs and is most active at dawn and
dusk. Forages on the ground for worms and insects, but also feeds
on berries. Call is a fluty whistle. Lays 2 or 3 eggs in a bulky cup
nest, disguised with moss, within a leafy shrub.
Best viewing: Cape Town, Garden Route, Wild Coast, Drakensberg,
KwaZulu-Natal Midlands, Mpumalanga escarpment

Albert Froneman/Images of Africa

KURRICHANE THRUSH   *Turdus libonyanus*

Habitat: open areas in bushveld, lawns in suburbia
Length: 22 cm **Status:** common resident

Grey-brown thrush with orange bill and orange-buff underparts.
Faintly speckled white throat has a pair of black, moustache-like
streaks. Immature is paler, mottled and streaked in buff. Forages on
the ground, flicking through leaf litter for insects and worms. Call is
a clear 'tseeeou' whistle. Up to 4 eggs are laid in a mud-and-grass cup
within a tree. Orange Ground-Thrush *Zoothera gurneyi* has white
wing spots; inhabits montane forest.
Best viewing: Pilanesberg, Kruger-Lowveld, Nylsvley

Duncan Butchart

GROUNDSCRAPER THRUSH   *Psophocichla litsitsirupa*

Habitat: open woodland with sparse ground cover,
lawns, fields and orchards **Length:** 22 cm
Status: common resident

Grey-backed thrush with white underparts boldly streaked in black.
Face is white with black stripes behind the eyes. Shows buffy-orange
wing panels in flight. Immature has a scaly back. Occurs in pairs
that forage for insects, running forward then standing in an upright
posture. Call is a sequence of whistled notes. Lays 2–4 eggs in a mud-
and-grass cup in tree fork. Spotted Ground-Thrush *Zoothera guttata*
has white wing spots; inhabits coastal forest.
Best viewing: Pilanesberg, Madikwe, Kruger-Lowveld

Albert Froneman

Nigel Dennis/Images of Africa

DARK-CAPPED BULBUL *Pycnonotus tricolor*

Habitat: woodland, forest edge, gardens, orchards
Length: 22 cm **Status:** common resident

Small, brown bird with dark head, pale underparts and distinctive, yellow vent. Black head has a small crest, giving a peaked appearance. Occurs in pairs or family groups. May become tame in gardens and parks. Call is a series of liquid whistles, but the raspy 'cheet-cheet-cheet' alarm call is better known. Forages in pairs or groups for small insects and berries. Lays 2 or 3 eggs in a neat cup attached to a branch with spider web.
Best viewing: widespread in suitable habitat

Albert Froneman/Images of Africa

CAPE BULBUL *Pycnonotus capensis*

Habitat: shrubby fynbos, succulent Karoo scrub, coastal bush and gardens **Length:** 21 cm
Status: common resident; endemic

Small, brown bird with pale underparts. White eye-rings and yellow vent are conspicuous. Occurs in pairs or family groups, foraging for berries and small insects. Call is a sharp, liquid whistle, or a raspy alarm made when predators are about, or when going to roost. Lays 2–5 eggs in an untidy cup of twigs and rootlets, concealed in a leafy bush.
Best viewing: West Coast, Cape Peninsula, Betty's Bay, Garden Route

Nigel Dennis/Images of Africa

AFRICAN RED-EYED BULBUL *Pycnonotus nigricans*

Habitat: wooded watercourses in Kalahari and Karoo
Length: 21 cm **Status:** common resident

Small, brown bird with pale underparts and black head with small crest giving a peaked appearance Red eye-rings and yellow vent are conspicuous. Forages in pairs or family groups for small insects and berries. May become tame in gardens and camps. Call is a series of liquid whistles. Lays 2 or 3 eggs in a flimsy cup placed in fork of a leafy bush. Bush Blackcap *Lioptilus nigricapillus* has red bill and legs; inhabits montane forest fringe.
Best viewing: Kgalagadi, Augrabies, Richtersveld, Namaqua, Kimberley

Albert Froneman/Images of Africa

SOMBRE GREENBUL *Andropadus importunus*

Habitat: coastal scrub, forest canopy and edge, densely wooded valleys and watercourses
Length: 20 cm **Status:** common resident

Drab, olive-brown bird with white eyes. Occurs singly or in pairs but is more often heard than seen as it keeps to dense cover. Feeds on berries and figs. Call is described as: 'Willie – come out and fight – scaaaaared', usually uttered from the top of a leafy tree. Up to 3 eggs are laid in a flimsy cup concealed in a leafy tree. Yellow-bellied Greenbul *Chlorocichla flaviventris* is bright yellow below; Terrestrial Brownbul *Phyllastrephus terrestris* has white throat.
Best viewing: widespread in suitable habitat

SPOTTED FLYCATCHER *Muscicapa striata*

 Habitat: open woodland, bushy koppies, wooded drainage lines **Length:** 14 cm **Status:** common non-breeding migrant (Sep–Apr)

Small, grey-brown bird with pale underparts. The name is misleading, as the breast and forehead are finely streaked, not spotted. Typically perches in an exposed position, low down on the outermost branches of a tree or shrub. Flicks wings on alighting from sallies to catch airborne insects. Solitary, quiet and inconspicuous. Individuals may return to the same foraging site each year. African Broadbill *Smithornis capensis* has black cap and broad, flat bill; forest dweller.
Best viewing: widespread in suitable habitat

Albert Froneman/Images of Africa

AFRICAN DUSKY FLYCATCHER *Muscicapa adusta*

 Habitat: forest fringe and clearings, wooded gardens and kloofs, fynbos and coastal bush **Length:** 12 cm **Status:** common resident; altitudinal migrant

Small, ashy-brown bird with indistinct, pale eyebrow. Underparts are pale with smudgy streaks, throat is white. Occurs singly or in pairs in well-wooded habitats, including forest edge and suburban gardens. Perches inconspicuously against foliage, launching out to capture winged insects. Lays 2 or 3 eggs in a nest cup of rootlets and moss, placed in a crevice. Ashy Flycatcher *M. caerulescens* is larger, blue-grey above with pale, unstreaked underparts.
Best viewing: Kirstenbosch, Garden Route, Magoebaskloof, Dwesa, Drakensberg

Albert Froneman/Images of Africa

MARICO FLYCATCHER *Bradornis mariquensis*

 Habitat: dry *Acacia* woodland with sparse ground cover **Length:** 18 cm **Status:** common resident

Small, brown-backed bird with snow-white underparts. Immature is heavily streaked and spotted. Occurs in pairs or small family groups in dry *Acacia* savanna. Hawks insect prey or forages on open ground in the manner of a scrub-robin. Lays 2 or 3 eggs in a small, flimsy cup placed in outer branches of a thorny tree. Pale Flycatcher *B. pallidus* is pale sandy-brown with less contrast between the back and underparts.
Best viewing: Kgalagadi, Kimberley, Madikwe, Pilanesberg

Nigel Dennis/Images of Africa

FAMILIAR CHAT *Cercomela familiaris*

 Habitat: stony hillsides, sparsely wooded drainage lines, villages **Length:** 15 cm **Status:** common resident

Small, pale brown bird with rusty-red tail conspicuous in flight. Has habit of flicking its wings briefly each time it lands. Forages in pairs, searching for small insects on the ground. May become tame. Call is a series of quiet warbles. Lays 2–4 eggs in a neat cup, lined with wool or feathers, placed in a crevice or hole, sometimes near houses, in sheds or on unused tractors. Karoo Chat *C. schlegelii* is slate-grey above with pale underparts.
Best viewing: widespread in suitable habitat

Duncan Butchart

Albert Froneman/Images of Africa

FISCAL FLYCATCHER *Sigelus silens*

Habitat: grassland, fynbos and scrubland with scattered trees, gardens **Length:** 18 cm **Status:** common resident and altitudinal migrant; near-endemic

Small, dark-backed bird with white underparts. Male is jet-black above; female is dusky brown; both have white wing bars and white-edged tail. Occurs in pairs, capturing insects in flight or on the ground. Call is a soft warble. Lays 2–4 eggs in a neat cup of rootlets and stems. Fairy Flycatcher *Stenostira scita* is much smaller, grey-backed with white eyebrows. Similar-coloured Common Fiscal has a longer tail, larger head, hooked bill and upright stance.
Best viewing: Addo, Gauteng, Drakensberg, Wakkerstroom, Cape Town

Albert Froneman/Images of Africa

CHINSPOT BATIS *Batis molitor*

Habitat: open woodland, wooded watercourses and hillsides in grassland **Length:** 12 cm **Status:** common resident

Tiny, black-and-white bird with yellow eyes and black mask. Male has a broad black bar on the breast; female a chestnut breast bar and spot on the throat. Immature is mottled. Usually seen in pairs. Feeds on caterpillars and insects. Joins mixed bird parties in winter. Song is a clear, three-note whistle 'three blind mice'. Up to 4 eggs are laid in a compact cup disguised with lichen. Male Pririt Batis *B. pririt* is alike but female lacks chin spot and is buffy below.
Best viewing: Kruger-Lowveld, Nylsvley, Pilanesberg, Hluhluwe-iMfolozi

Albert Froneman/Images of Africa

CAPE BATIS *Batis capensis*

Habitat: montane and coastal forest, wooded kloofs, watercourses and gardens, orchards **Length:** 12 cm **Status:** common resident; near-endemic

Tiny, multi-coloured bird. Both sexes have an olive-grey mantle and bold black face mask. Male has a pure white throat, bold, black chest bar and yellow eyes; female is chestnut on the throat and flanks with dark red eyes. Usually seen in pairs, moving restlessly in search of small insects and caterpillars. Joins mixed bird parties in winter. Song is a rippling whistle, or two bell-like notes. Lays 2 or 3 eggs in a compact cup nest disguised with lichen.
Best viewing: Kirstenbosch, Garden Route, Woodbush, Dwesa, Giant's Castle, Mpumalanga escarpment

Nigel Dennis/Images of Africa

WHITE-CRESTED HELMET-SHRIKE *Prionops plumatus*

Habitat: woodland, especially broad-leaved **Length:** 20 cm **Status:** common resident

Black-and-white shrike with short, forward-facing head plumes. Yellow eyes are ringed with yellow eye wattles. Gregarious, in restless flocks of up to 12 individuals. Feeds on insects gleaned from branches, also forages on the ground. Call is a muffled 'chiroo'. Cooperative breeder with several nest helpers. Up to 5 eggs are laid in a neat cup nest bound with spider web. Retz's Helmet-Shrike *P. retzii* is mainly black with scarlet bill and eye wattles.
Best viewing: Kruger-Lowveld, Marakele, Nylsvley, Mkhuze

COMMON FISCAL *Lanius collaris*

Habitat: grassland with scattered bushes, roadsides, coastal bush, Karoo and fynbos **Length:** 23 cm
Status: common to abundant resident

Black-and-white shrike with long tail and white 'V'-pattern on the back. Female has a rust wash on flanks. Some have white eyebrows. Immature is mottled and barred in brown. Perches conspicuously, in upright posture like a miniature hawk. Feeds mostly on large ground insects or small birds, pounced upon from perch. Often impales prey onto thorns or barbed wire for later retrieval. Lays 3 or 4 eggs in a deep cup concealed within a bush.
Best viewing: widespread in suitable habitat

Albert Froneman

SOUTHERN BOUBOU *Laniarius ferrugineus*

Habitat: forest edge, coastal bush, fynbos, wooded watercourses, koppies and gardens **Length:** 22 cm
Status: common resident; near-endemic

Black-and-white shrike with buffy underparts. Female is darker below. With a white 'V'-pattern on the back it is superficially similar to the Common Fiscal, but the body is held in a horizontal posture. Occurs in pairs, keeping mostly to the interior of low shrubs and dense foliage. Feeds on insects and nestling birds. Calls are varied, including liquid or grating notes usually uttered in duet. Lays 2 or 3 eggs in an untidy bowl concealed by foliage. Olive Bush-shrike *Telephorus olivaceus* has olive-green upperparts; no white on wing.
Best viewing: widespread in suitable habitat

Albert Froneman/Images of Africa

BLACK-BACKED PUFFBACK *Dryoscopus cubla*

Habitat: forest edge, open woodlands, wooded watercourses, coastal bush **Length:** 18 cm
Status: common resident

Small, black-backed shrike with snow-white underparts and white-edged wing feathers. The eyes are bright red. Displaying male erects a puffy ball of white feathers over his back. Female is duller, with a pale face. Noisy, restless and usually in pairs or mixed bird parties. Feeds on small insects. One of the calls from its repertoire is a sharp 'tjick-wheeou'. Up to 3 eggs are laid in a neat cup disguised with lichen. Brubru *Nilaus afer* has chestnut flank patches.
Best viewing: Ndumo, Mkhuze, Nature's Valley, Wild Coast, Pilanesberg, Kruger-Lowveld

Albert Froneman/Images of Africa

AFRICAN PARADISE-FLYCATCHER *Terpsiphone viridis*

Habitat: forest fringe, wooded kloofs and gardens, watercourses in grassland **Length:** 23 cm (plus 18 cm tail breeding ♂) **Status:** common breeding migrant (Sep–Apr); one race resident on KwaZulu-Natal coast

Small, chestnut-backed bird with indigo-blue head and smoky-grey underparts merging to pale vent. Bill and eye wattles are turquoise-blue. Breeding male differs from female in extravagant, ribbon-like tail. Usually seen in pairs, hawking small insects on the wing. Up to 4 eggs are laid in a tiny, lichen-camouflaged, cup nest. Call is a rippling 'wee-we-diddly' or a harsh 'jweet' alarm. Blue-mantled Crested Flycatcher *Trochocercus cyanomelas* has blue-grey back.
Best viewing: widespread in suitable habitat

Albert Froneman/Images of Africa

Duncan Butchart

BOKMAKIERIE *Telophorus zeylonus*

Habitat: open areas with rocks and scattered shrubs in grassland, Karoo and fynbos **Length:** 23 cm **Status:** common resident; near-endemic

Medium-sized shrike with bright, sulphur-yellow underparts; black gorget leading to eyes and bill. Immature is duller with no black gorget. Occurs in pairs. Calls stridently from bush tops, boulders and fence poles – a loud, ringing duet, beginning 'bok-bok-cheet'. Feeds on beetles and other insects. Lays 2–5 eggs in an open cup concealed in a dense shrub. Gorgeous Bush-shrike *T. viridis* has blood-red throat; is a secretive inhabitat of lowland thickets.
Best viewing: Cape Peninsula, Addo, Gauteng, Augrabies, Wakkerstroom, Drakensberg

Federico Veronesi

GREY-HEADED BUSH-SHRIKE *Malaconotus blanchoti*

Habitat: woodland, riverine forest, wooded kloofs and gardens **Length:** 26 cm **Status:** uncommon resident

Large shrike with yellow underparts, grey head and olive-green upperparts. The eye is pale yellow. The massive bill is used to tackle prey up to the size of chameleons and small snakes. Occurs singly or in pairs. Call is a drawn-out 'whooooo' leading to the alternate name of 'Ghostbird'. Lays 2–4 eggs in a cup nest concealed within a leafy tree. Orange-breasted Bush-shrike *Telophorus sulfureopectus* is smaller, with dark eyes and yellow eyebrows.
Best viewing: Kruger-Lowveld, Ndumo, Mkhuze, Pilanesberg, Marakele

Albert Froneman/Images of Africa

CRIMSON-BREASTED SHRIKE *Laniarius atrococcineus*

Habitat: open dry woodland with sparse ground cover **Length:** 23 cm **Status:** common resident

Dazzling, red and black shrike with white wingbars. Immature is ashy-grey with barring on the underparts. A rare yellow form exists. Occurs in pairs. The call is a strident 'quiquip'. Forages on ground below thorn trees, or among low branches. Beetles and other large insects are the main prey. Lays 2 or 3 eggs in a nest bowl made of bark strips and concealed within a thorn tree.
Best viewing: Kgalagadi, Madikwe, Pilanesberg, Marakele, Mapungubwe

Albert Froneman

RED-BACKED SHRIKE *Lanius collurio*

Habitat: open woodland, grassland with scattered bushes **Length:** 18 cm **Status:** common non-breeding migrant (Oct–Apr)

Small shrike. Male has a rich chestnut back, pale grey head and rump and black mask. Female is duller with finely barred underparts. Occurs singly in open habitats, perching low on outer branches. Insects are taken on the ground. Silent in non-breeding range. Lesser Grey Shrike *L. minor* has pale grey back. Black-crowned Tchagra *Tchagra senegalus* and Brown-crowned Tchagra *T. australis* have broad, white eyebrows; forage on ground or within shrubs.
Best viewing: widespread in suitable habitat

BLACK-HEADED ORIOLE *Oriolus larvatus*

Habitat: riverine forest, woodland, canopy of montane and coastal forest, wooded gardens **Length:** 25 cm
Status: common resident

Bright, sulphur-yellow bird with greenish back and black head. Bill and eyes are coral-red. Immature has a speckled head. Occurs singly or in pairs, joins mixed bird parties in winter. Varied diet includes insects, berries and nectar. Call is a liquid 'pleeoo' whistle, or a harsh nasal alarm. Lays 2or 3 eggs in a cup nest suspended from a branch and disguised with lichen. Eurasian Golden Oriole *O. oriolus* has yellow head and black wings; non-breeding migrant.
Best viewing: widespread in suitable habitat

Nigel Dennis/Images of Africa

SOUTHERN BLACK TIT *Parus niger*

Habitat: broad-leaved woodland, forest edge, wooded gardens **Length:** 16 cm **Status:** common resident

Small, black bird with white shoulder patches and edges to the wing feathers. Female is dusky-grey rather than black. Pairs or small family groups clamber through tangled vegetation, hang from bark or seed pods in search of insects and their larvae. Joins mixed bird parties in winter. Call is a harsh 'cherr-cherr-cherr'. Up to 6 eggs arc laid in a grass lined tree cavity. Grey Tit *P. afer* and Ashy Tit *P. cinerascens* are grey-backed with white facial streaks.
Best viewing: Kruger-Lowveld, Marakele, Nylsvley, Hluhluwe-iMfolozi, Dwesa

Albert Froneman/Images of Africa

SOUTHERN WHITE-CROWNED SHRIKE *Eurocephalus anguitimens*

Habitat: open woodland with sparse ground cover
Length: 25 cm **Status:** common resident

Large, brown and white shrike. Gregarious, family groups of up to ten perch in exposed positions on outer branches of trees, dropping to the ground to capture beetles and other insects. Call is a thin whistle or harsh chatter. Roosts in huddled groups on cold winter nights. Cooperative breeder with several nest helpers. Lays 2–4 eggs in a neat bowl nest bound with spider web on an exposed branch.
Best viewing: Kruger-Lowveld, Madikwe, Mapungubwe, Marakele

Tony Camacho/Images of Africa

MAGPIE SHRIKE *Corvinella melanoleuca*

Habitat: open woodland with sparse ground cover
Length: 50 cm (including 25 cm tail)
Status: common resident

Large, black shrike with extremely long tail; wing bars and tips of the flight feathers are white. Female is duller, with a shorter tail and white flanks. Gregarious, family groups of up to ten perch conspicuously and launch down to capture beetles, grasshoppers and other insects on the ground. Call is a squeaky 'pruuit-preeuo' whistle. Cooperative breeder with several nest helpers. Lays 2–4 eggs in a bulky cup on the outer branches of a thorny tree.
Best viewing: Kruger-Lowveld, Mapungubwe

Nigel Dennis/Images of Africa

Nigel Dennis/Images of Africa

CAPE GLOSSY STARLING *Lamprotornis nitens*

Habitat: grassland with scattered trees, wooded drainage lines, gardens, farmlands
Length: 23 cm **Status:** common resident

Iridescent, blue-green starling with pale yellow eyes. Not as glossy as Greater Blue-eared Starling and lacks dark ear-patches. Dark wing spots are not prominent, underbelly is the same colour as the back. Occurs in pairs or small flocks. Feeds on berries, figs and small insects. Call is a slurred whistle. Lays 2–4 eggs in tree hole lined with grass. Black-bellied Starling *L. corruscus* has dull plumage with black belly; inhabits coastal forest and fringe.
Best viewing: widespread in suitable habitat

Nigel Dennis/Images of Africa

GREATER BLUE-EARED STARLING *Lamprotornis chalybaeus*

Habitat: open woodland with sparse ground cover
Length: 23 cm **Status:** common resident

Iridescent, blue-green starling with pale yellow eyes and dark, almost black, ear-patches. Dark wing spots are prominent, the underbelly is royal blue. Occurs in pairs or large, noisy flocks. Call is a nasal 'squerr', similar to that of White-fronted Bee-eater. Gregarious, flocks gather to feed on insects and berries, or scavenge at camp sites. Lays 2–5 eggs in a tree hole lined with grass.
Best viewing: Kruger-Lowveld, Mapungubwe

Albert Froneman

BURCHELL'S STARLING *Lamprotornis australis*

Habitat: open woodland with sparse ground cover
Length: 32 cm **Status:** common resident

Glossy, purple-blue starling with dark eyes in dark mask, and long legs. Long tail is broad and kite-shaped. Spends much time on ground in an upright posture, flying for cover on broad wings. Occurs in pairs or small groups, often in the company of hornbills. Beetles and other insects are the main food. Call is a squeaky 'tjerrik'. Lays 2–4 eggs in a tree hole lined with grass.
Best viewing: Kruger-Lowveld, Mapungubwe, Nylsvley

VIOLET-BACKED STARLING *Cinnyricinclus leucogaster*

Habitat: open woodland, wooded koppies and watercourses **Length:** 18 cm **Status:** common breeding migrant (Sep–May)

Small, sexually dimorphic starling. Male is iridescent, violet-magenta above with snow-white belly. Female is thrush-like in plumage, with brown back and heavily streaked underparts. Occurs in pairs, small groups or flocks of up to 30, feeding on berries or insects such as winged termites. Call is a plaintive whistle. Lays 2–4 eggs in tree cavity or hollow metal fence post lined with grass, leaves and feathers.
Best viewing: Nylsvley, Marakele, Pilanesberg, Kruger-Lowveld, Hluhluwe-iMfolozi

Albert Froneman/Images of Africa

PIED STARLING   *Spreo bicolor*

Habitat: open grassland, Karoo scrub and fynbos, farmlands **Length:** 25 cm **Status:** common resident; endemic

Olive-brown starling with yellow gape, off-white vent and pale eyes. Occurs in groups of a dozen or more, but may form large flocks in winter. Feeds on grasshoppers and other insects as well as berries. Call is a loud screech. Lays 2–4 eggs in a hole in an earthen bank or erosion gulley, less often in eaves of houses and sheds. Wattled Starling *Creatophora cinerea* is pale grey with black wings; male develops yellow head and black wattles when breeding.
Best viewing: widespread in suitable habitat

Albert Froneman

RED-WINGED STARLING   *Onychognathus morio*

Habitat: rocky outcrops, cliffs, forest canopy, urban areas **Length:** 26 cm **Status:** common resident

Blue-black starling with distinctive, rusty-red wings most visible in flight. Female has an ashy grey head and is streaked on the chest. Occurs in pairs or small flocks in rocky habitats but has adapted to breeding on buildings, fuel stations and under bridges. Call is a sweet, fluty whistle. Feeds on insects and berries. Pale-winged Starling *O. nabouroup* has buffy wings and pale yellow eyes; occurs in rocky habitats of the dry west.
Best viewing: widespread in suitable habitat

Marietjie Oosthuizen

COMMON MYNA   *Acridotheres tristis*

Habitat: man-made structures in towns, roadsides, near buildings on farms **Length:** 24 cm **Status:** alien species, locally abundant resident, expanding range

Dark, starling-like bird with orange bill, legs and facial patch. White wing patches are conspicuous in flight. Occurs in pairs or small flocks, in close proximity to humans; dependent on man-made sites for nesting. Feeds on insects, berries and scraps. Common Starling *Sturnus vulgaris* has greenish-black plumage with small white spots, and sharply pointed bill (yellow when breeding); an invasive alien species from Europe, present in Cape Town and southern Cape.
Origin: native to Southeast Asia; first in Durban around 1900; in Johannesburg 1938

Peter Pickford/Images of Africa

RED-BILLED OXPECKER   *Buphagus erythrorhynchus*

Habitat: open woodland with large herbivores **Length:** 20 cm **Status:** common resident

Brown, starling-like bird with bulbous, waxy, red bill. Red eyes are surrounded by yellow eye wattles. Immature has dark eyes and bill. Gregarious, rides on the back of Giraffe, Buffalo and larger antelope; also cattle. Ticks are cleaned from mammal coats with a scissor motion of the bill. Call is a rasping hiss. Lays 2–5 eggs in a tree hole lined with dry grass. Yellow-billed Oxpecker *B. africanus* has bulbous, yellow and red bill, no eye wattles and a pale rump.
Best viewing: Kruger-Lowveld, Hluhluwe-iMfolozi, Mkhuze, Pilanesberg

Albert Froneman/Images of Africa

Nigel Dennis/Images of Africa

SOUTHERN BLACK FLYCATCHER *Melaenornis pammelaina*

Habitat: clearings in woodland, coastal scrub
Length: 19 cm **Status:** common resident

Unobtrusive, glossy black bird with square or slightly notched tail. Eyes are dark brown. Occurs in pairs, perching conspicuously and capturing insects on the ground. Call is a soft twitter. Lays 2–4 eggs in a shallow bowl placed in a tree cavity. Unlike the similar Fork-tailed Drongo, does not have strongly hooked bill. Black Cuckooshrike *Campephaga flava* has bright orange gape (male); moves unobtrusively through tree canopies.
Best viewing: widespread in suitable habitat

Peter Pickford/Images of Africa

FORK-TAILED DRONGO *Dicrurus adsimilis*

Habitat: woodland, forest edge, grassy clearings, farmlands **Length:** 25 cm **Status:** common resident

Glossy black bird with deeply forked tail, red eyes and pale wings. Occurs singly or in pairs, hawking insects from an exposed perch, often alongside large mammals that flush insects. Bold and aggressive, it frequently mobs or strikes hawks and eagles. Call is a jumble of grating metallic notes; also a good mimic. Lays 2–5 eggs in a shallow cup nest placed on a horizontal tree fork. Square-tailed Drongo *D. ludwigii* is smaller; inhabits coastal forest.
Best viewing: widespread in suitable habitat

Albert Froneman

PIED CROW *Corvus albus*

Habitat: any open country, industrial sites, waste dumps, farmlands **Length:** 50 cm
Status: common resident

Black-and-white crow with hooked, black bill. Immature is duller. Usually in pairs but larger numbers may gather at bountiful food sources. Bold and well adapted to feeding on human waste. Scavenges on road kills and carrion. Up to 7 eggs are laid in a bulky stick nest built on the branch of a tall tree, telephone pole or electricity pylon. White-necked Raven *C. albicollis* has deeper, black bill with pale tip; favours mountainous country.
Best viewing: widespread in suitable habitat

Nigel Dennis/Images of Africa

CAPE CROW *Corvus capensis*

Habitat: open grassland, Karoo scrub, Kalahari savanna, cultivated lands **Length:** 50 cm **Status:** common resident

Glossy black crow with thin, grey bill. Immature is browner and duller. Occurs in pairs or flocks of 50 or more. Feeds predominantly on insects and spilt grain, but will scavenge carrion occasionally. Up to 6 eggs are laid in a bulky stick nest built on a telephone pole, gum tree or windmill frame. House Crow *C. splendens* has greyish nape; it is an alien species that has invaded Durban and other east coast cities.
Best viewing: widespread in suitable habitat

RED-BILLED BUFFALO-WEAVER *Bubalornis niger*

Habitat: open woodland with sparse ground cover **Length:** 24 cm **Status:** common resident; seasonally nomadic

Large, dark weaver. Male is black with pink bill and white wing 'windows'. Female is pale ash-brown with a scaly breast. Feeds on seeds and insects. Call is a jumbled chatter of grating notes. Gregarious, flocks nest communally. Lays 2–4 eggs in a massive structure of thorny twigs, set in outer branches of large trees such as Baobab; or in pylon frames. Thick-billed Weaver *Amblyospiza albifrons* has deep, cone-shaped bill, black in male, yellow in female. **Best viewing:** Kruger-Lowveld, Mapungubwe

Albert Froneman/Images of Africa

WHITE-BROWED SPARROW-WEAVER *Plocepasser mahali*

Habitat: dry, open woodland with sparse ground cover, fringes of cultivation **Length:** 18 cm **Status:** common resident

Conspicuous, rusty-brown weaver with white underparts, broad, white eyebrows, and white rump visible in flight. Gregarious, small flocks forage in the vicinity of their breeding colonies. Feeds on grass seeds and termites. Call is strident jumble of liquid notes. Lays 2 or 3 eggs in a straw-ball nest suspended from outer branches of a thorny tree. Yellow-throated Petronia *Petronia superciliaris* lacks bold markings, has tiny, yellow spot on throat. **Best viewing:** Kgalagadi, Kimberley, Pilanesberg, Nylsvley, Marakele

Albert Froneman/Images of Africa

SOCIABLE WEAVER *Philetairus socius*

Habitat: dry Kalahari savanna **Length:** 14 cm **Status:** common resident; near-endemic

Small, buff-coloured weaver with spangled back, brown head and black facial mask. Bill is pale slate-blue. Feeds on seeds on the ground, flying up into cover if disturbed. Gregarious, flocks build a large, often enormous, thatched nest in Camel Thorn tree, windmill or telephone pole. Lays 3 or 4 eggs in chamber within a communal nest. Pygmy Falcon *Polihierax semitorquatus* depends upon thatched nest for breeding; lives alongside the weavers. **Best viewing:** Kgalagadi, Augrabies, Namaqualand

Nigel Dennis/Images of Africa

SCALY-FEATHERED FINCH *Sporopipes squamifrons*

Habitat: dry Kalahari woodland **Length:** 10 cm **Status:** common resident

Tiny, grey-brown finch with pink bill and bold face markings. Adult has bold, black moustachial streaks that resemble a beard, and a scaly appearance to crown and wing coverts. Gregarious, small flocks gather on ground to feed on seeds and termites. Lays 2–7 eggs in a grassy nest bowl within thorny *Acacia* tree or bush. African Quailfinch *Ortygospiza atricollis* has white around eyes, barred underparts; forages on ground and rarely perches in trees. **Best viewing:** Kgalagadi, Augrabies, Kimberley, Madikwe

Albert Froneman

Marietjie Oosthuizen

VILLAGE WEAVER *Ploceus cucullatus*

Habitat: woodland and coastal bush, gardens and parks, always breeds near water **Length:** 17 cm
Status: common to abundant resident

Medium-sized weaver with stout, pointed bill. Breeding male has the back boldly spotted with black. Red eyes are set in a black mask that extends as an arrow on the chest. Female and non-breeding male are drab, but yellow throat contrasts with whitish belly. Gregarious and conspicuous during summer, when activity is centred around noisy breeding colonies; often in thorn trees. Lays 2–4 eggs in a woven nest.
Best viewing: Kruger-Lowveld, Durban, St Lucia, Wild Coast

Chris van Rooyen

SOUTHERN MASKED-WEAVER *Ploceus velatus*

Habitat: grassland and scrub with scattered trees, parks and gardens, drainage lines in arid areas, woodland **Length:** 15 cm **Status:** common resident

Small weaver with stout, pointed bill and red eyes. Bright coloration is only assumed by the male during breeding season. Non-breeding male and female are drab olive-yellow. Seeds make up the bulk of the diet, but nestlings are fed insects. Call is a swizzling buzz. Lays 2–4 eggs in a woven nest often placed above water. Lesser Masked-Weaver *P. intermedius* has pale yellow eyes.
Best viewing: widespread in suitable habitat

Nigel Dennis/Images of Africa

CAPE WEAVER *Ploceus capensis*

Habitat: open country with scattered trees, marshes and riversides, gardens **Length:** 17 cm
Status: common resident; endemic

Large weaver with pointed bill and pale yellow eyes. Breeding male is golden yellow with ginger forehead and throat. Female and non-breeding male are pale olive. Pairs or groups feed on seeds and insects. Call is a swizzling buzz. Lays 2–4 eggs in a woven nest built among reeds or suspended from branches over water. Golden Weaver *P. xanthops* has plain yellow mantle and shorter bill; Yellow Weaver *P. subaureus* has bright red eyes.
Best viewing: widespread in suitable habitat

Albert Froneman/Images of Africa

SPECTACLED WEAVER *Ploceus ocularis*

Habitat: woodland, forest edge, coastal bush, wooded gardens **Length:** 16 cm
Status: common resident

Medium-sized weaver with pale eyes and long, black bill. Male has a narrow, black mask and a black stripe extending down the throat, with an orange-tinged face. Female lacks the black throat. Forages singly or in pairs, often in mixed bird parties, inspecting bark and gleaning foliage for insects. Call is a descending whistle. Lays 2–4 eggs in a woven nest with extremely long entrance tunnel. Dark-backed Weaver *P. bicolor* has dark brown head and back.
Best viewing: Kruger-Lowveld, Wild Coast, KwaZulu-Natal coast, Ndumo, Mkhuze, Addo

RED-HEADED WEAVER *Anaplectes melanotis*

Habitat: mixed woodland, gardens of farmsteads
Length: 15 cm **Status:** common resident

Small weaver. Male in breeding plumage has dazzling scarlet head, orange bill, white underbelly. Female and non-breeding male differ from other weavers in having orange bill. Occurs in pairs or small groups. Feeds mostly on insects. Lays 2 or 3 eggs in an untidy woven nest that incorporates dry leaves, suspended from branches or overhead wires.
Best viewing: Kruger-Lowveld, Mapungubwe, Marakele

Albert Froneman/Images of Africa

SOUTHERN RED BISHOP *Euplectes orix*

Habitat: open grassveld, marshes, cultivated farmlands **Length:** 13 cm **Status:** common to abundant resident

Brilliant red and black finch conspicuous only during spring and summer breeding season. Male in breeding plumage is unmistakable. Female and non-breeding male are drab, sparrow-like and easily overlooked. Gregarious, feeding primarily on grass seeds and grain. Displaying male puffs into a ball shape and hangs from reed stems, calling with an excited swizzle. Up to 5 eggs are laid in a woven nest built between upright reeds.
Best viewing: widespread in suitable habitat

Nigel Dennis/Images of Africa

YELLOW-CROWNED BISHOP *Euplectes afer*

Habitat: marshes, open grasslands, cultivated farmlands **Length:** 11 cm **Status:** common resident

Golden-yellow finch conspicuous only during spring and summer breeding season. Male in breeding plumage is black with brilliant yellow crown and rump; flies like a large bumblebee. Female and non-breeding male are drab, sparrow-like and easily overlooked. Occurs in small groups during summer, but forms larger flocks in winter. Lays 2–4 eggs in a woven nest placed among tall grass or reeds. Yellow Bishop *E. capensis* is larger, with all-black head.
Best viewing: Wakkerstroom-Highveld, Drakensberg, Golden Gate

Albert Froneman/Images of Africa

LONG-TAILED WIDOWBIRD *Euplectes progne*

Habitat: open grasslands, cultivated lands
Length: 18 cm plus 40 cm tail in summer
Status: common resident

Medium-sized seed-eater. Unmistakable when male is in black breeding plumage with extraordinarily long tail; red and white shoulder patches. Non-breeding male resembles drab female, but retains red shoulder. Occurs in small flocks in grassland and reedbeds. Lays up to 4 eggs in a nest hidden among grass. Red-collared Widowbird *E. ardens* has thin tail with red throat bar; Fan-tailed Widowbird *E. axillaris* has shorter, broad tail, with red wing patches.
Best viewing: widespread in suitable habitat

Nigel Dennis/Images of Africa

Nigel Dennis/Images of Africa

CAPE SPARROW *Passer melanurus*

Habitat: open grassland with scattered bushes, Karoo scrubland, fynbos, farms, gardens and towns
Length: 15 cm **Status:** abundant resident; near-endemic

Small, chestnut-backed sparrow with white underparts. Male has black face mask with prominent, white C-shape on side of head. Female is paler with grey and white face. Occurs in pairs during breeding season but forms flocks in winter. Feeds on ground, on seeds and scraps. Familiar bird in gardens, city parks and streets. Lays 2–6 eggs in an untidy straw nest built within a bush or under an eave.
Best viewing: widespread in suitable habitat

Albert Froneman/Images of Africa

SOUTHERN GREY-HEADED SPARROW *Passer diffusus*

Habitat: open woodland, wooded drainage lines in dry west, farmlands **Length:** 15 cm
Status: common resident

Chestnut-backed sparrow with plain grey head, pale underparts and narrow, white wing bar. Bill is dark when breeding, paler in winter. Occurs in pairs or family groups but may form flocks in winter. Seeds and small insects are gathered from the ground; also feeds in trees. Call is a soft 'chirrp-chirrp'. Lays 3 or 4 eggs in a tree cavity lined with grass and feathers. Streaky-headed Seedeater *Crithagra gularis* has distinct, white eyebrows.
Best viewing: widespread in suitable habitat

Albert Froneman

HOUSE SPARROW *Passer domesticus*

Habitat: towns, industrial sites, farms **Length:** 14 cm
Status: alien species; abundant resident

Small, chestnut-backed sparrow with pale grey underparts. Male has grey crown, brown face mask with prominent white patch on side of dark brown throat. Female is sandy brown with pale bill. Occurs in pairs or small flocks. Feeds on ground, on seeds and scraps. Familiar bird in gardens, city parks and streets. Lays 2–6 eggs in an untidy nest of straw, rags and string, placed in a cavity. Great Sparrow *P. motitensis* is larger, more rufous; native species.
Origin: arrived from Europe or India; first in Durban in late 1800s

Albert Froneman/Images of Africa

RED-BILLED QUELEA *Quelea quelea*

Habitat: *Acacia* woodland, grassland with scattered bushes, marshlands, cultivated lands **Length:** 13 cm
Status: common to abundant resident or nomad

Small, highly gregarious finch. Male in breeding plumage has black mask surrounded by pink or ochre wash, and a coral-red bill. Female and non-breeding male are sparrow-like, but have red bill. Swarms in great flocks of several thousand, even millions. Breeds colonially; up to 5 eggs are laid in a woven nest hung from a thorn tree. Raptors, storks and other predators are drawn to noisy breeding colonies, where nestlings are easy prey.
Best viewing: Nylsvley, Kruger-Lowveld

CAPE CANARY *Serinus canicollis*

Habitat: fynbos heathland, montane grassland, vegetated dunes, drainage lines in Karoo **Length:** 13 cm
Status: common resident; near-endemic

Small, yellow canary with grey nape. Male is brighter than female. Immature is duller, with streaks on breast. Occurs in pairs or small flocks, feeding on seeds and grasses, usually on the ground, but also in *Protea* bushes. Sings beautifully, with a typical canary warble. Lays 3 or 4 eggs in a small cup placed within a bush. Yellow Canary *Crithagra flaviventris* is bright golden yellow.
Best viewing: widespread in suitable habitat

Albert Froneman/Images of Africa

YELLOW-FRONTED CANARY *Crithagra mozambicus*

Habitat: open woodland, riverine thickets, coastal bush, gardens and farmlands **Length:** 12 cm
Status: common resident

Small, yellow canary with greyish back, bold, yellow eyebrows and dark, moustache-like streak. Yellow rump is obvious in flight. Occurs in small flocks, feeding quietly on the ground or in tree canopies. Feeds on seeds, flower buds and nectar. Call is soft swizzle or chirpy song. Lays 3 or 4 eggs in a deep cup concealed within a bush. Brimstone Canary *C. sulphuratus* has large, deep bill. Forest Canary *C. scotops* has heavily streaked underparts.
Best viewing: widespread in suitable habitat

Marietjie Oosthuizen

CINNAMON-BREASTED BUNTING *Emberiza tahapisi*

Habitat: rocky hillsides and koppies with scattered bush, open woodland **Length:** 15 cm
Status: common resident; seasonally nomadic

Small, rust-brown seed-eater with black-and-white head. Male is darker and more boldly marked, with rich cinnamon underparts. Occurs in pairs and small groups, foraging on ground for small seeds and insects. Call is a grating swizzle, made from an exposed perch. Lays 2–4 eggs in a shallow cup nest at base of grass tuft or rock. Cape Bunting *E. capensis* has pale buffy underparts. Lark-like Bunting *E. impetuani* lacks bold black-and-white face markings.
Best viewing: widespread in suitable habitat

Albert Froneman/Images of Africa

GOLDEN-BREASTED BUNTING *Emberiza flaviventris*

Habitat: broad-leaved woodland **Length:** 16 cm
Status: common resident

Small, sparrow-like bird with golden-yellow underparts and chestnut back. Head is black with two bold white stripes above and below the eye. White wing bars are conspicuous in flight. Female is paler yellow below. Usually in pairs, but may form small flocks when not breeding. Feeds on seeds and small insects. Call is lively, nasal song. Lays 3 or 4 eggs in a cup nest concealed within foliage.
Best viewing: Pilanesberg, Kruger-Lowveld, Marakele, Ithala, Mkhuze

Nigel Dennis/Images of Africa

Nigel Dennis/Images of Africa

RED-HEADED FINCH *Amadina erythrocephala*

Habitat: dry grassland, Karoo scrubland, Kalahari savanna **Length:** 14 cm **Status:** common resident; near-endemic

Small finch with scaly underparts and stout, pink bill. Male has a bright orange-red head. Pairs or small flocks feed mostly on the ground. Diet consists primarily of fallen grass seeds, also insects. Drinks regularly, in flocks of 100 or more outside the breeding season. Lays 4–6 eggs in a grass ball nest placed in weaver's nest or woodpecker hole. Cut-throat Finch *A. fasciata* has blood-red band on throat.
Best viewing: Kgalagadi, Augrabies, Pilanesberg, Wakkerstroom, Golden Gate

Albert Froneman/Images of Africa

VIOLET-EARED WAXBILL *Granatina granatina*

Habitat: dry, open woodland with sparse ground cover **Length:** 14 cm **Status:** common resident

Tiny, multi-coloured finch with long tail. Male is mostly cinnamon, with dazzling violet face, blue forehead and bright red bill. Female is ashy-brown with muted facial colours. Both sexes have bright blue rump and tail. Feeds mostly on grass seeds. Drinks regularly, often alongside other waxbills. Lays 2–7 eggs in a ball of dry grass, concealed within a thorny bush.
Best viewing: Kgalagadi, Pilanesberg, Madikwe, Marakele

Nigel Dennis/Images of Africa

COMMON WAXBILL *Estrilda astrild*

Habitat: rank vegetation near water, fynbos heathland, bracken at forest edge **Length:** 13 cm **Status:** common resident

Tiny, pinkish-grey finch with finely barred body, rosy underparts and long tail. Bill and eye mask are bright waxy red. Occurs in small flocks. Prefers fresh grass seeds stripped from inflorescence. Lays 4–6 eggs in a grass ball nest placed in low vegetation. Black-faced Waxbill *E. erythronotos* has black face and bill; Swee Waxbill *Coccopygia melanotis* has green back; Orange-breasted Waxbill *Sporaeginthus subflavus* has orange eyebrows and vent.
Best viewing: widespread in suitable habitat

Albert Froneman

GREEN-WINGED PYTILIA *Pytilia melba*

Habitat: flowering grasses in bushveld and arid scrubland **Length:** 13 cm **Status:** common resident

Tiny, multi-coloured finch. Male has brilliant scarlet bill, forehead, throat and tail. Back is olive, head pale grey and the underparts are barred. Female is duller, lacks red on the face. Occurs in pairs, often with waxbills or firefinches. Feeds on seeds and insects. Usual call is single 'wik' note, but it sometimes warbles a lively song. Lays 2–5 eggs in a grass ball nest, concealed within a bush. Green Twinspot *Mandingoa nitidula* has black belly with white spots.
Best viewing: Kruger-Lowveld, Pilanesberg, Nylsvley, Marakele

RED-BILLED FIREFINCH *Lagnosticta senegala*

Habitat: *Acacia* thickets in woodland **Length:** 10 cm
Status: common resident

Tiny, rose-red finch with yellow eye-rings. Female is dull sandy-brown. Both sexes have pink bill, crimson rump and tiny white spots on breast and flanks. Feeds on seeds, often with waxbills, in pairs or small flocks. Lays 3 or 4 eggs in a grass ball nest concealed within a thorny bush. African Firefinch *L. rubricata* has blue-grey bill, with grey back to head; Jameson's Firefinch *L. rhodopareia* has red head with blue-grey bill.
Best viewing: widespread in suitable habitat

Albert Froneman/Images of Africa

BRONZE MANNIKIN *Spermestes cucullatus*

Habitat: grassy clearings in woodland, forest edge,
gardens **Length:** 9 cm **Status:** common resident

Tiny, chocolate-brown finch with black head and pale lower bill. Iridescent, green-bronze shoulders are not always obvious. Immature is pale buffy-fawn. Gregarious, occurring in flocks of up to 30. Feeds on fresh grass seeds, stripped from stems or picked from the ground. Call is a soft, rasping warble. Lays 2–8 eggs in an untidy ball nest of grass inflorescences, often near an active paper-wasp nest. Red-backed Mannikin *S. bicolor* has chestnut back.
Best viewing: widespread in suitable habitat

Albert Froneman/Images of Africa

BLUE WAXBILL *Uraeginthus angolensis*

Habitat: *Acacia* thickets in woodland **Length:** 13 cm
Status: common resident

Tiny, powder-blue and fawn finch. Female has pale blue only on face and tail. Occurs in pairs or small flocks, feeding on the ground, often in the company of other waxbills and firefinches. Diet consists of grass seeds. Drinks regularly. Call is a soft but high-pitched whistle. Lays 2–7 eggs in an oval ball of grass seedheads concealed in a thorny bush, sometimes near nest of paper wasps.
Best viewing: widespread in suitable habitat

Albert Froneman/Images of Africa

PIN-TAILED WHYDAH *Vidua macroura*

Habitat: all open habitats including gardens and
coastal bush **Length:** 12 cm plus 22 cm tail of
breeding male **Status:** common resident

Tiny, black-and-white finch with extremely long tail and scarlet bill. Male loses long, ribbon-like tail feathers when not breeding. Female is drab, sparrow-like. Feeds mostly on grass seeds. Male is usually accompanied by a harem of up to six females. Brood parasite, the eggs – up to 25 per season – laid in the nest of the Common Waxbill. Shaft-tailed Whydah *V. regia* is buffy below with red legs; Long-tailed Paradise-Whydah *V. paradisaea* has broad tail feathers.
Best viewing: widespread in suitable habitat

Albert Froneman/Images of Africa

Nigel Dennis/Images of Africa

WHITE-BELLIED SUNBIRD *Cinnyris talatala*

Habitat: woodland, wooded watercourses and hillsides in grassland, gardens, coastal bush
Length: 12 cm **Status:** common resident

Tiny, metallic blue-green sunbird with purple-blue throat and snow-white belly. Female is grey above, with unstreaked, white underparts. Feeds primarily on nectar of aloes and other tubular flowers. Call is a strident, rippling warble. Up to 3 eggs are laid in an untidy purse of leaves bound with spider web, and suspended from a branch. Dusky Sunbird *C. fuscus* has dull, blackish-green head and grey breast; restricted to semi-arid Karoo and Kalahari.
Best viewing: Kruger-Lowveld, Pilanesberg, Marakele, Nylsvley, Hluhluwe-iMfolozi

Albert Froneman/Images of Africa

AMETHYST SUNBIRD *Chalcomitra amethystina*

Habitat: woodland, forest edge, coastal bush, gardens
Length: 15 cm **Status:** common resident

Completely black sunbird, with iridescent amethyst throat and rump, and emerald forehead. Female is pale brown on the back with dark throat and yellowish, streaked underparts. Feeds on nectar of plants such as *Strelitzia*, *Erythrina*, *Aloe* and *Kniphofia* but also insects and spiders. Aggressively chases rivals. Call is a series of fast, high-pitched, canary-like notes. Lays 2 eggs in an untidy purse nest bound with spider web, suspended from a branch.
Best viewing: Garden Route, Wild Coast, KwaZulu-Natal Midlands, Kruger-Lowveld, Pilanesberg

Nigel Dennis/Images of Africa

SCARLET-CHESTED SUNBIRD *Chalcomitra senegalensis*

Habitat: open woodland, coastal bush, gardens
Length: 15 cm **Status:** common resident

Dark brown sunbird, that appears black, with dazzling scarlet chest and iridescent turquoise forehead. Female is dark above, with dark bands below. Feeds on nectar of *Erythrina*, *Aloe*, *Leonotis*, *Schotia* and others, but also insects and spiders. Call is a repetitive 'cheep-chip-chop'. Lays 2 eggs in an untidy purse nest suspended from an outer branch.
Best viewing: Kruger-Lowveld, Ndumo, Mkhuze, Mapungubwe

Margaret Westrop/Images of Africa

GREATER DOUBLE-COLLARED SUNBIRD *Cinnyris afer*

Habitat: forest fringe, *Protea* grassland, wooded watercourses in dry areas
Length: 15 cm **Status:** common resident; endemic

Metallic, emerald-green sunbird with broad, scarlet chest patch. Female is olive-brown above, buffy-yellow below. Occurs singly or in pairs, or with other sunbirds at abundant nectar sources. Lays 2 eggs in an oval purse bound to vegetation with spider web. Southern Double-collared Sunbird *C. chalybeus* has narrower red chest patch. Marico Sunbird *C. mariquensis* has magenta chest, with black belly.
Best viewing: Drakensberg, Eastern Escarpment, Tsitsikamma, Garden Route, De Hoop

ORANGE-BREASTED SUNBIRD *Anthobaphes violacea*

Habitat: fynbos heathland and dunes; gardens
Length: 15 cm (♂); 12 cm (♀) **Status:** common
resident; endemic

Small, metallic green sunbird with long tail and orange underparts.
Female is uniformly pale olive-brown. Occurs in pairs or groups at
nectar-rich *Erica, Protea* or *Leonotis*, often in the company of
other sunbirds. Also feeds on spiders and insects. Lays 2 eggs in an
oval purse nest on the edge of a bush. Collared Sunbird *Hedydipna
collaris* has short tail, short bill and canary-yellow underparts; occurs
in well-wooded habitats of eastern lowlands.
Best viewing: Cape Peninsula, Garden Route, Plettenberg Bay

Albert Froneman

MALACHITE SUNBIRD *Nectarinia famosa*

Habitat: montane grassland with *Protea* bushes,
fynbos, Karoo **Length:** 25 cm (♂); 14 cm (♀)
Status: common resident

Large, emerald-green sunbird with long tail feathers. Male displays
yellow shoulder 'epaulettes' when breeding, but becomes olive-
brown with green blotches in winter 'eclipse' plumage. Female is pale
olive with yellowish, lightly-streaked underparts. Occurs singly or in
pairs. Feeds on nectar of plants such as *Protea, Mimetes, Kniphofia,
Leonotis, Watsonia* and *Gladiolus*. Call is a series of twittering notes.
Lays 2 eggs in a dome-shaped nest concealed in bush.
Best viewing: Drakensberg, Cape Peninsula, Garden Route,
Wakkerstroom, Magaliesberg

Rita Meyer/Images of Africa

CAPE SUGARBIRD *Promerops cafer*

Habitat: fynbos hillsides and dunes, gardens with
Protea **Length:** 40 cm (♂); 28 cm (♀)
Status: common resident; endemic

Long-tailed, sunbird-like bird with long, curved bill. Mostly rufous-
brown with white moustachial streak and throat, yellow vent. Sexes
are alike but female has shorter tail. Feeds on nectar of *Protea* and
other fynbos plants, as well as some ornamentals in gardens. Sings
from an exposed perch. Lays 2 eggs in a cup-shaped nest placed
within a dense bush. Gurney's Sugarbird *P. gurneyi* has shorter tail
and rufous chest; restricted to Drakensberg.
Best viewing: Cape Peninsula, Garden Route, Plettenberg Bay

Nigel Dennis/Images of Africa

CAPE WHITE-EYE *Zosterops virens*

Habitat: forests, wooded watercourses and hillsides in
grassland, wooded gardens, coastal bush
Length: 12 cm **Status:** common resident; endemic

Tiny, green bird with distinctive ring of small, white feathers around
eyes; eastern birds are brighter; Cape race has grey underparts.
Occurs in pairs during summer but forms flocks in winter. Feeds on
small insects, such as aphids, as well as berries. Call is a soft, musical
warble. Lays 2–4 eggs in a deep cup, concealed within foliage.
Orange River White-eye *Z. pallidus* has peachy underparts; African
Yellow White-eye *Z. senegalensis* is golden yellow below.
Best viewing: widespread in suitable habitat

Nigel Dennis/Images of Africa

Albert Froneman/Images of Africa

TAWNY-FLANKED PRINIA *Prinia subflava*

Habitat: rank growth on fringes of rivers and streams, wooded hillsides **Length:** 14 cm
Status: common resident

Tiny, long-tailed bird with russet wings and white eyebrows. Has the habit of raising its tail vertically. When disturbed, perches in an exposed position and utters its scolding 'sbee-sbee' call. Feeds on small insects and spiders. Lays 2–5 eggs in a purse nest, woven of grass blades, in a low bush. Black-chested Prinia *P. flavicans* has black chest bar; Karoo Prinia *P. maculosa* and Drakensberg Prinia *P. hypoxantha* are streaked below.
Best viewing: widespread in suitable habitat

Albert Froneman/Images of Africa

RATTLING CISTICOLA *Cisticola chiniana*

Habitat: open *Acacia* woodland **Length:** 13 cm
Status: abundant resident

Small, warbler-like bird with rufous upperparts streaked in black, pale underparts. Noisy and conspicuous, it perches on low bushes or in rank grass. Call is distinctive 'tchi-tchi-tchi-trrrrrrrr', showing black gape. Feeds on small insects and spiders. Lays 2–5 eggs in an oval ball nest of grass and plant fibres, placed in a grass tuft or *Acacia* bush. Other cisticola species distinguished by tail length, back pattern and habitat preference.
Best viewing: Kruger-Lowveld, Pilanesberg, Hluhluwe-iMfolozi

Albert Froneman/Images of Africa

CHESTNUT-VENTED TIT-BABBLER *Parisoma subcaeruleum*

Habitat: dry *Acacia* savanna, Karoo scrubland, fynbos
Length: 14 cm **Status:** common resident

Small, warbler-like bird with ashy-grey back, streaked throat and chestnut vent. Eyes and tail tip are white. Occurs in pairs or mixed bird parties when not breeding. Feeds on small insects and caterpillars. Restless and very vocal; call is a melodious whistle but it also mimics other birds. Lays 2 or 3 eggs in a flimsy cup nest bound with spider web, hidden within a shrub. Layard's Tit-Babbler *P. layardi* lacks chestnut vent.
Best viewing: widespread in suitable habitat

Albert Froneman/Images of Africa

CAPE GRASSBIRD *Sphenoeacus afer*

Habitat: rank growth near water, damp areas in fynbos, bracken at forest fringe **Length:** 20 cm
Status: common resident; near-endemic

Small, warbler-like bird with heavily streaked back and rufous head. Black moustache-like streaks and ragged-tipped tail are distinctive. Occurs singly or in pairs. Keeps within cover for long periods, but sings with a melodious jumble of notes from tall grass or bush tops. Feeds on insects and spiders. Lays 2 or 3 eggs in a bowl of grass, concealed within tangled growth. Levaillant's Cisticola *Cisticola tinniens* is smaller with plain underparts.
Best viewing: Kirstenbosch, Betty's Bay, Wakkerstroom, Drakensberg

BAR-THROATED APALIS *Apalis thoracica*

Habitat: forest, wooded kloofs and gardens, coastal scrub and fynbos **Length:** 13 cm
Status: common resident

Tiny, warbler-like bird with long-tail; plumage varies according to region (there are 10 races in South Africa). Back is olive or grey, underparts cream or buffy. Pale eyes and bold throat bar are distinctive. Usually forages in pairs, feeding on spiders and insects. Typical call is urgent 'philip-philip, philip'. Lays 2–4 eggs in a dome-shaped nest concealed within a leafy shrub. Yellow-breasted Apalis *A. flavida* has red eyes, lemon-yellow underparts.
Best viewing: widespread in suitable habitat

Albert Froneman/Images of Africa

GREEN-BACKED CAMAROPTERA *Camaroptera brachyura*

Habitat: forest fringe, wooded watercourses and kloofs, coastal bush **Length:** 12 cm
Status: common resident

Tiny, warbler-like bird with green back and pale underparts. Lively and restless, the short tail is held upwards to reveal the white vent. Occurs singly or in pairs in dense undergrowth, often near or on the ground. Feeds on insects and other invertebrates. Extremely vociferous, call is a strident 'bleeep-bleeep'. Lays 2–4 eggs in a ball of living leaves, stitched together with spider web. Grey-backed Camaroptera *C. brevicaudata* has grey mantle.
Best viewing: Dwesa-Wild Coast, Eshowe-Dlinza, Nature's Valley, Nelspruit

Mike Karantonis

WILLOW WARBLER *Phylloscopus trochilus*

Habitat: any woodland, including groves of exotic trees and gardens **Length:** 11 cm **Status:** common non-breeding migrant (Oct–Apr)

Tiny warbler. May be olive-brown above with creamy-yellow underparts *P. t. trochilus*, or greyish-brown above, with whitish underparts *P. t. acredula*. In both races the pale yellow eyebrows are distinctive. Keeps to leafy cover as it moves restlessly in search of small insects. Forages alone or with other birds, but mostly quiet and easily overlooked. The most common of several rather similar migratory warblers.
Best viewing: widespread in suitable habitat

Albert Froneman/Images of Africa

LONG-BILLED CROMBEC *Sylvietta rufescens*

Habitat: mixed woodland, coastal bush, wooded drainage lines in dry west **Length:** 10–12 cm
Status: common resident

Tiny, warbler-like bird with buffy underparts and short, almost invisible tail, and thin, down-curved bill. Occurs in pairs, often joins mixed bird parties. Moves restlessly among foliage, often hanging upside-down to explore bark for insects. Call is persistent 'chirrit-chirrit-chirrit''. Up to 3 eggs are laid in a deep purse nest, disguised with lichen, suspended within a bush. Penduline-Tits *Anthoscopus* spp and eremomelas *Eremomela* spp have longer tails and straight bills.
Best viewing: widespread in suitable habitat

Albert Froneman/Images of Africa

REPTILES

An extremely rich diversity of reptiles occurs in South Africa, with many endemic species occurring in the semi-arid west and the Cape mountains. The precise number of reptile species is difficult to establish, as taxonomists continue to find new forms or revise existing families, but there are over 110 snakes (of which 58 are endemic or near-endemic), 25 chelonians (including at least 10 endemic tortoises), 12 worm lizards and more than 170 lizards (most of which are endemic, including 15 localized species of dwarf chameleon).

The majority of reptiles are secretive and seldom seen. Most are encountered by chance, but certain species are restricted to particular habitats and may be actively sought. Many lizards favour exposed rocky areas, while geckos favour walls or tree bark.

All reptiles are cold-blooded and require food less frequently than mammals or birds. Many become dormant and hibernate during the cool winter months. Reptiles are among the most misunderstood and feared of all animals, which is a great pity, as most are fascinating and harmless.

Most snakes are nocturnal and are seldom seen. Since they are smaller than humans, they actively avoid us and will only bite when cornered or surprised. Among the potentially dangerous snakes are the adders that have large, hinged front fangs containing cytotoxic (tissue damaging) venom, and the elapids (cobras and mambas) that have short, rigid frontal fangs with neurotoxic (nerve destroying) venom. The arboreal Boomslang and Vine Snake have very dangerous haemotoxic (causing haemorrhaging) venom, but they are back-fanged and would be unlikely to bite anyone other than a handler. If confronted by a potentially dangerous snake, the best strategy is to remain calm and allow it to escape; any attempt to catch or kill the snake will increase your chances of being bitten.

Featured here are 44 of the more conspicuous or widespread reptiles, including two marine turtles and the Nile Crocodile. Not included, are fossorial (ground-living) blind snakes and worm lizards, which are rarely encountered by the casual bush-walker or naturalist.

The names used here follow those in *A Guide to the Reptiles of Southern Africa* by Alexander & Marais (Struik Publishers, 2007). Length measurements are taken from nose tip to tail tip.

SOUTHERN AFRICAN PYTHON *Python natalensis*

Habitat: rocky outcrops, wetlands, sugar cane plantations **Length:** 3–4 m (rarely 5 m) **Status:** uncommon

Huge, muscular snake with geometrically patterned skin. Adult is able to capture, constrict and swallow prey up to the size of small antelope. Cane-rats and hyrax feature prominently in the diet. Although not poisonous, it may inflict a severe ripping bite. Swims well. Most active at dusk and after dark. Up to 60 large eggs are laid in a burrow.
Best viewing: Hluhluwe-iMfolozi, Ndumo, Thembe, Kruger-Lowveld, Pilanesberg, Marakele

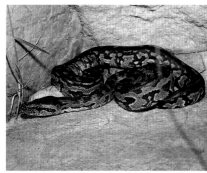

Leonard Hoffmann/Images of Africa

PUFF ADDER *Bitis arietans*

Habitat: rocky hillsides, stony plains, grassland **Length:** 90–120 cm **Status:** common

Short, stocky snake with chevron patterns in ochre, tan and black. Scales are keeled, giving a rough appearance and texture. Most active at dusk and after dark, but may bask in sun. Rodents, frogs and ground birds are the main prey. Will bite humans readily if threatened; the venom is cytotoxic and potentially fatal. Litters consist of 20–40 young.
Best viewing: widespread in suitable habitat

Nigel Dennis/Images of Africa

RHOMBIC NIGHT ADDER *Causus rhombeatus*

Habitat: fallen logs and termite mounds, often near water **Length:** 30–60 cm **Status:** fairly common

Short, stocky snake with chevron patterns in fawn and brown. Has a distinct V-mark on the head. Hunts mostly after dark but basks in the open during the day. Feeds exclusively on frogs and toads. Venom is cytotoxic but rarely fatal to humans. A clutch of up to 25 eggs is laid in a hole or burrow.
Best viewing: widespread in suitable habitat

Leonard Hoffmann/Images of Africa

RHOMBIC EGG-EATER *Dasypeltis scabra*

Habitat: trees, termite mounds and rocky outcrops **Length:** 45–75 cm **Status:** fairly common

Small, boldly patterned snake, closely resembling the Rhombic Night Adder. Strictly nocturnal. Feeds exclusively on birds' eggs, unhinging the almost toothless jaws to swallow larger eggs, which are then crushed by bony projections from the vertebrae. Climbs well, so most bird nests are vulnerable. When disturbed it may coil and uncoil itself, making a rasping sound with its rough scales. Lays up to 25 eggs in summer.
Best viewing: widespread in suitable habitat

Hein von Hörsten/Images of Africa

Leonard Hoffmann/Images of Africa

BROWN HOUSE SNAKE *Lamprophis capensis*

Habitat: rocky outcrops, termite mounds, houses
Length: up to 150 cm **Status:** fairly common

Medium-sized snake with variable coloration, ranging from pale pinkish-brown to rust. Squared-off head shows its close relationship to pythons; the two pale lines on either side of the amber eyes are diagnostic. Nocturnal. Preys mostly on rodents, which are constricted, then swallowed headfirst. Up to 15 eggs are laid in summer.
Best viewing: widespread in suitable habitat

Leonard Hoffmann/Images of Africa

MOLE SNAKE *Pseudaspis cana*

Habitat: most habitats, including farmlands
Length: up to 150 cm **Status:** common

Large, thick-bodied snake with short, chisel-shaped snout. Variably coloured from pale brown to brick red; Cape race is pitch-black. Juvenile is attractively patterned in tan and black. Active by day, it preys on burrowing mammals such as mole-rats, which are constricted, then swallowed. Non-venomous, but able to inflict severe bites. Gives birth to up to 50 young.
Best viewing: widespread in suitable habitat

BLACK MAMBA *Dendroaspis polylepis*

Habitat: termite mounds, rocky outcrops, marsh fringes **Length:** 240–300 cm (rarely over 400 cm)
Status: fairly common

Large, sleek snake with coffin-shaped head. Body colour varies from dusky-olive to ash-grey; only the inside of the mouth is black. Diurnal, feeding mostly on birds and small mammals. Strongly territorial. Will strike repeatedly if cornered; a small dose of its neurotoxic venom may be fatal. A clutch of up to 17 eggs is laid in a termite mound or burrow.
Best viewing: Kruger-Lowveld, Ndumo, Mkhuze, Marakele, Mapungubwe

Duncan Butchart

OLIVE GRASS SNAKE *Psammophis mossambicus*

Habitat: usually in damp places near water
Length: 100–180 cm **Status:** fairly common

Olive-brown snake with dark-edged scales; pale yellowish below. May lift front third of the body, so sometimes confused with Black Mamba, which has a blunter head. Active by day; pursues prey of lizards, frogs, small mammals and other snakes. Bites readily if handled, but venom is mild. Lays up to 30 eggs among dead leaves in summer.
Best viewing: widespread in suitable habitat

Bryan Maritz

RINKHALS *Hemachatus haemachatus*

Habitat: grassland and open scrub close to water
Length: 100–150 cm **Status:** common; endemic

Large, variably coloured, cobra-like snake. Charcoal-grey, brown, olive and tiger-banded forms occur; some have white bars on the throat. Spreads hood when threatened but may also sham death. Neurotoxic venom may be sprayed or injected. Active by day or night. Feeds on toads, rodents and other snakes. Up to 30 young are born in summer.
Best viewing: widespread in suitable habitat

Leonard Hoffmann/Images of Africa

MOZAMBIQUE SPITTING COBRA *Naja mossambica*

Habitat: rocky outcrops, termite mounds and hollow logs **Length:** up to 120 cm **Status:** common

Fairly large, thick-bodied snake. Colour varies from olive-brown to pale grey, with a salmon-pink and black throat. Active by day or night, preying on rodents and toads. Spreads its hood when threatened and sprays neurotoxic venom into the eyes of the adversary. Often takes up residence around homesteads. A clutch of up to 20 eggs is laid in summer.
Best viewing: widespread in suitable habitat

Leonard Hoffmann/Images of Africa

CAPE COBRA *Naja nivea*

Habitat: dry river courses and open areas
Length: 120–140 cm (rarely over 200 cm)
Status: fairly common; near-endemic

Large, slender snake with numerous colour forms. Kalahari population is bright yellow, fynbos population is reddish-brown with darker speckles. Active mainly by day. Spreads its hood when threatened and will bite; neurotoxic venom; accounts for most snake-bite fatalities to humans in its range. Feeds on rodents and bird nestlings. Up to 20 eggs are laid in a burrow.
Best viewing: Kgalagadi, Namaqua, Augrabies, Mokala, Karoo

Leonard Hoffmann/Images of Africa

SNOUTED COBRA *Naja annulifera*

Habitat: termite mounds and hollow logs
Length: 150–250 cm **Status:** fairly common

Large, variably coloured snake that may be sandy-yellow, dark brown or blue black; broad-banded individuals also occur. Head is blunt with a darker top. Most active after dark, preying on toads, rodents and other snakes. May bask in the morning sun. Neurotoxic venom is potentially lethal to humans. Up to 30 eggs are laid in a burrow or in loose soil.
Best viewing: Nylsvley, Marakele, Hluhluwe-iMfolozi, Kruger-Lowveld

Leonard Hoffmann/Images of Africa

Leonard Hoffmann/Images of Africa

BOOMSLANG *Dispholidus typus*

Habitat: trees, shrubs and bushes
Length: 120–200 cm **Status:** common resident

Slender, arboreal snake with huge eyes and a stubby head. Variable in colour: male is usually bright green with pale blue markings; female is olive-brown. Distinctive juvenile is greyish with yellow throat and lime-green eyes. Active by day, feeding mostly on birds and chameleons. Haemotoxic venom is potentially fatal to humans. Up to 20 eggs are laid in a tree hollow.
Best viewing: widespread in suitable habitat

Leonard Hoffmann/Images of Africa

SOUTHERN VINE SNAKE *Thelotornis capensis*

Habitat: trees, shrubs and bushes
Length: 80–120 cm **Status:** fairly common

Slender, arboreal snake with distinctive lance-shaped head. Skin is intricately patterned and serves as superb camouflage. Constantly flicks its black-tipped, red tongue and inflates throat if molested. Active by day, preying on chameleons, geckos and small birds. Haemotoxic venom is potentially fatal to humans. Up to 18 eggs are laid in a tree hollow.
Best viewing: Kruger-Lowveld, Ndumo, Mkhuze

Duncan Butchart

SPOTTED BUSH SNAKE *Philothamnus semivariegatus*

Habitat: trees, shrubs and bushes
Length: 60–90 cm **Status:** common

Slender, arboreal snake varying in colour from olive to emerald, with small black spots and bars. Active by day, it preys upon geckos, chameleons and tree-frogs. When agitated or threatened, it may inflate its neck to reveal bright blue skin, and strike out. Lacks fangs and venom glands and is harmless to humans. A clutch of up to 12 eggs is laid in a tree hollow.
Best viewing: widespread in suitable habitat

Leonard Hoffmann/Images of Africa

HERALD SNAKE *Crotaphopeltis hotamboeia*

Habitat: damp or marshy grassland, reeds, suburban gardens **Length:** 45–70 cm **Status:** common

Small, slender snake with glossy, blue-black head and distinctive, orange-red upper lip. Body is olive-brown above, usually with small white spots; the underbelly is off-white. Nocturnal, it feeds primarily on small frogs. Belligerent if cornered, it bites readily but the venom is not dangerous to humans. A clutch of up to 20 eggs is laid in leaf litter.
Best viewing: widespread in suitable habitat

WATER (NILE) MONITOR *Varanus niloticus*

Habitat: fringes of freshwater rivers and dams
Length: 100–200 cm **Mass:** 12–20 kg
Status: common

Massive, semi-aquatic lizard with an elongated snout. Adult is dark olive-brown or grey-brown above, paler below. Juvenile is strikingly patterned in yellow and black. Feeds on anything it can overpower, including crabs, frogs, birds and crocodile eggs. Preyed upon by the Martial Eagle. Up to 60 soft-shelled eggs are laid in a hole excavated in an active termite mound.
Best viewing: widespread in suitable habitat

Lanz von Hörsten/Images of Africa

ROCK MONITOR *Varanus albigularis*

Habitat: thickets, woodland and koppies
Length: 100–150 cm **Mass:** 12–15 kg
Status: fairly common

Massive, dry-land lizard with a rounded snout. Adult is grey-brown above; pale yellow below with dark spots and bands. Juvenile is more brightly coloured. Often climbs trees. Feeds on anything it can overpower, and also scavenges. Preyed upon by the Martial Eagle. Up to 30 soft-shelled eggs are laid in a hole excavated in an embankment or termite mound.
Best viewing: Marakele, Kruger-Lowveld, Hluhluwe-iMfolozi

Johan Marais

GIANT PLATED LIZARD *Gerrhosaurus validus*

Habitat: crevices in rocky outcrops
Length: 50–60 cm **Status:** fairly common

Large, flat-bodied lizard with short limbs, long tail and comparatively small head. Scales are plate-like with small spots creating a barred pattern. Juvenile is boldly patterned in black and pinkish-yellow. Active by day but rarely ventures far from its rocky retreat. Insects, agamas, geckos, figs and berries feature in the diet. Lays 2–5 eggs in a crevice.
Best viewing: Kruger-Lowveld, Mapungubwe

Duncan Butchart

ROUGH-SCALED PLATED LIZARD *Gerrhosaurus major*

Habitat: crevices in rocky outcrops, termite mounds
Length: 25–30 cm **Status:** fairly common

Medium-sized, flat-bodied lizard with short limbs and long tail. Scales are ridged and rough, giving a strongly armoured appearance. Adult is dull straw-coloured; the immature is brighter. Rarely moves far from rocky retreat or termite mound. Insects, agamas, figs and berries feature in the diet. Lays 2–6 eggs in a hole or crack.
Best viewing: Kruger-Lowveld, Mkhuze, Hluhluwe-iMfolozi, Mapungubwe

Marius Burger

Duncan Butchart

SOUTHERN TREE AGAMA *Acanthocercus atricollis*

Habitat: woodland **Length:** 20–26 cm
Status: common to abundant

Medium-sized, arboreal lizard with box-shaped head. Breeding male has a bright cobalt-blue head. Female and non-breeding male have grey-brown skin that provides cryptic camouflage against the bark of trees. Active by day, feeding on termites and ants. Comes to ground only to move from one tree to another or to lay a clutch of up to 14 eggs in soft soil.
Best viewing: Kruger-Lowveld, Hluhluwe-iMfolozi, Mkhuze, Mapungubwe

Leonard Hoffmann/Images of Africa

SOUTHERN ROCK AGAMA *Agama atra*

Habitat: rocky outcrops and hillsides
Length: 10–16 cm **Status:** common to abundant; endemic

Plump, ground-dwelling lizard with box-shaped head and dark, charcoal-grey body. Male is conspicuous during summer when sitting in exposed situations, showing the blue sides of his head. Active by day, feeding on ants, termites and other small invertebrates. Lays up to 18 eggs in a shallow hole dug in sandy soil.
Best viewing: Suikerbosrand, Magaliesberg, Marakele

Graham Alexander

BLACK GIRDLED LIZARD *Cordylus niger*

Habitat: cracks in rocky outcrops in coastal fynbos, stone walls **Length:** 12–14 cm **Status:** fairly common; endemic

Small, jet-black lizard with compressed body and flat, triangular head. Back is covered in rows of keeled scales and the tail is spiny. Most active in mornings and evenings when it feeds on beetles, grasshoppers and other insects. Basks in the sun on boulders or walls. Three to seven young are born in late summer.
Best viewing: Cape Peninsula

Leonard Hoffmann/Images of Africa

SUNGAZER *Cordylus giganteus*

Habitat: sandy clearings and termite mounds in flat grassland **Length:** 24–28 cm **Status:** uncommon; vulnerable due to loss of grassland; endemic

Large, sandy-brown lizard with spiny scales. Groups live in colonies, with individuals occupying their own self-excavated burrow. Typically emerges from burrow to sun itself in exposed positions. Ambushes beetles, grasshoppers, termites and spiders. Hibernates during cold Highveld winter. May live up to 20 years. One or two live young are born in summer.
Best viewing: Golden Gate, Wakkerstroom

DRAKENSBERG CRAG LIZARD *Pseudocordylus melanotus*

Habitat: boulder outcrops on mountain slopes
Length: 20–28 cm **Status:** fairly common; endemic

Medium-sized lizard with compressed body and large, triangular head; the scales on the tail are spiky. Male is brighter than female, with brilliant orange or yellow flanks. Active by day; frequently seen basking on boulders. Insects, spiders, berries and flowers feature in the diet. May become comatose on cold winter nights. Two or three babies are born in midsummer.
Best viewing: Drakensberg, Golden Gate, Naudé's Nek, Wakkerstroom

Johan Marais

AUGRABIES FLAT LIZARD *Platysaurus broadleyi*

Habitat: exposed granite boulders **Length:** 15–17 cm
Status: common to abundant; endemic

Slender, compressed lizard with long tail. Male is brilliantly coloured with turquoise head, orange flanks and inky-blue throat. Female is brown with three pale stripes on the back. Feeds mostly on ants. Lays 2 elongate eggs in a communal nursery site. Common Flat Lizard is one of several other *Platysaurus* species with restricted distributions in South Africa.
Best viewing: Augrabies

Johan Marais

FLAP-NECK CHAMELEON *Chamaeleo dilepis*

Habitat: woodland, Karoo scrub and grassland
Length: 12–17 cm **Status:** common

Distinctive reptile with large head, conical eyes and prehensile tail. Adult is pale to dark green, often with white blotches, but is able to change colour. Active by day, preying on flies and other insects captured with the long, sticky tongue. Vine Snake, Boomslang and Grey-headed Bushshrike are the main predators. Buries up to 60 eggs in soil.
Best viewing: widespread in suitable habitat

Duncan Butchart

CAPE DWARF CHAMELEON *Bradypodion pumilum*

Habitat: shrubs and forest edge in fynbos
Length: 6–8 cm **Status:** fairly common; endemic

Small, arboreal reptile with conical eyes and prehensile tail. Colour varies from leaf-green to pale grey, usually with a pink or orange lateral stripe. Active by day, preying on flies and other insects captured with the sticky tongue. Snakes, coucals and shrikes are among the predators. Litters of up to 8 young are born during summer.
Best viewing: Cape Peninsula, Betty's Bay, West Coast

Leonard Hoffmann/Images of Africa

Lex Hes

EASTERN STRIPED SKINK *Trachylepis striata*

Habitat: rock outcrops, stone walls and pathways, woodland **Length:** 16–20 cm
Status: common to abundant

Slender, glossy lizard, with a long, tapered tail. Body is blackish-brown, with a pale band running from above the eye to the tail tip. Active by day, it keeps mostly to trees and rocks. Beetles and other insect prey are captured after a chase. Preyed upon by goshawks and snakes. Litters of 3–9 babies are born in summer.
Best viewing: widespread in suitable habitat

Johan Marais

RAINBOW SKINK *Trachylepis margaritifer*

Habitat: rocky outcrops **Length:** 18–28 cm
Status: fairly common

Sleek, medium-sized lizard with long tail. Male is bronze-green above with an orange tail; the whole body glitters in the sun. Female is smaller and darker, with striped flanks and electric-blue tail. Immature resembles the female. Active by day, capturing beetles and other insects. Goshawks and snakes are the predators. Lays up to 10 eggs in a crevice.
Best viewing: Kruger-Lowveld, Hluhluwe-iMfolozi, Mapungubwe

Leonard Hoffmann/Images of Africa

CAPE SKINK *Trachylepis capensis*

Habitat: sandy clearings, logs, aloe stems and boulders **Length:** 16–20 cm **Status:** common; near-endemic

Chubby, medium-sized lizard with blunt head. Body is speckled in tan, black and cream, while the underbelly is uniform yellowish or grey. Three pale stripes run from the back of the head to the tail. Active by day, hunting beetles, grasshoppers and other insects. Goshawks and snakes are its main predators. Usually gives birth to up to 18 babies.
Best viewing: widespread in suitable habitat

GIANT LEGLESS SKINK *Acontias plumbeus*

Habitat: forest and woodland with extensive leaf litter and loose soil **Length:** 30–50 cm **Status:** fairly common; near-endemic

Large, limbless lizard with a blunt-tipped tail. Body is glossy, plum-black or dark-brown with a pale, pinkish snout. Fossorial, so rarely seen, but comes to the surface when ground is waterlogged after heavy rain. Feeds on centipedes, earthworms, beetles and frogs. Mole Snake and Honey Badger are among the predators. Up to 14 babies are born in midsummer.
Best viewing: widespread in suitable habitat

Duncan Butchart

MOREAU'S TROPICAL HOUSE GECKO *Hemidactylus mabouia*

Habitat: under eaves and on walls of houses, rough barked trees **Length:** up to 12 cm
Status: common

Slender, flat-bodied lizard with greyish-pink, almost translucent skin. Flat toes have retractable claws and adhesive pads. Strictly nocturnal, capturing moths and other insects around lights. Male makes a soft 'tic-tic-tic' call when rivals approach. Preyed upon by owls and snakes. Lays 2 hard-shelled eggs in a crevice, often at a communal site.
Best viewing: Kruger-Lowveld, Ndumo, St Lucia, Durban, Nelspruit

Graham Alexander

WAHLBERG'S VELVET GECKO *Homopholis wahlbergii*

Habitat: under eaves and on walls of houses, under bark, rocky outcrops **Length:** up to 20 cm
Status: fairly common

Chubby, round-nosed lizard with velvety scales. Toes are slightly webbed with fixed claws and flat, adhesive pads. Strictly nocturnal, capturing moths and other insects around lights, usually on outside walls. Territorial males may fight vigorously. Preyed upon by owls and snakes. Lays 2 hard-shelled eggs in a crevice.
Best viewing: Kruger-Lowveld, St Lucia, Ndumo, Nelspruit, Tzaneen

Johan Marais

CAPE DWARF GECKO *Lygodactylus capensis*

Habitat: tree trunks, walls, rocky outcrops
Length: 5–7 cm **Status:** common to abundant

Tiny, greyish lizard with broken stripes running down the flanks. Most active by day, feeding on termites, ants, small moths and other insects. Males are territorial and frequently fight rivals. Predators include snakes, rain-spiders and shrikes. Lays 2 small, hard-shelled eggs in a crack or crevice, often in a communal site with a hundred or more eggs.
Best viewing: widespread in suitable habitat

Johan Marais

COMMON BARKING GECKO *Ptenopus garrulus*

Habitat: sandy flats with sparse vegetation
Length: 8–9 cm **Status:** common to abundant; near-endemic

Small, large-headed lizard with bulging eyes; body is sand-coloured. Terrestrial and strictly nocturnal, it is rarely seen but often heard. Individuals excavate burrow systems. Calls at sunset with a repetitive 'chip'. Ants, termites and beetles make up the diet. Meerkats, owls and snakes are the main predators. Lays 1 or 2 hard-shelled eggs in spring.
Best viewing: Kgalagadi, Augrabies, Namaqua

Johan Marais

Duncan Butchart

LEOPARD TORTOISE *Stigmochelys pardalis*

Habitat: stony hillsides and grassy plains
Length: 30–50 cm (max 75 cm) **Mass:** 10–20 kg (up to 40 kg in E. Cape) **Status:** fairly common resident

Large tortoise with dome-shaped carapace that is neither hinged nor serrated on its rim. Active by day, feeding on plant foliage and berries; drinks regularly. Young are vulnerable to predators such as Southern Ground-Hornbill; adults are vulnerable to grass fires. Clutches of up to 18 ping-pong ball-sized eggs are laid in a shallow burrow.
Best viewing: widespread in suitable habitat

KALAHARI TENT TORTOISE *Psammobates oculiferus*

Habitat: arid Kalahari savanna, wooded grassland
Length: 12–14 cm (♀ larger) **Mass:** 300–480 g
Status: fairly common; near-endemic

Small tortoise with dome-shaped carapace with dark bands arranged in a striking, radial pattern. Carapace margin is serrated; beak is strongly hooked. Active by day, feeding mostly on succulent plants. Hornbills and Honey Badgers are among the predators. The closely related Karoo Tent Tortoise *P. tentorius* has several colour forms. Up to 6 eggs are laid in a burrow.
Best viewing: Kgalagadi, Augrabies, Pilanesberg, Madikwe, Mokala

Duncan Butchart

SPEKE'S HINGED TORTOISE *Kinixys spekii*

Habitat: woodland **Length:** 17–20 cm (♀ larger)
Mass: up to 1.5 kg **Status:** fairly common

Medium-sized tortoise with flattened carapace that has a distinctive hinge, affording protection to the rump. Active by day, feeding on berries, grass, fungi, termites, snails and millipedes. Hibernates during winter. Spotted Hyaena and Southern Ground-Hornbill are among the predators. Up to 6 eggs are laid in a burrow.
Best viewing: Kruger-Lowveld, Mapungubwe, Nylsvley, Pilanesberg, Ndumo

Graham Alexander

SERRATED HINGED TERRAPIN *Pelusios sinuatus*

Habitat: seasonal pans, waterholes and rivers
Length: 30–40 cm (♀ larger) **Mass:** up to 7 kg
Status: common to abundant

Large, blackish-brown terrapin with a domed carapace. Shields on the hind portion of the shell are serrated. Basks in the sun on branches or rocks with outstretched neck. Able to bury itself and remain in a torpid state during dry conditions. Diet includes freshwater mussels, frogs and carrion, as well as ticks on Hippopotamus and African Buffalo. Up to 25 eggs are laid in summer.
Best viewing: Kruger-Lowveld, Ndumo, Mkhuze, St Lucia

Nigel Dennis/Images of Africa

MARSH TERRAPIN *Pelomedusa subrufa*

Habitat: seasonal pans, dams and waterholes
Length: 25–32 cm (♀ larger) **Mass:** 2.5 kg
Status: common to abundant

Medium-sized terrapin with relatively compressed carapace. Head has pig-like nostrils and is retracted sideways into the shell. Basks in the sun on sandbanks. Able to bury itself and remain in a torpid state during dry conditions. Diet includes carrion, insects, tadpoles, ducklings and doves, which are ambushed while drinking. Up to 30 eggs are laid in summer.
Best viewing: Barberspan, Karoo, Addo, Marievale, Nylsvley

Johan Marais

LOGGERHEAD TURTLE *Caretta caretta*

Habitat: shallow coastal waters, subtropical beaches
Length: 700–1 000 cm **Mass:** 80–140 kg
Status: uncommon seasonal visitor (Nov–Jan)

Large marine turtle with a sharp parrot-like beak. Adult has smooth shell, but young have keeled scales. Young drift at sea for first three years of life, feeding mostly on bluebottles. Adult feeds on crabs, sea urchins and molluscs in coastal shallows. Breeds on Maputaland beaches; female emerges at night to excavate a nesting hole and lasy approximately 100 eggs.
Best viewing: Maputaland beaches between St Lucia and Kosi Bay

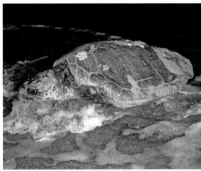

Martin Harvey/Images of Africa

LEATHERBACK TURTLE *Dermochelys coriacea*

Habitat: surface waters of tropical and temperate oceans **Length:** 1.3–1.7 m **Mass:** up to 800 kg
Status: uncommon seasonal visitor (Nov–Jan)

Huge marine turtle that may weigh as much as an African Buffalo. Smooth, barrel-shaped shell has a rubbery appearance. Adult feeds exclusively on jellyfish, while young has a more varied diet. Undertakes long sea journeys, often entering cold sea currents. Female emerges at night to excavate a nesting hole and lays 100 or more eggs.
Best viewing: Maputaland beaches between St Lucia and Kosi Bay

Roger de la Harpe/Images of Africa

NILE CROCODILE *Crocodylus niloticus*

Habitat: freshwater rivers and dams **Length:** 3–4 m (larger individuals rare) **Mass:** 70–150 kg **Status:** fairly common resident; locally threatened by water pollution

Massive, unmistakable, aquatic predator. Active by day or night. Juvenile feeds on small animals such as frogs, while adult takes large fish and mammals up to the size of Impala. Reaches maturity at about 15 years, and may live to a great age. Clutches of up to 80 eggs are laid in a sand burrow, and young are guarded by the female.
Best viewing: Ndumo, St Lucia, Kruger, Hluhluwe-iMfolozi, Pilanesberg

Duncan Butchart

FROGS

Frogs are elusive but interesting amphibious creatures that depend on fresh water for breeding, although several species spend most of their life out of water. South Africa has over 100 species of frog, at least half of which are endemic or near-endemic. On the following pages, 20 of the more widespread or interesting South African frogs are featured. There are two other kinds of amphibians – newts and salamanders – but they do not occur south of the Sahara.

Frogs have two life stages: the tadpole (larval), which is usually totally aquatic, and the four-limbed adult, which is active in and out of water. Though not often seen, frogs, like birds, have distinct vocalizations and this facilitates their identification and study. Male frogs call repeatedly at the onset of the breeding season, which usually begins after the first rains and may continue throughout summer. Most species hibernate during the dry winter months.

Most frogs are nocturnal and are best found at night with the aid of a strong torch. It is also worth venturing out in rain or drizzle, as many species are active in wet weather. Be vigilant when out 'frogging' at night, as snakes are the chief predators of frogs. Frogs are also preyed upon by herons, storks, kingfishers and other birds by day. The tadpoles of various species form an important link in the aquatic food chain for predatory crabs, fishes and dragonfly larvae.

Several species have tiny distribution ranges and are vulnerable to habitat destruction. Some, such as the Red Toad and Foam-nest Frog, regularly inhabit buildings, while the Guttural Toad often colonizes garden ponds.

In recent years, frogs around the world have suffered dramatic population declines, with several species becoming extinct. Amphibians have highly permeable skins, making them susceptible to toxins such as chemical pesticides in the environment. Their numbers are also affected by climate change caused by global warming, and increased radiation due to ozone depletion. A virulent chytrid fungus has been found to be the cause of frog extinctions in Tropical America and eastern Australia and this may have originated in Africa (where it is thought to be endemic, and therefore not harmful, among platanas).

The names used here follow those in *Frogs and Frogging in Southern Africa* by Vincent Carruthers (Struik Publishers, 2001) and *Complete Guide to Frogs of Southern Africa* by Vincent Carruthers and Louis du Preez (Random House Struik, 2009) which is highly recommended for anyone wishing to learn more about these fascinating animals.

COMMON PLATANNA *Xenopus laevis*

Habitat: permanent waterbodies including dams, pools and rivers **Length:** 6–10 cm **Status:** common

Extraordinary frog with eyes on the top of its head and a compressed body. Forelimbs are short and slender, hind legs are large and powerful with webbing between the clawed toes. Usually seen suspended just below the water surface. Almost totally aquatic, but will move on land during rain. Preys upon aquatic insects, tadpoles and small fish; also scavenges. Small, jelly-capsuled eggs are attached individually to submerged objects.
Best viewing: widespread in suitable habitat

Louis du Preez

GIANT BULLFROG *Pyxicephalus adspersus*

Habitat: poorly drained soils and seasonal pans in grassland **Length:** 15–20 cm **Status:** seasonally locally common, but threatened in parts of range; near-endemic

Massive, olive-green frog with orange-yellow underparts. Remains underground during dry winter, but emerges after heavy summer rains to occupy temporary pans in grassland; adult males then fight for the right to mate. Preys on insects as well as smaller frogs and rodents. Call is a deep, slow bellow. Adult bites if handled. Numerous eggs are laid individually. Numbers are greatly reduced on Highveld.
Best viewing: Chrissiesmeer, Marievale, Addo, Nylsvley, Kgalagadi

Roger de la Harpe

BANDED RUBBER FROG *Phrynomantis bifasciatus*

Habitat: seasonal pans **Length:** 6 cm **Status:** seasonally fairly common

Medium-sized, fairly compressed-looking frog. Very distinctive: shiny black body with broad bands of red, pink or yellow on the back and legs. These bright colours serve to warn potential predators that the skin exudes powerful toxins. Most frequently seen when on the move after summer showers. Male takes cover at the water's edge and calls with a loud, telephone-like trill. Ants are the main prey. Clusters of jelly-coated eggs are attached to vegetation.
Best viewing: Pilanesberg, Marakele, Nylsvley, Kruger-Lowveld

Leonard Hoffmann/Images of Africa

BUBBLING KASSINA *Kassina senegalensis*

Habitat: seasonal pans and vleis, permanent pools **Length:** 4–5 cm **Status:** seasonally common

Small, boldly patterned frog. Back is variable in colour, being fawn, yellow or olive, with distinctive, bold, dark stripes. Sides are mottled and the underbelly is off-white. Call is a loud liquid 'quoip', made during the day or night from the base of a grass tuft, often some distance from water. Usually very difficult to locate the source of the call. Insects are the main prey. Clusters of jelly-coated eggs are attached to vegetation.
Best viewing: widespread in suitable habitat

Duncan Butchart

Duncan Butchart

GUTTURAL TOAD *Amietophrynus gutturalis*

Habitat: seasonal pans, man-made dams, garden ponds **Length:** 8–10 cm
Status: seasonally abundant

Sandy-brown or grey frog with lumpy skin. Differs from Raucous Toad in having red flecks on the thighs. Breeds in permanent water, including garden ponds, but often forages some distance away and can be seen around outdoor lights after dark. Insects and worms are the main prey. Call is a loud, reverberating snore, usually uttered in chorus by numerous males at the water's edge. Eggs are contained in paired, jelly-coated strings, entangled on aquatic plants.
Best viewing: widespread in suitable habitat

Louis du Preez

RAUCOUS TOAD *Amietophrynus rangeri*

Habitat: grassland and bushveld above 900 m
Length: 8–10 cm **Status:** seasonally common; endemic

Sandy-brown or grey frog with lumpy skin. Distinguished from Guttural Toad by the absence of red flecks on the thighs. More often found alongside running water than at ponds or dams, but may venture into dry, rocky habitats. Insects and worms are the main prey. Call is a duck-like 'kwaak', repeated at intervals. Does not call in large choruses. Eggs are contained in paired, jelly-coated strings, entangled on aquatic plants.
Best viewing: widespread in suitable habitat

Louis du Preez

KAROO TOAD *Vandijkophrynus gariepensis*

Habitat: seasonal rain pools **Length:** 7–9 cm
Status: common to abundant; endemic

Mottled or plain khaki-coloured frog with lumpy skin. Underbelly is off-white, often with small spots. Often found in gardens and may hibernate in homes. Breeds in temporary pans and dams. Insects and worms are the main prey. Call is a series of rasping squawks given from hiding places at the water's edge. Eggs are contained in paired, jelly-coated strings, entangled on aquatic plants.
Best viewing: widespread in suitable habitat

Duncan Butchart

RED TOAD *Schismaderma carens*

Habitat: leaf litter, pools and dams **Length:** 7–9 cm
Status: common to abundant

Brick-red frog distinguished by a raised dark line down its flank from eye to groin. Two dark spots may be present on the back. Often found in gardens and may hibernate in homes. Breeds in temporary pans and dams. Insects and worms are the main prey. Males call in chorus, often while afloat; the repetitive call can be likened to the revs of a powerful motorbike. Eggs are contained in paired, jelly-coated strings, entangled on aquatic plants.
Best viewing: widespread in suitable habitat

NATAL SAND FROG *Tomopterna natalensis*

Habitat: seepages in grassland, vleis and streambanks
Length: 4–5 cm **Status:** seasonally common; endemic

Small, burrowing frog with a toad-like shape and posture. A small, flat disc is present on each hind foot. Mostly nocturnal, but may call on overcast days in spring. Feeds on insects. One of the noisiest of all frogs; male calls with a loud, monotonous piping note from an exposed position on sandbanks or around pools. Similar Tremelo Sand-Frog *T. cryptotus* ranges west to the dry Kalahari. Eggs are contained in individual jelly capsules.
Best viewing: widespread in suitable habitat

Duncan Butchart

BUSHVELD RAIN FROG *Breviceps adspersus*

Habitat: sandy soils in dry savanna **Length:** 3–4 cm
Status: seasonally common to abundant

Tiny, rotund frog with a down-turned mouth that gives it a 'grumpy' appearance. Back is mottled in various shades of brown, tan and buff, and the underparts are white. It spends most of its life underground in a torpid state, emerging, often in large numbers, after rain. Termites are the main prey. A small clutch of eggs is laid in damp soil or humus, and the tadpoles live in moist chambers until they change into froglets.
Best viewing: Kruger-Lowveld, Pilanesberg

Louis du Preez

SOUTHERN FOAM NEST FROG *Chiromantis xerampelina*

Habitat: seasonal pans and waterholes
Length: 7–9 cm **Status:** seasonally common

Medium-sized frog with slender, webbed toes tipped with adhesive pads. Body is grey or tan, but the skin turns a chalky white in sunlight. It lives in the branches of trees but frequently enters buildings or vehicles. Termites and other insects are the prey. Eggs are laid in a distinctive, white foamy nest that is whipped up by the mating couple and a gaggle of unpaired males and hung from an overhanging branch above a pool or pan.
Best viewing: Ndumo, Mkhuze, Phinda, Hluhluwe-iMfolozi, Kruger-Lowveld

Duncan Butchart

BROWN-BACKED TREE FROG *Leptopelis mossambicus*

Habitat: open woodland, pan fringes
Length: 5–6 cm **Status:** seasonally fairly common

Small frog with broad head and large, bulging eyes. Adult is tawny-brown on the back with dark flanks. Immature is pale green. Limbs are slender with toes and fingers terminating in discs. Strictly nocturnal. Call is a loud, nasal 'kwarck', repeated at intervals from a perch in a tree or bush. Feeds on insects. Eggs are laid among damp vegetation near water.
Best viewing: Kruger-Lowveld, Ndumo, Mkhuze

Duncan Butchart

Duncan Butchart

COMMON RIVER FROG *Amietia angolensis*

Habitat: streams, pools, garden ponds
Length: 6–8 cm **Status:** common

Streamlined, green or brown with dark spots and blotches. Snout is pointed and the hind legs are long and powerful. One of the few frogs active in the winter months. Active by day and night. Often sits on emergent stones or at the water's edge, but is quick to dive in with a splash if disturbed. Call is a distinctive rattle and croak, uttered mostly on cool winter nights. Feeds mostly on insects. Individual eggs are surrounded by a large jelly capsule.
Best viewing: widespread in suitable habitat

Leonard Hoffmann/Images of Africa

CAPE RIVER FROG *Amietia fuscigula*

Habitat: fast-flowing streams **Length:** 8–12 cm
Status: common; near-endemic

Streamlined frog with pointed snout. Hind legs are long and powerful, with well-webbed toes. Back is variable in colour, often with a thin middle stripe. Active by day and night. Occurs in still or flowing water, usually resting on the banks or rocks. Leaps into water with a loud splash when approached. Call is a series of taps followed by a sharp grunt. Feeds mostly on insects. Individual eggs are surrounded by a large jelly capsule.
Best viewing: widespread in suitable habitat

Louis du Preez

CLICKING STREAM FROG *Strongylopus grayii*

Habitat: edges of streams and pools in montane and coastal grassland or fynbos **Length:** 4–5 cm
Status: fairly common; endemic

Streamlined frog with sharply pointed snout. Hind legs are extremely long and slender, with toes only slightly webbed. Back is variable in colour, usually blotched with a narrow middle stripe; the underbelly is plain white. Occurs in fringing vegetation alongside still or flowing water. Call is a sharp, repetitive snapping sound, like the clicking of your tongue. Feeds mostly on insects. Individual eggs are surrounded by a large jelly capsule.
Best viewing: widespread in suitable habitat

Louis du Preez

PLAIN GRASS FROG *Ptychadena anchietae*

Habitat: vleis and moist grassland **Length:** 4–5 cm
Status: fairly common

Streamlined frog with pointed snout. Back is plain, brick red, with paler underparts and dark eyes. Hind legs are extremely long and slender, with toes only slightly webbed. Capable of prodigious leaps and all members of this genus are sometimes known as 'rocket-frogs'. Call is a high-pitched trill. The several other South African *Ptychadena* species are more boldly patterned. Feeds mostly on insects. Individual eggs are surrounded by jelly capsules.
Best viewing: Kruger-Lowveld, Ndumo, Mkhuze, St Lucia

PAINTED REED FROG *Hyperolius marmoratus*

Habitat: reedbeds and rank growth on the edge of wetlands and rivers **Length:** 2–3 cm **Status:** common to abundant

Tiny, brightly coloured frog. Adult is variable with three dominant colour forms: Eastern Lowveld form is boldly striped in black, yellow and red; KwaZulu-Natal and Eastern Cape form is cream-coloured with darker speckles; southern Cape form is dark with pale spots and stripes; a plain fawn-brown form occurs throughout. Monotonous, sharp whistle call is made by day or night; many males call simultaneously. Feeds on small insects. Clusters of eggs are attached to submerged plants.
Best viewing: widespread in suitable habitat

Duncan Butchart

ARUM LILY REED FROG *Hyperolius horstocki*

Habitat: lilies and sedges around pans in fynbos **Length:** 2–3 cm **Status:** fairly common; endemic

Tiny, putty-coloured frog with bright orange toes and inner limbs. Male has an orange throat. Pale line runs from the nose, above the eye, and down the flank. Flattened discs on the toe tips enable it to climb on slippery surfaces. Active by day or night. Call is a repetitive, nasal bleat. Feeds on small insects. Clusters of individual eggs are attached to submerged plants.
Best viewing: Cape Peninsula, Betty's Bay, De Hoop

Michael Langford

BOETTGER'S CACO *Cacosternum boettgeri*

Habitat: damp or inundated grassland, seasonal rain pools **Length:** 2–3 cm **Status:** seasonally common

Tiny, squat-bodied frog with variable coloration, ranging from emerald-green to dull brown. Stripes, blotches and spots may be present. White underbelly with dark spots is diagnostic. Most active after rain; numbers gather at temporary pans and pools to breed. Call is piercing click, uttered monotonously at night and on cloudy days. Feeds on small insects. Clusters of individual eggs are attached to submerged plants.
Best viewing: widespread in suitable habitat

Nature Picture Library/Photo Access

SNORING PUDDLE FROG *Phrynobatrachus natalensis*

Habitat: vleis, seasonal pans, rain puddles, fringes of dams **Length:** 2–3 cm **Status:** seasonally common

Small, blunt-nosed, slender-limbed frog with toes webbed for half their length. Skin is mottled, brown or green, with wart-like bumps. Adult usually has an orange or pale stripe down the centre of its back. Active by day or night, feeding on small insects. Call is a rapidly repeated nasal snore. Feeds on small insects. Clusters of eggs float in a layer of the water surface.
Best viewing: widespread in suitable habitat

Leonard Hoffmann/Images of Africa

TREES AND SHRUBS

South Africa has over 1 000 species of woody plants, comprising trees, shrubs and lianas (vines). Some of these are distinctive and easy to recognize, particularly when flowering or in fruit, but most require careful study as they often belong to complex plant families comprising numerous similar species.

The following pages feature 136 of the more eye-catching, widespread or interesting indigenous trees and shrubs. This amounts to about 15% of the country's woody plant diversity, so becoming familiar with these will be a good grounding for more detailed study. The majority of the species selected are common within their range and can be found with ease if you use the individual distribution maps as a guide.

Except where a species has a unique and distinctive growth form, the accompanying photograph depicts the leaves, flowers or other noteworthy features close-up, rather than the whole plant. Description of bark, fruit, growth habit and flowering periods will further aid identification.

To identify woody plants, it is necessary to become familiar with some basic botanical terminology relating to the individual parts. In particular, it is important to determine whether the leaves of the species you are looking at are simple or compound (divided into leaflets), and how they are arranged on the branch (opposite or alternate).

In addition to the more distinctive and widespread indigenous species, 28 alien trees and shrubs are also featured. These troublesome invaders reproduce so rapidly that they out-compete native plant communities. Parts of Australia share a similar climate to South Africa, so it is not surprising that many species of *Eucalyptus* ('gums') and thornless *Acacia* ('wattles') have flourished in this country where their natural control mechanisms, such as seed-parasites, are absent. The same is true for several South American and Asian plants. In addition to these subtropical species, a number of temperate zone, northern hemisphere trees – such as pines, poplars, oaks and willows – have become an integral, though often unwanted, part of local landscapes. The control or removal of these invasive alien trees and shrubs is an ongoing battle; being able to identify them is the first step.

Not included here are the many ornamental alien trees that are grown in towns and around farm homesteads. Species such as the spectacularly flowered Kapok, Frangipani, Bougainvillea, Flamboyant, African Flame and Golden Trumpet will catch the eye of any traveller, but they originate in other parts of the world. So far, these species have not become naturalized (self-reproducing) in this country.

It is important to learn the scientific names of plants, as this knowledge facilitates comparison between related species. The names used here follow those in *Trees of Southern Africa* revised by Coates Palgrave (Struik Publishers, 2002).

GRASSLAND TREE FERN *Cyathea dregei*

Habitat: along streams in temperate grassland, forest fringes **Height:** up to 4 m **Status:** locally common, but much habitat lost to timber plantations

Striking tree fern with thick stem and distinctive feathery fronds up to 2 m long. Stout, black stem is fire resistant. Grows in full sun but is dependent on frequent mist and high rainfall. Most specimens lose their leaves in winter, with new fronds unfurling in spring. The similar *C. capensis* has a slender stem and grows only within the shade of forest.
Best viewing: Blyde Canyon-Graskop, Drakensberg

Duncan Butchart

COASTAL STRELITZIA *Strelitzia nicolai*

Habitat: coastal sand dunes, swamp forest
Height: up to 6 m **Status:** common to abundant; near endemic

Tall, banana-like plant with huge, broad leaves. Leaf blades may be over a metre long and are usually spliced into strips by the wind. Trunk becomes exposed in older specimens as dried leaves fall off. Usually grows in dense, impenetrable clumps. Spectacular white and lilac flowers are produced throughout the year. Black seeds are capped with a woolly, orange aril. Sunbirds and monkeys relish the nectar. Similar Cape Strelitzia *S. alba* and Mountain Strelitzia *S. caudata* have exclusive distribution ranges.
Best viewing: Wild Coast, KwaZulu-Natal coast

Duncan Butchart

WILD DATE PALM *Phoenix reclinata*

Habitat: riversides and swamp forest, termite mounds
Height: up to 6 m **Status:** common to abundant

Bushy palm with dark green, feather-shaped leaves up to 4 m long. Often forms dense clumps along rivers and streams. Clusters of creamy-white flowers are held in orange sheaths (Aug–Oct). Edible fruits appear in late summer; yellow ripening to brown. Birds, monkeys, African Civet and humans relish the fruit. Weavers strip the leaves for nest building.
Best viewing: Kruger-Lowveld, Ndumo, Mkhuze, Hluhluwe-iMfolozi, St Lucia, Wild Coast

Duncan Butchart

LALA PALM *Hyphaene coriacea*

Habitat: coastal sandflats, Lowveld savanna (south of Olifants River) **Height:** up to 7 m **Status:** common but heavily utilized for palm wine in northern KwaZulu-Natal

Slender palm with large, grey-green, fan-shaped leaves up to 120 cm wide. Leaf petioles are armed with black spines. Fully grown, unbranched specimens are uncommon. Usually forms impenetrable clumps in low-lying areas but not always along rivers. Clusters of large, bell-shaped fruits hang on the tree throughout the year. The very similar *H. petersiana* replaces this species north of the Olifants River, where it may reach a height of 18 m.
Best viewing: Kosi Bay, St Lucia, Phinda, Umthamvuna, Kruger

Duncan Butchart

Duncan Butchart

BROAD-LEAVED YELLOWWOOD   *Podocarpus latifolius*

Habitat: coastal and montane forest **Height:** up to 30 m, but stunted on exposed hillsides **Status:** uncommon

Small to large, bushy, evergreen tree related to conifers. Simple leaves (about 10 cm long) are grey-green, leathery, sickle-shaped, held in spirals at the tips of stems. Male cones are pinkish, female receptacle is fleshy, maroon. Large, fleshy berries, blue-grey to purple, are joined to the receptacles. The related *P. falcatus* has much smaller leaves (up to 5 cm) while *P. henkelii* has longer, drooping leaves (up to 17 cm). Timber of all yellowwoods is valued for furniture production.
Best viewing: Tsitsikamma, Table Mountain, Dwesa (Wild Coast), Giant's Castle, Woodbush

Duncan Butchart

WILLOW BEECHWOOD   *Faurea saligna*

Habitat: sandy soils of stony hillsides or open woodland **Height:** up to 15 m **Status:** fairly common

Small to medium-sized, deciduous, upright tree. Bark is dark brown and deeply fissured. Leaves are simple, narrowly oblong, almost sickle-shaped; begin as pink buds which open then turn from pale green to orange in autumn. Rows of small, puffy flowers are held on slender, drooping spikes (Aug–Feb); often harbour ants. Fruit is a small nutlet with a persistent style. Similar *F. rochetiana* has broad leaves and *F. galpinii* has upright flower stalks.
Best viewing: Marakele, Pilanesberg, Magaliesberg, Mpumalanga escarpment

Duncan Butchart

MOUNTAIN CYPRESS   *Widdringtonia nodiflora*

Habitat: rocky outcrops and gullies on mountain sides **Height:** 4–6 m (larger specimens lost to lumber industry) **Status:** locally common

Evergreen conifer that may be a small bush or cone-shaped tree. Typically grows in colonies. Bark is greyish-brown, becoming fissured and flaky to reveal orange underbark. Leaves are scale-like, clinging to stems; young growth is thinner, more needle-shaped. Lacks flowers. Male and female cones appear on the same tree; female cone is more rounded with 4 scales.
Best viewing: Giant's Castle (Drakensberg), Table Mountain, Blyde Canyon eastern escarpment

SILVER-TREE   *Leucadendron argenteum*

Habitat: gravel soils on hillsides **Height:** up to 7 m **Status:** locally common in very restricted range; endemic

Slender, evergreen tree with distinctive silvery foliage. Most striking in summer when leaves shimmer vividly in the sunlight. Bark is smooth with distinctive leaf scars. Leaves are elliptic, covered in silvery hairs, and crowded at stem tips. Flowers appear in cone-like heads (Aug–Sep). Seeds are enclosed within a small black nut. Able to withstand strong winds, resistant to fierce fires.
Best viewing: eastern slopes of Table Mountain

Nigel Dennis/Images of Africa

TREE PINCUSHION *Leucospermum conocarpodendron*

Habitat: mountain sides, coastal dunes
Height: up to 5 m **Status:** locally common, but one subspecies confined to Table Mountain; endemic

Large, bushy, evergreen shrub or small, single-stemmed tree. Often forms a rounded shape. Bark is smooth or deeply fissured if fire-scorched. Branches are usually tangled and interlocking. Oblong leaves with several teeth on the tip face upwards on branches in a scale-like manner. Leaves may be greyish and hairy or green and smooth. Large yellow flower heads (Aug–Dec) attract nectar-seeking sugarbirds.
Best viewing: Table Mountain, De Hoop

Duncan Butchart

COMMON PROTEA *Protea caffra*

Habitat: rocky hillsides, often on cooler, south-facing slopes **Height:** up to 6 m
Status: common to abundant; near endemic

Short, gnarled tree with rough, almost black bark. Typically grows in colonies on hillsides. Leaves are simple, narrowly oblong, leathery, blue-grey and arranged in clusters at branch tips. Attractive, long-lasting flowers lure nectar-feeding Malachite Sunbird and Gurney's Sugarbird, and are often inhabited by ants (Nov–Mar). Old, dry flower heads remain on the tree for several months. Silver Protea *P. roupelliae* shares much of this species' range, but new leaves of this tree are covered in distinctive silvery hairs.
Best viewing: widespread in suitable habitat

Duncan Butchart

SUGARBUSH *Protea repens*

Habitat: base of hillsides in fynbos
Height: up to 5 m **Status:** locally common but colonies often cleared for farming; endemic

Small, thickset tree with angular stems. Bark is greyish-brown, smooth with leaf scars. Leaves are simple, upright, leathery, thinly oblong, clustered at stem tips. Flowers open white but turn yellow within days; blooms at different times of year within its range. Dried seed-head is a ribbed cone. Nectar-rich flowers are visited by bees and sunbirds. A wide variety of similar *Protea* species occurs in the fynbos biome of the south-western Cape.
Best viewing: Cape Peninsula

Duncan Butchart

WABOOM *Protea nitida*

Habitat: rocky mountain slopes **Height:** up to 7 m
Status: common; endemic

Small, open-branched tree or multi-stemmed shrub. Leaves are simple, blue-green, oval, and held at right angles to the stem. Large, creamy-white flowers appear throughout the year. Waboom means 'Wagon Tree' and it was so-named because it provided hard wood for making wagon wheels for the first European settlers. Flowers are visited by Cape Sugarbird and Malachite Sunbird. A wide variety of similar *Protea* species occurs in the fynbos biome of the south-western Cape.
Best viewing: Cape Peninsula

Braam van Wyk

Walter Knirr/Images of Africa

QUIVER-TREE *Aloe dichotoma*

Habitat: rocky hillsides **Height:** up to 6 m
Status: common; distribution may be contracting
due to climate change; near endemic

Large, thickset tree aloe with broad trunk and tangled branch
structure. Whorls of stiff, sap-filled leaves appear at the branch
tips. Bark is smooth, yellowish-bronze, flaking off in sheets. Bright
yellow flowers appear in dense clusters on short spikes (Jun–Aug).
Birds and baboons relish the nectar. Sociable Weavers often build
their thatched nests in the branches. Giant Quiver-Tree *A. pillansii*
is taller and more slender; confined to Richtersveld.
Best viewing: Augrabies, Richtersveld, Namaqua

Duncan Butchart

EASTERN TREE ALOE *Aloe barberae*

Habitat: sheltered kloofs of east and south-facing
hillsides **Height:** up to 18 m **Status:** fairly common;
near endemic

Large, slender-stemmed tree aloe with ornate branching structure;
the tallest of aloes. Whorls of leathery, sap-filled leaves appear at
the branch tips. Bark is pale grey and smooth. Pinkish-red tubular
flowers appear on impressive candelabra-shaped spikes (May–Jun).
Sunbirds and white-eyes relish the nectar. Easily grown from
cuttings, and often planted in towns and around kraals.
Best viewing: Hluhluwe-iMfolozi, KwaZulu-Natal Midlands,
Kosi Bay, Port Edward, Barberton

Duncan Butchart

MOUNTAIN ALOE *Aloe marlothii*

Habitat: rocky hillsides **Height:** up to 6 m
Status: common to abundant; near endemic

Large, single-stemmed aloe. A whorl of stiff, sap-filled leaves
appears at the branch tip. Margins and undersides of the leaves are
heavily toothed. Bright, yellow-orange tubular flowers appear in
horizontal spikes, on a branched flower head (Jun–Aug). Birds and
baboons feed on the nectar. Widely cultivated in towns, gardens and
roadsides. Most widespread of several similar species, including
A. ferox, A. africana, A. excelsa, A. littoralis and *A. thraskii.*
Best viewing: Marakele, Pilanesberg, Magaliesberg, Kruger-
Lowveld, Hluhluwe-iMfolozi, Mkhuze

Duncan Butchart

KRANTZ ALOE *Aloe arborescens*

Habitat: mountain sides, coastal dunes
Height: 2–3 m **Status:** common to abundant

Large, multi-stemmed bush or small tree with 'bearded' appearance
due to old, dry leaves persisting on stems. Slender, sap-filled leaves
arch downwards and are bluish or greyish green, with conspicuous
teeth on the margins. Bright, pink-red, tubular flowers form a
triangular shape on an unbranched spike (May–Jul). Sunbirds,
starlings and baboons relish the nectar. Often cultivated as a hedge.
Best viewing: widespread in suitable habitat

Duncan Butchart

NABOOM *Euphorbia ingens*

Habitat: rocky hillsides, koppies, termite mounds
Height: up to 10 m **Status:** common to abundant

Medium to massive, cactus-like tree with a dense, multi-branched crown. Leafless, but has green, succulent branchlets, four-angled in oblong segments. Paired spines are situated on the rims. Small yellow flowers appear alongside spines on rims (Apr–May). The three-lobed fruits turn reddish when ripe. All parts exude poisonous, white latex, sticky to the touch.
Best viewing: widespread in suitable habitat

Duncan Butchart

BUSHVELD CANDELABRA EUPHORBIA *Euphorbia cooperi*

Habitat: koppies, rocky hillsides, open woodland
Height: up to 5 m **Status:** common

Single-stemmed, cactus-like tree with outstretched crown of succulent branches. Leafless, but has green, succulent branches, five-angled in heart-shaped segments. Paired spines are situated on rims of the angled branchlets. Masses of yellow flowers attract great numbers of wasps and other pollinating insects (Jun–Oct). The three-lobed fruits turn reddish when ripe. All parts exude poisonous, white latex, sticky to the touch.
Best viewing: Kruger-Lowveld, Pilanesberg, Marakele, Ithala

Duncan Butchart

ELEPHANT'S TRUNK *Pachypodium namaquanum*

Habitat: among boulders in rocky desert
Height: up to 4 m **Status:** locally fairly common;
near endemic

Distinctive, single-stemmed, succulent tree with a crown of foliage confined to growth tips. Trunk is usually unbranched, with warty, spine-tipped bumps across the surface. Large, crinkled, grey-green leaves are crowded at the ends of the stems. Tubular, red flowers appear among the leaves (Sep–Dec). Hair-tipped seeds are released from a paired pod. When seen on the skyline, this strange plant has an almost human form, hence the Afrikaans common name '*Halfmens*'.
Best viewing: Richtersveld

Braam van Wyk

IMPALA-LILY *Adenium multiflorum*

Habitat: among rocks or sandy flats in open woodland
Height: up to 2 m (usually much smaller)
Status: fairly common

Stocky shrub or small tree with thick, succulent stems. Trunk is smooth, greyish-green. Leaves are simple, arranged in spirals at branch tips; glossy dark or blue-green. Spineless. Showy flowers are star-shaped, pink with crimson margins (May–Aug). Fruit is cigar-shaped, paired pod that splits to release silky-tufted seeds. Widely cultivated in hot, dry climates.
Best viewing: Kruger-Lowveld, Mkhuze, Ndumo, Mapungubwe

Duncan Butchart

SYCAMORE FIG *Ficus sycomorus*

Habitat: riverbanks in dry savanna **Height:** up to 20 m
Status: locally common (but many swept away by
flooding rivers during cyclones)

Massive, spreading tree with smooth, pale yellow trunk and
branches. Trunk is often buttressed with roots exposed. Simple
leaves are heart-shaped and coarse in texture. All parts contain
sticky, milky-white latex. Large figs are green, ripening to orange,
and borne on branchlets of main stems in all months. Birds, fruit-bats
and monkeys relish the figs and serve as seed dispersers.
Best viewing: Ndumo, Mkhuze, Kruger-Lowveld, Mapungubwe

Duncan Butchart

RED-LEAVED FIG *Ficus ingens*

Habitat: koppies and rocky hillsides **Height:** up to 10 m
Status: fairly common

Small to medium-sized tree, often broader than tall, with smooth,
pale trunk and branches. Germinates in crevices and is able to
split rocks. Forms low mats on north-facing rocks on cool, windswept Highveld. Simple leaves are heart-shaped, smooth and
shiny. New leaf growth is coppery-red, which gives the tree its
common name. Small, greenish figs attract birds and monkeys.
The similar *F. glumosa* has soft, hairy leaves.
Best viewing: widespread in suitable habitat

Duncan Butchart

COMMON WILD FIG *Ficus burkei*

Habitat: riverbanks and termite mounds, coastal bush,
forest **Height:** up to 15 m **Status:** common

Large, spreading tree with smooth, pale grey bark. Often has aerial
roots hanging from branches and is usually a strangler of other
trees. Leaves simple, dull or glossy with long petiole; in droopy
spirals around stems. Contains milky latex. Small, stalkless figs
are massed along stems, and relished by birds and fruit-bats. Very
similar *F. natalensis* and *F. petersii* are restricted to KwaZulu-Natal
and the Lowveld, respectively.
Best viewing: widespread in suitable habitat

Duncan Butchart

LARGE-LEAVED ROCK FIG *Ficus abutilifolia*

Habitat: koppies and rocky hillsides **Height:** up to 8 m
(usually much smaller) **Status:** fairly common

Small tree that grows among rocks; one of several 'rock-splitting'
figs. Milky-white or yellowish-grey stem and roots are exposed in
crevices. Bark is smooth. Leaves are simple, large, heart-shaped or
round; dark glossy green above with conspicuous pinkish-yellow
veins and midrib. Pale green figs ripen to red and are borne in small
groups in the leaf axils. Barbets and other birds feed on the figs.
Similar *F. cordata* has smaller leaves; occurs in dry west.
Best viewing: Marakele, Pilanesberg, Magaliesberg, Ithala

Duncan Butchart

BROOM-CLUSTER FIG *Ficus sur*

Habitat: forest fringe, streambanks, termite mounds
Height: up to 12 m **Status:** fairly common

Small to large tree with spreading crown. Bark is smooth, greyish-ochre. Leaves are simple, oval, with pointed tip and wavy margin. New leaves are wine-red, turning apple-green with time. Clusters of large, greenish-pink figs are borne on branched panicles on the trunk, main branches or even exposed roots. Birds, primates and humans relish the juicy figs.
Best viewing: widespread in suitable habitat

Duncan Butchart

WONDERBOOM FIG *Ficus salicifolia*

Habitat: koppies and rocky hillsides, wooded kloofs
Height: up to 9 m **Status:** fairly common

Small to large, widely spreading tree. Bark of young trees is pale grey and smooth, becoming dark and rough with age. Leaves are simple, oblong with almost parallel sides. Figs are whitish-green ripening to pink with white dots; borne in the leaf axils. The famous 'Wonderboom' near Pretoria is a huge and complex tree, with pendulous branches rooting to cover a large area; this tree is estimated to be over 1 000 years old.
Best viewing: Wonderboom (Pretoria), Marakele, Magaliesberg, Blyde Canyon

Duncan Butchart

SHEPHERD'S TREE *Boscia albitrunca*

Habitat: arid and semi-arid plains and hillsides
Height: up to 7 m **Status:** common

Stout, evergreen tree with white or pale grey trunk and branches. Distinctive browse line often at the base of the rounded crown of leaves. Simple leaves are small, grey-green and leathery, very nutritious. Sheep and goats may depend upon this tree during times of drought, hence the common name. Small, sweetly scented flowers appear in dense clusters (Aug–Oct). Small yellow berries are eaten by birds.
Best viewing: widespread in suitable habitat

Duncan Butchart

WHITE STINKWOOD *Celtis africana*

Habitat: riverbanks, wooded kloofs and montane forest **Height:** up to 20 m **Status:** common; often a pioneer species

Tall, deciduous tree with smooth, pale grey trunk, sometimes buttressed at the base. Simple leaves are heart-shaped, finely toothed and alternate. Leaves are soft and lime-green in spring, leathery and dark green in summer, yellow in autumn. Small, greenish flowers appear in leaf axils (Aug–Oct). Small, yellow berries relished by Thick-billed Weavers. Pigeonwood *Trema orientalis* has similar foliage.
Best viewing: widespread in suitable habitat

Duncan Butchart

Duncan Butchart

UMBRELLA THORN *Acacia tortilis*

Habitat: clay soils on flats Height: up to 12 m
Status: common to abundant

Large, flat-topped, deciduous tree with bare, low-branching trunk.
This is the archetypal tree of African savannas. Largest specimens
grow on alluvial soils near rivers. Bark is dark grey and vertically
grooved. Leaves are bipinnately compound with tiny leaflets.
Both straight and hooked thorns are present. Flowers are cream
balls in spring and early summer (Sep–Nov). Seedpods are small,
coiled in clusters.
Best viewing: Mkhuze, Kruger-Lowveld, Pilanesberg, Madikwe

PAPERBARK THORN *Acacia sieberiana*

Habitat: sandy soils of eastern escarpment foothills
Height: up to 12 m Status: common to abundant

Large, umbrella-shaped tree, often with low-branching trunk. Bark
is corky, pale yellow, peels off in large, papery sections. Leaves
are bipinnately compound with tiny leaflets. Thorns are straight
and white, up to 9 cm. Cream, ball-shaped flowers cover the tree
(Sep–Nov). Seedpods are large and woody, pale sandy-brown. Rough
bark harbours geckos and insects, which attract wood-hoopoes, tits
and other birds.
Best viewing: Nelspruit-Barberton-Badplaas, KwaZulu-Natal
Midlands

Duncan Butchart

SCENTED THORN *Acacia nilotica*

Habitat: poorly drained clay soils on flats
Height: up to 7 m Status: common to abundant

Small, bushy tree that may form an umbrella shape; often grows
in dense thickets. Bark is dark grey and deeply grooved. Leaves
are bipinnately compound. Thorns are straight, paired, distinctly
backward-pointing, up to 9 cm long. Bright yellow, ball-shaped
flowers appear in profusion (Sep–Apr). Distinctive 'beaded'
seedpods are sweet scented. Similar *A. gerrardii* has reddish bark
and narrow, flattened pods.
Best viewing: widespread in suitable habitat

Duncan Butchart

COMMON HOOK THORN *Acacia caffra*

Habitat: rocky hillsides and along streams
Height: up to 12 m Status: common; near endemic

Open-branched, deciduous tree, with feathery foliage. Often has
branches low down, frequently in a contorted shape. Bark is dark
brown, deeply furrowed with age. Thorns are in hooked pairs.
Bipinnately compound leaves have 21–50 pairs of tiny leaflets.
Flowers appear in creamy-yellow spikes, often when tree is leafless
(Aug–Nov). Seedpods are narrow, sickle-shaped. Similar *A. galpinii*
assumes much larger size (up to 25 m) and has larger, thicker pods.
Best viewing: widespread in suitable habitat

Duncan Butchart

SWEET THORN *Acacia karroo*

Habitat: clay soils **Height:** up to 7 m
Status: common to abundant

Rounded tree with bright green foliage; deciduous in drier parts of
its range. Bark of older trees is dark and rough, while saplings have
brick-red trunks. Straight, white thorns are in pairs, most abundant
on new growth, up to 10 cm long. Bipinnately compound leaves.
Flowers are sweetly scented, golden balls (Dec–Jan). Pods are sickle-
shaped. Waxbills and other small birds build grass-ball nests within
the armed branches.
Best viewing: widespread in suitable habitat

Duncan Butchart

CAMEL THORN *Acacia erioloba*

Habitat: sandy soils, often along seasonal drainage
lines **Height:** up to 20 m **Status:** common

Large tree with low, lateral branches and spreading crown. Bark
is very rough, deeply furrowed, blackish-brown. Large, paired
thorns are straight, white, up to 6 cm, sometimes swollen at
their base. Bipinnately compound leaves with up to 15 pairs of
leaflets. Flowers are golden-yellow balls (Jul–Sep). Seedpods are
thick, curved and covered in velvety grey hairs; much relished by
antelope and livestock.
Best viewing: Kgalagadi, Augrabies, Mokala, Kimberley

Duncan Butchart

KNOB THORN *Acacia nigrescens*

Habitat: sandy soils, hillsides, alluvial flats
Height: up to 16 m **Status:** common to abundant

Tall, upright, deciduous tree with rounded crown. May be the
dominant tree in flat or undulating country. Bark is fissured and
bears large, thorn-tipped knobs. Thorns are short, hook shaped.
Leaves are bipinnately compound with 2–4 pairs of leaflets, larger
than those of any other *Acacia*. Masses of creamy-white flower
spikes cover the canopy, attracting bees and other insects (Aug–
Nov). Seedpods are flat and papery.
Best viewing: Kruger-Lowveld, Mapungubwe, Phongola, Mkhuze

Duncan Butchart

BLACK THORN *Acacia mellifera*

Habitat: sandy soils on flats **Height:** up to 6 m (but
usually shorter) **Status:** common to abundant

Multi-stemmed shrub or small tree, with an impenetrable tangle
of thorny branches. Bark is smooth and grey, but fissured on older
trees. Thorns are dark brown or black, hooked, in pairs like claws.
Leaves are bipinnately compound with 3 or 4 pairs of leaflets.
Flowers are produced in massed spikes, turning the whole tree
creamy-white (Sep–Nov) and attracting hordes of bees. Seedpods
are flat and papery.
Best viewing: Pilanesberg, Kgalagadi, Augrabies, Mokadi

Duncan Butchart

Duncan Butchart

FEVER-TREE ACACIA *Acacia xanthophloea*

Habitat: clay soils of alluvial flats **Height:** up to 15 m
Status: common to abundant

Tall, upright tree with sparse, feathery foliage. Sulphur-yellow bark, powdery to the touch, renders it unmistakable. Leaves are bipinnately compound. Thorns are straight, paired, white, up to 7 cm long. Flowers are dense, golden-yellow balls (Sep–Nov). Seedpods are sickle-shaped. Prefers the same moist habitat as the malaria-carrying mosquito, hence the name.
Best viewing: Ndumo, Mkhuze, St Lucia, Hluhluwe-iMfolozi, Kruger, Mapungubwe

Duncan Butchart

ANA-TREE *Faidherbia albida*

Habitat: alluvial soils of river valleys **Height:** up to 25 m
Status: uncommon

Tall, upright tree that may reach massive proportions. Older trees often have drooping branches. Unusually, this tree is typically leafless in summer, hence the alternative name 'Winter Thorn'. Young stems are white with distinctive zigzag growth pattern. Short spines are straight and in pairs. Leaves are bipinnately compound. Small, cream flowers appear in spikes (May–Sep). Thick, coiled pods are relished by Elephant, antelope and baboons.
Best viewing: Kruger, Mapungubwe

Duncan Butchart

SICKLE-BUSH *Dichrostachys cinerea*

Habitat: most soils types, often invades disturbed areas **Height:** up to 5 m **Status:** abundant

Small, deciduous tree or shrub with *Acacia*-like appearance. Usually multi-stemmed, often forms thickets. Bark is grey-brown, deeply grooved. Branches are armed with straight spines. Leaves are bipinnately compound with tiny leaflets. Flowers are attractive pink and yellow hanging catkins resembling Christmas tree decorations (Oct–Jan). Pods appear in dense, tangled clusters that fall to the ground.
Best viewing: widespread in suitable habitat

FLAT-CROWN ALBIZIA *Albizia adianthifolia*

Habitat: sandy soils on coastal flats **Height:** up to 20 m
Status: common

Tall, widely spreading, deciduous tree with flat crown. Bark is greyish-ochre and rough. Leaves are bipinnately compound with rectangular leaflets. Masses of greenish-white flower heads cover the canopy to attract butterflies, bees, wasps and sunbirds (Jul–Sep). Pods are papery and twisted, splitting to release the seeds. Broad umbrella shape offers exceptional shade.
Best viewing: Ndumo, Thembe, Kosi Bay, Wild Coast

Duncan Butchart

MOPANE *Colophospermum mopane*

Habitat: clay soils of eastern Lowveld
Height: up to 18 m **Status:** common to abundant

Multi-stemmed shrub or large, deciduous tree with rounded crown. Often dominant on poorly drained clay soils as tall, single-species woodland or low scrub. Bark is dark grey and deeply furrowed. Leaves are divided into a butterfly shape, bright green when young, ageing to coppery-red. Flowers are inconspicuous. Fruit is a thin, sand-coloured, kidney-shaped pod. Mopane worms (caterpillars of a large moth) feed on the foliage during summer.
Best viewing: Kruger (north), Mapungubwe

Duncan Butchart

POD MAHOGANY *Afzelia quanzensis*

Habitat: sandy soils of eastern Lowveld, sandforest
Height: up to 20 m **Status:** fairly common; larger specimens targeted by woodcutters

Large, deciduous tree with spreading crown. Bark is pale grey, flaking off in older trees. Leaves are compound with 4–7 pairs of glossy green leaflets with wavy margins. The strange flowers have a single pink petal, appearing with the new growth (Oct–Nov). Large, woody pods house striking, black seeds with waxy yellow or red arils; eaten by baboons and Trumpeter Hornbills.
Best viewing: Kruger (especially far north), Ndumo, Thembe, Mapungubwe

Duncan Butchart

BURKEA *Burkea africana*

Habitat: coarse, sandy soils **Height:** up to 10 m
Status: common

Medium-sized, deciduous tree with attractive spreading crown. Often forms single-species stands or mini-woodlands. Bark is grey, rough and flaky. Bipinnately compound leaves are grey-green with 5–9 alternate leaflets, and an off-centre terminal one. Small, creamy-white flowers are arranged in pendulous spikes (Sep–Nov). Thin, papery pods hang in clusters at stem tips, often remaining on the tree for months.
Best viewing: Magaliesberg, Marakele, Nylsvley

Duncan Butchart

NYALA-TREE *Xanthocercis zambesiaca*

Habitat: alluvial soils of river valleys, termite mounds
Height: up to 30 m **Status:** uncommon

Large, evergreen tree with rounded crown. Younger branchlets hang vertically from larger branches. Bark is brown and rough. Leaves are compound, with up to 7 pairs of leaflets; dark green and glossy. Flowers are small, pea-shaped in short sprays (Sep–Dec). Pod resembles a berry with just one shiny black seed. Provides abundant shade for large mammals during the heat of the day.
Best viewing: Kruger-Lowveld, Mapungubwe

Duncan Butchart

Duncan Butchart

KIAAT *Pterocarpus angolensis*

Habitat: sandy soils, rocky hillsides **Height:** up to 16 m
Status: fairly common; larger specimens in demand
for timber

Tall, deciduous tree with sparse, spreading crown of drooping
leaves. Most distinctive in winter when leafless and decorated with
round, papery-fringed pods with spiky centres. Bark is dark brown,
furrowed in older trees; wood exudes a blood-red sap. Leaves are
compound with terminal leaflet. A profusion of small, yellow,
pea-shaped flowers is produced on branched sprays (Aug–Dec).
Best viewing: Kruger-Lowveld, Blyde Canyon, Ithala

Duncan Butchart

ROUND-LEAVED BLOODWOOD *Pterocarpus rotundifolius*

Habitat: open woodland, hillsides
Height: usually 8–10 m (may be larger)
Status: common to abundant

Medium-sized tree with pendulous foliage, or shrub that forms
scrubby thickets. Bark is grey to brown, becoming fissured with
age. Leaves are compound with a terminal leaflet; the leaflets are
almost round in shape. A profusion of bright yellow, pea-shaped
flowers form large, showy heads (Sep–Jan). A single seed is held
in a flattened pod.
Best viewing: Kruger-Lowveld, Marakele, Pilanesberg

Duncan Butchart

WEEPING WATTLE *Peltophorum africanum*

Habitat: sandy soils, vlei margins, termite mounds
Height: up to 10 m **Status:** common

Medium-sized, deciduous tree with *Acacia*-like foliage, but without
thorns. Branches low down or may be multi-stemmed. Bark
becomes rough, grey-brown with age. Bipinnately compound
leaves are fern-like. Yellow, pea-shaped flowers are showy with
crinkled petals in erect sprays (Sep–May). Seedpods are oval, flat,
pale brown, held in bunches.
Best viewing: widespread in suitable habitat

Duncan Butchart

LONG-TAIL CASSIA *Cassia abbreviata*

Habitat: termite mounds, open woodland
Height: up to 6 m **Status:** fairly common

Small, deciduous tree with open, spreading crown. Remarkable for
its extremely long, tail-like pods that split and twist to reveal seeds
embedded in green pulp. Bark is dark brown to black, divided into
ridged blocks. Leaves are compound, with up to 11 pairs of leaflets.
Clusters of showy, yellow flowers appear on long spikes (Aug–Sep).
Seedpods host parasitic beetles, which attract tits, crombecs and
other birds.
Best viewing: Kruger-Lowveld, Mapungubwe

TREE WISTERIA *Bolusanthus speciosus*

Habitat: poorly drained clay soils **Height:** up to 7 m
Status: common

Medium-sized, upright, deciduous tree with drooping foliage. Often branches low down or may be multi-stemmed. Bark is dark brown and deeply fissured. Leaves are compound, 3–7 pairs of elliptic leaflets plus a terminal one. Flowers are deep purple, pea-shaped in long, terminal sprays (Aug–Nov). Flat, narrow seedpods are borne in clusters, remaining on the tree for many months.
Best viewing: Mkhuze, Kruger-Lowveld

Duncan Butchart

CORK-BUSH *Mundulea sericea*

Habitat: sandy flats, rocky hillsides **Height:** up to 4 m
Status: common

Small, deciduous tree or shrub with silvery-green foliage. Bark is rough and corky with age, often blackened by fire (to which it is resistant). Leaves are compound with 6–10 pairs of opposite leaflets covered with silky hairs. Attractive purple, pea-like flowers appear in hanging sprays (Oct–Feb). Flat, velvety, pale-brown pods split to release seeds.
Best viewing: widespread in suitable habitat

Duncan Butchart

KEURBOOM *Virgilia oroboides*

Habitat: forest fringe, river valleys **Height:** 5–15 m
Status: common; endemic

Small, upright tree with fine, wispy foliage. Bark is pale grey-brown and smooth. Leaves are compound with 5–10 pairs of leaflets. Masses of lilac, pea-shaped flowers hang in terminal sprays (Aug–Jan). Seedpods are sandy-brown and velvety. Beautiful, fast-growing tree ideal for cultivation, but not long-lived. Can be used as a pioneer species to create a forest clump.
Best viewing: Cape Town, De Hoop, Garden Route

Kristo Pienaar/Images of Africa

UMZIMBEET *Millettia grandis*

Habitat: coastal forest, often on fringe **Height:** up to 13 m **Status:** common; endemic

Medium-sized, evergreen tree with attractive foliage. Bark is grey-brown, smooth or flaky. Leaves are compound with 3–7 pairs of pointed leaflets; dark green above, pale and hairy below. Veins are conspicuous. Beautiful, purple, pea-shaped flowers held in upright spikes above the leaves (Dec–Jan). Seedpod is flat and woody, covered with velvety hairs, splitting into a spiral when ripe.
Best viewing: Dwesa (Wild Coast), KwaZulu-Natal coast

Duncan Butchart

Duncan Butchart

SACRED CORAL-TREE *Erythrina lysistemon*

Habitat: rocky hillsides, koppies **Height:** up to 12 m
Status: fairly common

Medium-sized tree with rounded crown. Spectacular when leafless and covered with scarlet flowers (Jun–Aug). Leaves are trifoliate with triangular leaflets. Individual flowers consist of one rolled petal enclosing other petals and stamens. Beaded pods contain scarlet 'lucky beans'. Bark is smooth with thorns on stems. The similar Coast Coral Tree *E. caffra* occurs from Port Shepstone to Humansdorp.
Best viewing: Marakele, Magaliesberg, Nelspruit, Barberton, Phongola

Duncan Butchart

WEEPING BOER-BEAN *Schotia brachypetala*

Habitat: drainage lines and termite mounds
Height: up to 12 m **Status:** common; near endemic

Large, deciduous tree with a spreading crown, often branching low down. Bark is rough, dark grey-brown. Compound leaves are shiny green with 4–6 pairs of leaflets. Masses of crimson, cup-shaped flowers literally 'weep' with nectar; sunbirds, orioles, parrots, monkeys and insects find the nectar irresistible (Aug–Sep). Seedpod is woody with a persistent rim.
Best viewing: Kruger-Lowveld, Mkhuze, Ndumo, Hluhluwe-iMfolozi

Duncan Butchart

KAROO BOER-BEAN *Schotia afra*

Habitat: drainage lines and termite mounds
Height: up to 12 m **Status:** common; near endemic

Small, multi-branched tree with gnarled trunk and stiff branches. Bark is pale grey on small branchlets, darker grey and rough on older trees. Leaves are compound with 6–18 pairs of small leaflets; dark green. Brilliant crimson flowers in dense clusters on branched heads provide a splash of colour in semi-arid landscapes (Aug–Oct). Seedpod is woody with a persistent rim.
Best viewing: Addo, Camdeboo, Karoo

Duncan Butchart

GLOSSY BOTTLEBRUSH *Greyia sutherlandii*

Habitat: well-drained soil on rocky hillsides, cliffs and forest fringe **Height:** up to 5 m
Status: common; endemic

Small, gnarled tree with open-branched appearance. Bark is rough and almost black on older specimens. Simple leaves are round, toothed and alternate, clustered towards ends of stems; glossy green above, hairless and sticky when young. Spectacular scarlet flowers in dense, brush-like spikes (Aug–Oct). Nectar favoured by sunbirds and white-eyes. Fruit is a cone-shaped tube that splits to release seeds.
Best viewing: Drakensberg

SAUSAGE TREE *Kigelia africana*

Habitat: alluvial soils of river valleys **Height:** up to 20 m
Status: fairly common

Large, deciduous tree with a squat trunk and thick branches. Bark is pale grey and smooth. Compound leaves have up to 4 pairs of leaflets and a terminal one, crusty in texture. Extravagant, tubular flowers have crinkly, crimson petals, rich in nectar and favoured by sunbirds and fruit-bats (Jul–Sep). The extraordinary sausage-shaped fruits are up to 0.5 m long and may weigh over 5 kg.
Best viewing: Kruger-Lowveld, Mapungubwe, Ndumo, Mkhuze

Duncan Butchart

APPLE-LEAF *Philenoptera violacea (Lonchocarpus capassa)*

Habitat: alluvial soils of river valleys **Height:** up to 18 m
Status: common to abundant

Tall, irregularly shaped tree with twisted trunk and sparse foliage. Pale bark flakes off in blocks. Leaves are compound, with 1 or 2 pairs of leaflets and a terminal leaflet; coarsely textured. Flowers are lilac, pea-shaped in terminal sprays (Sep–Nov). Seedpods thin and papery, in clusters. Thousands of small froghopper insects feed on the sap and exude a frothy foam sunshade; this fluid drips from the tree like rain.
Best viewing: Kruger-Lowveld, Mapungubwe

Duncan Butchart

PAPERBARK CORKWOOD *Commiphora marlothii*

Habitat: koppies, cliffs, rocky hillsides
Height: up to 5 m **Status:** locally common

Small tree with striking green trunk and branches. Branches are angular and contorted. An aromatic sap (myrrh) occurs in all parts. Yellowish, papery barks peels off trunk and branches. Leaves are compound with 3–5 pairs of soft, woolly leaflets and a terminal one, clustered at branch tips. Small, yellow flowers are on short stalks in clusters (Sep–Oct). Small, black berries have a waxy scarlet cap; relished by birds.
Best viewing: Marakele, Pilanesberg, Blyde Canyon

Duncan Butchart

OLDWOOD *Leucosidea sericea*

Habitat: mountains and streambanks
Height: up to 5 m **Status:** common to abundant;
near endemic

Bushy shrub or small, gnarled tree with distinctive, coarsely-flaking bark. Evergreen and able to withstand bitter cold and frosts. Compound leaves are greyish-green, velvety and shaped like those of a rose bush (to which family it belongs). Young stems are hairy. Clusters of small, greenish-yellow flowers produced in a spray (Aug–Dec). Small nuts are encased in the old, dry flowers.
Best viewing: Drakensberg, Golden Gate, Suikerbosrand, Blyde Canyon, Wakkerstroom

Duncan Butchart

Duncan Butchart

MARULA *Sclerocarya birrea*

Habitat: well-drained sandy soils
Height: up to 15 m **Status:** common to abundant;
protected species

Large, deciduous tree with spreading crown. Branchlets and twigs have thick, rounded growth points. Bark is pale grey, peeling off in disc-shaped flakes. Leaves are compound with 3–7 pairs of pointed leaflets, and a terminal one, on long petioles. Flowers are tiny; male and female on separate trees. Juicy yellow fruits ripen on the ground (Feb–Apr); relished by Elephant, baboons and humans.
Best viewing: widespread in suitable habitat

Duncan Butchart

MOBOLA-PLUM *Parinari curatellifolia*

Habitat: well-drained sandy soils **Height:** up to 13 m
Status: fairly common

Large, evergreen tree with a spreading crown. Often forms single-species clumps or mini-woodlands in suitable habitat. Bark is dark, grey-brown and rough. Simple, elliptic leaves are dark green above, hairy and yellowish below with distinctive lateral veins. Inconspicuous pink flowers appear in leaf axils (Jul–Oct). Fruit is a fleshy, greyish-yellow berry, scaly and pitted on the surface.
Best viewing: Eastern escarpment foothills, Kruger-Lowveld

Duncan Butchart

LIVE-LONG *Lannea discolor*

Habitat: koppies, sandy soils on hillsides, termite
mounds **Height:** up to 13 m **Status:** common

Medium-sized, open-branched, deciduous tree. Often the first species to shed leaves in autumn, last to show new growth in spring. Bark is coppery-grey, rough on older trees. Leaves are compound with 2–5 pairs of oval leaflets, plus a terminal one. Foliage turns rusty-red in autumn. Small, sweetly scented flowers appear on long spikes (Sep–Oct). Fruit is a fleshy, grape-sized berry.
Best viewing: Magaliesberg, Nylsvley, Pilanesberg, Blyde Canyon, Kruger-Lowveld

Duncan Butchart

TARWOOD *Loxostylis alata*

Habitat: koppies, cliffs, forest fringe, streambanks
Height: up to 5 m **Status:** fairly common; endemic

Small, evergreen tree with attractive, feathery foliage. Trunk and branches are often contorted. Bark is pale grey with leaf scars persisting on branchlets. Leaves are compound with 2–5 pairs of lance-shaped leaflets and a terminal one. Male and female flowers on separate trees; white, pink or brick-red in dense terminal clusters (Sep–Feb). Fruit is a small berry with a black, tar-like fluid in its skin.
Best viewing: Eastern Cape mountains

WHITE KIRKIA *Kirkia acuminata*

Habitat: rocky hillsides **Height:** up to 20 m
Status: common

Large, single-stemmed, deciduous tree with main branches radiating high up. Compound leaves with 6–10 pairs of elliptic leaflets, clustered at stem tips with a wispy appearance. Leaves turn gold and coppery-red in autumn. Small, greenish flowers appear in leaf axils (Oct–Dec). Fruit is a small, four-lobed capsule, splitting to release seeds. Related Mountain Kirkia *K. wilmsii* has fine, feathery foliage.
Best viewing: Marakele, Soutpansberg, Kruger (Lebombo ridges in east)

Duncan Butchart

WILD-PLUM *Harpephyllum caffrum*

Habitat: coastal and montane forest **Height:** up to 10 m
Status: common; endemic

Evergreen tree with low lateral branches; may take on a widely spreading shape in exposed seaward situations. Bark is smooth, pale grey with a satin sheen, darkening with age. Leaves are compound with 4–8 pairs of elliptic, sickle-shaped leaflets and a terminal one; bright red leaflets persist on the tree for weeks. Small, greenish flowers are inconspicuous (Nov–Feb). Fruit is a scarlet, grape-sized berry relished by turacos.
Best viewing: widespread in suitable habitat

Duncan Butchart

CAPE-ASH *Ekebergia capensis*

Habitat: coastal and montane forest, riversides
Height: up to 20 m **Status:** common

Large, semi-deciduous tree which may be evergreen in moister climates. Crown is dense with hanging foliage. Beautiful, coppery-red autumn foliage. Leaves are compound with up to 7 pairs of pointed leaflets, plus a terminal one. Flowers pinkish-white, small and inconspicuous (Sep–Nov). Round berries are pale yellow, becoming red when ripe; relished by turacos and other birds.
Best viewing: Kirstenbosch, Garden Route, Wild Coast, KwaZulu-Natal coast, Drakensberg

Duncan Butchart

NATAL MAHOGANY *Trichilia emetica*

Habitat: riversides and coastal forest **Height:** up to 20 m
Status: common

Large, evergreen tree with a dense rounded crown. Usually grows near water. Trunk is dark, usually low-branching and covered in scaly bark. Leaves are compound with up to 11 leaflets plus a terminal one; dark green and glossy above, paler and hairy below. Small greenish flowers appear in leaf axils; heavily scented (Aug–Oct). Spherical fruits split to reveal large, black and red seeds eaten by turacos and other birds.
Best viewing: KwaZulu-Natal coast and Midlands, Ndumo, St Lucia, Kruger-Lowveld

Duncan Butchart

Duncan Butchart

RIVER BUSHWILLOW *Combretum erythrophyllum*

Habitat: riversides **Height:** up to 12 m
Status: common

Tall, open-branched, deciduous tree. Shape is often contorted with larger branches arching down and sometimes touching the ground. Bark is smooth, pale ochre-brown. Simple leaves are opposite, narrowly oval with pointed tips; rusty-red in autumn. Pale yellow flowers appear in dense spikes (Sep–Nov). Small, four-winged fruits are pale brown and persist on the tree for months.
Best viewing: widespread in suitable habitat

Duncan Butchart

RED BUSHWILLOW *Combretum apiculatum*

Habitat: sandy soils of hillsides **Height:** up to 8 m
Status: abundant

Small, deciduous tree with crooked branches and spare crown, often multi-stemmed. Leaves are broad with tips pointed and twisted, in opposite pairs. Bark is greyish, cracking into small flakes. Small, yellowish flowers appear on dense spikes, together with new foliage (Sep–Feb). Small, four-winged fruits are reddish-green, drying to brown. Is often the dominant woody plant on dry slopes.
Best viewing: widespread in suitable habitat

Braam van Wyk

RUSSET BUSHWILLOW *Combretum hereroense*

Habitat: poorly drained clay soils
Height: up to 8 m **Status:** common

Small, deciduous tree with crooked branches frequently trailing close to the ground, often multi-stemmed. Leaves are simple, small, dark green above and paler below; in opposite pairs. Bark is variable, fissured in older trees. Pale yellow flowers appear in dense terminal spikes, usually with new leaves (Sep–Nov). Small, four-winged fruits are bright rusty-red and cover the entire tree (Jan–Jun).
Best viewing: widespread in suitable habitat

Duncan Butchart

LEADWOOD *Combretum imberbe*

Habitat: poorly drained soils of alluvial flats, woodland
Height: up to 20 m **Status:** fairly common but in
demand for carving and construction

Large, deciduous tree with a straight trunk and sparse crown. Leaves are simple, small, grey-green, in opposite pairs. Young stems are spine-tipped. Bark is pale grey, with texture of elephant skin. Creamy-yellow flowers appear in slender spikes (Nov–Mar). Four-winged fruits are yellowish. May live for thousands of years, even skeletal specimens provide nesting sites and refuges for owls, starlings, rollers, bats and other wildlife.
Best viewing: Kruger-Lowveld, Mapungubwe

SILVER CLUSTER-LEAF *Terminalia sericea*

Habitat: well-drained sandy soils, often on 'seep-lines' where clay and sandy soils meet **Height:** up to 20 m **Status:** common to abundant

Tall, graceful, deciduous tree with distinctive, silvery-green foliage. Often forms single-species stands or mini-woodlands. Bark is dark and deeply furrowed. Leaves are simple, elongate and borne in clusters at stem tips. Small, yellowish flowers are in spikes and have a pungent, urine-like scent (Sep–Dec). Papery seedpods are oval, pinkish-grey. Branchlets are often covered in swollen galls caused by larvae of small insects.
Best viewing: widespread in suitable habitat

Duncan Butchart

PURPLE-POD CLUSTER-LEAF *Terminalia prunioides*

Habitat: poorly drained clay soils, rocky hillsides **Height:** up to 8 m **Status:** common

Small, deciduous tree or dense, tangled shrub; may be single or multi-stemmed. Bark is brownish-grey, striated on older trees. Paired or single spines present at the base of lateral branchlets. Leaves are simple, arranged in spirals at ends of dwarf branchlets. Masses of tiny white flowers, arranged in spikes, are clustered on branchlets (Oct–Jan). Papery seedpods are bright plum red (Jan–Jul).
Best viewing: Kruger-Lowveld, Mapungubwe

Duncan Butchart

AFRICAN OLIVE *Olea europaea africana*

Habitat: hillsides and riverbanks, drainage lines in dry west **Height:** up to 7 m (rarely up to 18 m) **Status:** common, widely cultivated

Densely foliaged, evergreen tree with rounded shape. Branches typically obscured by foliage. Trunk is gnarled with rough, dark bark. Leaves are simple, elliptic, opposite, leathery, pale below and with pointed tips. Greenish-white flowers are small and inconspicuous (Oct–Feb). Fruit is a small, oval berry, purplish when ripe; relished by African Olive-Pigeon and other birds.
Best viewing: widespread in suitable habitat

Duncan Butchart

SAND-OLIVE *Dodonaea viscosa*

Habitat: tolerant of virtually all habitats **Height:** 3–5 m (rarely up to 10 m) **Status:** common to abundant

Small, evergreen tree or bushy shrub; often multi-stemmed. Bark is dark grey and stringy in older trees. Leaves are simple, elliptic, arranged in spirals; shiny, pale green with a sticky, resinous surface. Small, greenish-yellow flowers appear in clusters (Apr–Aug). Fruit is a two- or three-lobed capsule that splits to release papery, winged seeds. Commonly cultivated as a hedge or dune-binder.
Best viewing: widespread in suitable habitat

Duncan Butchart

Duncan Butchart

MATUMI *Breonadia salicina*

Habitat: riverbanks, sometimes growing in streams
Height: up to 20 m **Status:** common

Medium-sized to large, evergreen tree, often forms a pointed pyramid shape. Trunk is grey-brown with ridged bark. Leaves are simple, oblong and shiny. Small, yellowish flowers are packed in ball-shaped heads (Dec–Mar). Fruit is a small, two-lobed capsule. The similar Quinine-Tree *Rauvolfia caffra* shares the same habitat but has drooping foliage and pale, fawn-coloured bark.
Best viewing: Kruger-Lowveld, Blyde Canyon

Duncan Butchart

QUININE-TREE *Rauvolfia caffra*

Habitat: riverine and coastal forest, alluvial soils of river valleys **Height:** up to 18 m **Status:** uncommon

Large, evergreen tree with straight trunk, usually branching high up. Bark is fawn-coloured, soft and corky with age. Simple leaves are narrowly oblong, dark, shiny green and smooth, with pale yellow midrib and veins. Foliage droops downwards. All parts contain milky latex. Small, trumpet-shaped flowers appear in clusters at branch tips; sweetly scented. Berries are glossy green, speckled with pale spots.
Best viewing: Ndumo, KwaZulu-Natal coast, Wild Coast, Kruger-Lowveld

Duncan Butchart

TOAD-TREE *Tabernaemontana elegans*

Habitat: riverine fringes, coastal scrub forest, rocky outcrops **Height:** 3–5 m (rarely up to 10 m)
Status: fairly common

Small or medium-sized, deciduous tree with open-branched appearance. Bark is fawn-coloured, thickly corky with deep, longitudinal fissures. Leaves are simple, oblong, crowded at branch tip; glossy dark green above, paler below. Sweetly scented, white flowers appear in terminal heads (Oct–Feb). Fruit is a pair of ball-shaped spheres that split to expose an orange pulp containing seeds; the dry fruit cases resemble a toad's head.
Best viewing: Mkhuze, St Lucia, Ndumo

FOREST BIG-LEAF *Anthocleista grandiflora*

Habitat: montane forest fringe, sheltered kloofs, riverbanks **Height:** up to 30 m **Status:** fairly common

Tall, slender, evergreen tree that usually branches high up. Bark is pale grey and smooth. Leaves are simple, very large (150 cm) and clustered at the branch tips; glossy, dark green above, paler below. Tulip-shaped, creamy-white flowers are jasmine-scented; displayed in large terminal clusters (Sep–Jan). Fruit is a green, grape-sized berry relished by fruit-bats, turacos and hornbills.
Best viewing: Hazyview, Magoebaskloof, Barberton

Duncan Butchart

BLACK MANGROVE *Bruguiera gymnorrhiza*

Habitat: intertidal mudflats **Height:** up to 10 m
Status: locally common

Medium-sized, evergreen tree; often conical-shaped. Grows on the
seaward side of mangrove swamps, often in association with White
Mangrove *Avicennia marina* and Red Mangrove *Rhizophora
mucronata*. Bark is reddish-brown, fibrous; distinctive, knee-like
prop-roots help anchor the buttressed trunk in mud. Leaves are
simple, elliptic, smooth; dark green, turning yellow before dropping.
Fruit is attached to a cigar-shaped cylinder (11 cm).
Best viewing: Kosi Bay, St Lucia, Durban, Wild Coast

Duncan Butchart

POWDER-PUFF TREE *Barringtonia racemosa*

Habitat: riverbanks, freshwater swamps, less saline
fringe of mangrove swamps **Height:** 4–8 m (rarely up
to 15 m) **Status:** fairly common

Small to medium-sized, evergreen tree; often multi-stemmed. Bark
is variably coloured, smooth or rough. Leaves are simple, oblong,
thick and leathery and crowded at branch tips; dull green above,
paler below with raised midrib. White or pale pink flowers are
spectacular, with a profusion of long, white stamens bursting from
the petals; open fully at night and fade during course of the day
(Nov–Jun). Fruit is a hard, buoyant drupe.
Best viewing: Kosi Bay, St Lucia, Mtunzini

Duncan Butchart

SNEEZEWOOD *Ptaeroxylon obliquum*

Habitat: montane and coastal forest, sheltered
kloofs, open woodland **Height:** up to 20 m
Status: fairly common

Shrub or large tree with attractive foliage. Bark is pale grey,
darkening and becoming deeply fissured with age. Leaves are
compound, with 3–7 pairs of opposite leaflets, crowded at branch
tips; dark or blue-green. Autumn foliage is golden yellow. Small, pale
yellow, sweetly scented flowers produced in branched heads; male
and female on separate trees (Aug–Dec). Fruit is an oblong capsule.
Sawdust is pungent and sneeze-inducing.
Best viewing: Tsitsikamma, Dwesa, Mkhuze, Woodbush, Addo

Braam van Wyk

SMALL KNOBWOOD *Zanthoxylum capense*

Habitat: sheltered kloofs, forest edge, rocky outcrops,
termite mounds **Height:** 4–7 m (rarely up to 10 m)
Status: fairly common

Small, evergreen, thorny-stemmed tree or shrub. Bark is grey,
smooth, armed with cone-shaped knobs tipped with sharp spines.
Leaves are compound with 4–8 pairs of leaflets and a terminal one;
smallest leaflets at the base. Inconspicuous, yellowish flowers appear
in short terminal sprays (Dec–Jan). Clusters of small brownish-red
berries resemble miniature lemons in shape and skin texture.
Best viewing: widespread in suitable habitat

Duncan Butchart

Duncan Butchart

TAMBOTI   *Spirostachys africana*

Habitat: poorly drained clay soils, riverbanks and termite mounds **Height:** up to 20 m **Status:** common

Medium-sized, deciduous tree that often forms groves. Main trunk is straight with almost black bark breaking up into small blocks. Leaves are small, alternate with scalloped margins; some turn scarlet in autumn. Small, inconspicuous flowers appear in spikes (Sep–Jan). Fruit is a three-lobed capsule. Contains poisonous white latex and burned wood produces nauseating smoke.

Best viewing: Kruger-Lowveld, Hluhluwe-iMfolozi, Mkhuze, Pilanesberg, Marakele

Duncan Butchart

POTATO-BUSH   *Phyllanthus reticulatus*

Habitat: alluvial soils of river valleys, riverbanks, termite mounds **Height:** up to 4 m (scrambles higher up tall trees) **Status:** common

Slender, multi-stemmed shrub, scrambler or twiggy tree. Often forms thickets. Bark is reddish-brown or grey, stringy and fissured with age. Leaves are simple, small, alternate, medium-green; evenly spaced along pendulous stems. Small, inconspicuous yellow flowers are clustered in leaf axils; strong cooked potato scent is characteristic of Lowveld evenings (Jul–Oct). Red-black berries are relished by bulbuls and other birds.

Best viewing: Kruger-Lowveld, Ndumo, Mkhuzu, Hluhluwe-iMfolozi

Duncan Butchart

TASSEL-BERRY   *Antidesma venosum*

Habitat: hillsides and termite mounds, vlei margins **Height:** up to 8 m **Status:** common

Small, open-branched tree, often with gnarled or contorted shape. Bark is greyish-brown becoming lightly fissured with age. Leaves are simple, oval, sharply pointed and alternate; apple-green above, paler below. Tiny flowers appear in pencil-shaped 'catkin' spikes; male and female flowers on separate trees. Spikes of small, fleshy berries occur in profusion; red to black when ripe, attracting hordes of birds and primates (Mar–May).

Best viewing: widespread in suitable habitat

MITZEERIE   *Bridelia micrantha*

Habitat: streambanks, near mountain springs **Height:** up to 20 m **Status:** fairly common

Medium to large tree with rounded crown of drooping foliage. Bark is flaky, becoming rough with age. Blunt spines appear irregularly. Leaves are simple, oval, sharply pointed; may be wavy or scalloped but usually with margin entire. Young leaves and autumn foliage coppery-red. Inconspicuous flowers appear in clusters in leaf axils (Jan–Mar). Small, fleshy berries, black when ripe, attract birds and monkeys.

Best viewing: widespread in suitable habitat

Duncan Butchart

RED IVORY *Berchemia zeyheri*

Habitat: riverbanks, termitaria, rocky ridges
Height: up to 15 m **Status:** uncommon

Large to medium-sized tree with dense, rounded crown. Single stemmed, often branching high up. Bark is dark and fissured with age. Simple leaves are oval and opposite; glossy dark green above, paler below, with the smooth texture of human skin. Inconspicuous flowers appear in clusters at leaf axils (Sep–Dec). Fruit is a small, oval berry, turning yellow when ripe; sweet and relished by birds. Related Brown Ivory *B. discolor* has larger, broader leaves.
Best viewing: Kruger-Lowveld, Pilanesberg, Marakele, Mkhuze

Duncan Butchart

JACKET-PLUM *Pappea capensis*

Habitat: rocky outcrops and termite mounds
Height: up to 7 m **Status:** fairly common

Gnarled, open-branched, deciduous tree. Bark is grey or pale brown (there are two distinct subspecies). Simple leaves are oval and arranged in spirals on stem tips. May have a parchment-like texture with fine serrations on edge, or be leathery with no serrations. Spikes of small cream flowers attract pollinating flies and wasps (Jan–May). Fruit is a small brown capsule that splits to reveal a seed covered in scarlet jelly.
Best viewing: widespread in suitable habitat

Duncan Butchart

LAVENDER CROTON *Croton gratissimus*

Habitat: rocky outcrops and hillsides, coastal dunes
Height: up to 12 m **Status:** common

Slender, open-branched, deciduous tree with drooping foliage. Bark is pale grey becoming darker and fissured with age. Leaves are simple, elliptic, alternate, with margin entire; dark green above, silvery-white below with orange spots (scales). Clear, watery latex runs from the stems. Small, yellowish flowers appear in clusters on pendulous spikes. Fruit is a small, three-lobed capsule.
Best viewing: widespread in suitable habitat

Duncan Butchart

LAVENDER-TREE *Heteropyxis natalensis*

Habitat: rocky hillsides, forest margins
Height: up to 4–10 m **Status:** common; endemic

Slender, open-branched, deciduous tree with drooping foliage. Bark is yellow-ochre or pale-grey; flaking off in large, stiff blocks to reveal salmon-pink underbark. Leaves are simple, elliptic, alternate; shiny green above, paler below. Freshly crushed leaves have a strong lavender scent. Small, yellowish flowers appear in terminal heads (Dec–Mar). Fruit is a capsule that splits to release small seeds; may persist on the tree for months.
Best viewing: Eastern escarpment foothills, Blyde Canyon

Duncan Butchart

Duncan Butchart

CAPE-CHESTNUT *Calodendrum capense*

Habitat: coastal and montane forest **Height:** up to 20 m
Status: common

Medium to large tree with rounded crown of dense foliage.
Evergreen in moist areas. Smooth bark is pale grey, darkening with
age, often patterned with lichen. Leaves are simple, oval; dark green
above, with prominent lateral veins. Puts on a magnificent display
of large, showy, pale pink flowers (Oct–Dec). Fruit is a small brown
capsule that splits to release the seeds.
Best viewing: Tsitsikamma, Garden Route, Wild Coast,
KwaZulu-Natal Midlands, Woodbush

Braam van Wyk

POMPON TREE *Dais cotinifolia*

Habitat: forest fringe, riverine thickets, rocky hillsides
Height: up to 6 m **Status:** common; near endemic

Small tree or shrub with single stem. Bark smooth, becoming
striated in older specimens. Simple leaves, oval, opposite, crowded
at stem tips; olive or blue-green above, paler below, with smooth,
waxy texture. Showy pink flowers appear in dense round clusters,
resembling pompons (Nov–Feb). Dried flower heads persist on the
tree for weeks.
Best viewing: widespread in suitable habitat

MOUNTAIN HARD-PEAR *Olinia emarginata*

Habitat: montane forest, rocky hillsides and kloofs,
mountain stream sides **Height:** 5–20 m
Status: fairly common

Gnarled shrub or tall, pale-barked tree with crooked trunk and
branches. Bark is creamy-yellow or pale grey, flaking off to reveal
brighter underbark; young stems are four-angled. Leaves are
simple, oblong, opposite; glossy dark green above, paler below.
Small, pinkish flowers appear in loose heads; sweetly scented
(Oct–Jan). Fruit is a thin-skinned berry, eaten by white-eyes,
bulbuls and other birds.
Best viewing: Giant's Castle (Drakensberg), Magaliesberg,
Blyde Canyon

Duncan Butchart

WILD-PEACH *Kiggelaria africana*

Habitat: streambanks and forest edge
Height: up to 5 m **Status:** common

Small to medium-sized, evergreen tree with dense foliage. Bark
is grey and smooth, becoming rougher with age. Simple leaves
are oval, alternate; dull greyish-green above, paler and velvety
below. Leaf margin is often serrated on new growth. Flowers are
inconspicuous. Fruit is a round, leathery capsule that splits into a
star shape to reveal bright orange seeds; relished by birds.
Best viewing: widespread in suitable habitat

Braam van Wyk

WATERBERRY *Syzygium cordatum*

Habitat: always near water: on riverbanks, at mountain springs, seeplines, swamp forest **Height:** up to 15 m **Status:** common

Medium-sized, evergreen tree with dense crown. Simple leaves are oval, waxy, blue-green; opposite with petioles very short or absent. Rough, corky bark varies in colour from pale grey to dark brown. Showy creamy-white flowers have long stamens and appear in dense clusters. Abundant nectar attracts bees and sunbirds. Ripe berries are purple-black; relished by barbets, turacos and monkeys.
Best viewing: widespread in suitable habitat

Duncan Butchart

WHITE MILKWOOD *Sideroxylon inerme*

Habitat: coastal forest and fringe, along rivers and termite mounds **Height:** up to 10 m **Status:** fairly common but larger specimens now rare; near endemic

Wide-crowned tree or dense, evergreen shrub, adapted to withstand coastal winds. Simple leaves oblong, waxy; darker above with pale midrib. Produces copious milky latex, hence the name. Green to purple berries appear (Jul–Jan); relished by monkeys and turacos. Differs from similar Red Milkwood *Mimusops zeyheri* in distribution, shape of berries and flowers.
Best viewing: widespread in suitable habitat

Duncan Butchart

COASTAL RED-MILKWOOD *Mimusops caffra*

Habitat: coastal dunes, fully exposed to salt spray and sea winds **Height:** 2–6 m (rarely up to 15 m) **Status:** locally abundant

Bushy, evergreen shrub or stunted tree. Simple leaves oval to round, waxy and leathery; blue-green and smooth above, pale and hairy below. The leaf margin is distinctly rolled under. Produces milky latex, hence the name. Oval, orange-red berries have a pointed tip (Apr–Sep); relished by humans, monkeys and birds. Related Red-Milkwood (Moepel) *M. zeyheri* has oblong leaves; inland distribution.
Best viewing: Wild Coast, KwaZulu-Natal coast

Duncan Butchart

STAMVRUG *Englerophytum magalismontanum*

Habitat: rocky hillsides, koppies **Height:** 2–4 m (rarely up to 10 m) **Status:** common

Small, evergreen bush or medium-sized tree; usually multi-stemmed with tangled branches. Bark is grey and smooth, becoming dark and rough with age; stems covered with spurs. Leaves are simple, oval, crowded at stem tips; dark, glossy green above, densely covered with golden hair below. Small flowers have a pungent odour. Grape-sized berries grow on spurs of old wood (Dec–Feb), contain milky sap.
Best viewing: widespread in suitable habitat

Duncan Butchart

Duncan Butchart

WILD-PEAR *Dombeya rotundifolia*

Habitat: sandy soils, hillsides, koppies
Height: up to 15 m **Status:** common to abundant

Crooked, deciduous tree with open branches and bushy crown.
Bark is dark brown and deeply furrowed with age. Round leaves
are alternate, irregularly toothed and coarsely textured; apple-
green turning yellow in autumn. Masses of papery white or pale
pink flowers put on a spectacular show (Aug–Sep); fade to russet-
brown and persist on the tree for months. Fruits are inconspicuous
capsules. Host to processionary caterpillars.
Best viewing: widespread in suitable habitat

Duncan Butchart

LOWVELD STAR-CHESTNUT *Sterculia murex*

Habitat: rocky hillsides, koppies **Height:** up to 10 m
Status: fairly common, but small range; endemic

Crooked, deciduous tree with bushy crown. Bark is grey and
smooth, becoming dark and furrowed with age. Leaves are digitately
compound, with lance-shaped leaflets forming a star shape; new
growth is soft and hairy, turns bright coppery-yellow in autumn.
Clusters of waxy, butter-yellow flowers appear in profusion
(Jul–Sep). Fruit is a large, spine-covered, boat-shaped pod, splitting
to reveal black, nut-like seeds.
Best viewing: Nelspruit, Barberton, Hazyview

Duncan Butchart

STAR-CHESTNUT *Sterculia rogersii*

Habitat: rocky outcrops, koppies **Height:** 2–5 m
Status: fairly common

Squat, multi-stemmed tree or shrub with bloated trunk. Deciduous
and often leafless for many months. Bark is pale grey, peeling to
reveal pink or yellow patches. Leaves are simple, three-lobed;
greyish-green above, paler and velvety below; turn yellow before
dropping. Flowers are greenish-pink, saucer shaped, in profusion
(Jul–Jan). Woody, boat-shaped pods, covered with golden hairs, split
to reveal black seeds.
Best viewing: Kruger-Lowveld, Mapungubwe, Ndumo

BAOBAB *Adansonia digitata*

Habitat: sandy soils of bushveld savanna
Height: up to 25 m **Status:** common

Gigantic, squat tree that may live for thousands of years.
Unmistakable when leafless in winter. Bark is smooth and fibrous,
much favoured by elephant. Leaves are digitately compound with
5 leaflets. Flowers are large and white, opening fully at night and
pollinated by fruit-bats; last just a single night. Seeds are in a dry,
white pulp ('cream-of-tartar') in a large, velvety pod. Owls, hornbills
and bushbabies live in trunk cavities.
Best viewing: Mapungubwe, Kruger (north)

Duncan Butchart

RED-ALDER *Cunonia capensis*

Habitat: montane and coastal forest, streambanks
Height: up to 30 m **Status:** fairly common; endemic

Broad-crowned, evergreen tree or dense shrub. Bark is pale and flaky at first, becoming dark and rough with age. Leaves are compound with 2–5 pairs of leaflets plus a terminal one; bud is enclosed in a distinctive paddle-shaped stipule. Clusters of small, creamy flowers appear in showy spikes at the branch tips (Mar–May). Fruit is a leathery, two-horned capsule (Apr–Jul).
Best viewing: Kirstenbosch, Garden Route, Tsitsikamma, Wild Coast

Duncan Butchart

COLDBARK OCHNA *Ochna arborea*

Habitat: montane and coastal forest, wooded kloofs, sandforest **Height:** 3–12 m
Status: uncommon; near endemic

Slender, deciduous tree or shrub. Bark is very smooth, pale-grey; peels off in layers to reveal pink or olive underbark, creating a beautiful, mottled pattern and distinctly cool to the touch. Leaves are simple, opposite, oval, leathery and shiny green above; margin may be toothed or entire; new growth is bronze. Bright yellow flowers are produced on terminal sprays (Aug–Nov). Attractive black and red seeds decorate the tree (Oct–Feb).
Best viewing: Tsitsikamma, Wild Coast, KwaZulu-Natal coast, Phinda, Woodbush

Estate of Piet van Wyk

CURRY-BUSH *Hypericum revolutum*

Habitat: streamsides and forest fringe at high altitudes
Height: 1–3 m **Status:** common

Bushy shrub or small, evergreen tree; often a pioneer species in forest patches. Bark is reddish-brown; branchlets are angular. Leaves are bluish-green, simple, elliptic, crowded at stem tips. Flowers are bright yellow, saucer-shaped with broad petals and central mass of stamens (throughout the year); buds are sticky to the touch. Seeds are contained in a reddish-brown capsule.
Best viewing: Blyde Canyon, Drakensberg

Duncan Butchart

SNUFF-BOX TREE *Oncoba spinosa*

Habitat: open woodland, rocky ridges, riverbanks
Height: 3–5 m **Status:** fairly common

Slender, deciduous shrub or small tree with pendulous, thorny branches. Bark is grey and mottled; stems are armed with straight spines up to 5 cm long. Leaves are simple, oval, with coarsely toothed margin; glossy dark green above. Flowers are large and showy with broad, white petals and a central mass of yellow stamens resembling a fried egg (Aug–Jan). Fruit is a woody capsule that splits into 8 valves.
Best viewing: widespread in suitable habitat

Duncan Butchart

Duncan Butchart

MOUNTAIN CABBAGE-TREE *Cussonia paniculata*

Habitat: rocky hillsides, koppies **Height:** up to 4 m
Status: common to abundant; endemic

Distinctive, lollipop-shaped tree; usually short and single-stemmed. Bark is dark brown, deeply furrowed, corky and fire resistant. Leathery leaves are very large, fan-shaped with 7–9 leaflets. Small, greenish flowers and fleshy fruits are held in clusters on spikes. Barbets feed on the fruits and may excavate nest holes in the soft wood. The Common Cabbage *C. spicata* is taller with branched crown and greener foliage.
Best viewing: widespread in suitable habitat

Duncan Butchart

FALSE CABBAGE-TREE *Schefflera umbellifera*

Habitat: fringe of montane and coastal forest, rocky ridges **Height:** 6–20 m **Status:** fairly common

Tall, upright, evergreen tree that branches high up to produce a rounded crown. Bark is grey-brown and smooth, becoming darker and fissured with age. Leaves are digitately compound, with 3–5 elliptic leaflets; glossy green above with wavy margin. Small flowers are greenish-yellow in loose terminal heads (Jan–May). Fruit is a small, round berry ripening to wine-red; eaten by birds.
Best viewing: Blyde Canyon, Drakensberg, Wild Coast, Tsitsikamma

Duncan Butchart

PARSLEY-TREE *Heteromorpha arborescens*

Habitat: rocky hillsides, koppies **Height:** 2–7 m
Status: fairly common

Open-branched shrub or small, deciduous tree with sparse foliage and pendulous branches. Distinctive bark is coppery-bronze, waxy, peeling off in papery flakes; older branches are ringed like bamboo stems. Leaves are variably compound, with 3–7 leaflets; aromatic parsley scent when crushed. Yellowish flowers are borne in dense, round heads, attractive to butterflies (Dec–Jan). Seeds are produced on branched heads.
Best viewing: widespread in suitable habitat

CARROT-TREE *Steganotaenia araliacea*

Habitat: rocky hillsides, koppies **Height:** 2–10 m
Status: fairly common

Open-branched shrub or small, deciduous tree with sparse foliage. Distinctive bark is pale green or yellowish, waxy, peeling off in papery strips. Leaves are compound with 2–3 pairs of widely spaced leaflets and a terminal one; the leaflet margins are conspicuously toothed with fine, hair-like points. Small flowers are greenish-yellow, in tight clusters (Aug–Oct). Seeds are contained in a flattened capsule with papery wings.
Best viewing: Blyde Canyon, Barberton mountains, Soutpansberg

Duncan Butchart

BUSHVELD GARDENIA *Gardenia volkensii*

Habitat: poorly drained soils in savanna
Height: up to 7 m **Status:** common

Small, thickset, evergreen tree or bushy shrub with angular stems. Bark is pale grey and smooth. Leaves are simple, leathery and borne in threes at stem tips; glossy green with wavy margins. Large, showy flowers open white but turn yellow within days and may cover the entire tree; sweetly scented, pollinated by hawk-moths (Jul–Oct). Fruit is an egg-shaped drupe, ribbed on the surface, and sometimes eaten by Greater Kudu.
Best viewing: widespread in suitable habitat

Duncan Butchart

COMMON ROTHMANNIA *Rothmannia capensis*

Habitat: coastal and montane forest, rocky outcrops in montane grassland, coastal bush
Height: 2–14 m **Status:** common; endemic

Small to medium-sized, evergreen tree with dense foliage; stunted on windswept mountains. Bark is greyish-brown, cracked into small segments on older trees. Leaves are simple, opposite, elliptic; glossy dark green above, paler below with distinctive glandular spots. Beautiful, bell-shaped flowers are creamy-white with wine-red streaks, and sweetly scented (Dec–Feb). Fruit is green, ball-shaped.
Best viewing: widespread in suitable habitat

Duncan Butchart

VELVET WILD-MEDLAR *Vangueria infausta*

Habitat: koppies, rocky hillsides, coastal scrub
Height: 1–6 m **Status:** common

Small tree or shrub with disproportionately large leaves and contorted trunk. Bark is smooth, yellowish-grey. Simple leaves are opposite, tough and velvety with prominent veins below; older leaves are rough and twisted. Inconspicuous yellowish flowers appear in leaf axils (Sep–Oct). Fruit is round, marble- or golfball-sized, shiny green ripening to yellow; relished by humans and animals.
Best viewing: widespread in suitable habitat

Duncan Butchart

ASSEGAI *Curtisia dentata*

Habitat: coastal and montane forest, grassy hillsides, coastal scrub **Height:** 6–20 m **Status:** fairly common

Medium-sized to large, evergreen tree with dense foliage. Bark is brown and smooth becoming darker and fissured in small square blocks with age. Leaves are simple, opposite, oval with sharp, teeth-like serrations; shiny apple-green above, pale and velvety below. Inconspicuous cream flowers appear in terminal head (Oct–Mar). Fruit is a round, fleshy berry. Timber was widely used for tool and spear (assegai) handles, hence the name.
Best viewing: Table Mountain, Tsitsikamma, Dwesa, Woodbush

Duncan Butchart

Duncan Butchart

BUFFALO-THORN *Ziziphus mucronata*

Habitat: alluvial soils, hillsides, termite mounds, coastal scrub **Height:** up to 6 m **Status:** common to abundant

Densely foliaged, deciduous tree with fierce thorns. Bark is smooth, becomes rough with age. Simple leaves are oval, serrated and glossy green above, dull green below; alternate leaves appear on distinctive zigzag stems. Small but prolific thorns are arranged in pairs, with one straight and one hooked. Tiny, green flowers are in clusters (Nov–Feb). Brick-red berries are relished by go-away-birds and starlings.
Best viewing: widespread in suitable habitat

GREEN-THORN *Balanites maughamii*

Habitat: open woodland, termite mounds, sandforest **Height:** 10–20 m **Status:** fairly common

Medium-sized to tall deciduous tree, reaching greatest size in sandforest. Bark is grey and smooth; larger trees have a distinctively fluted trunk. Branches have a zigzag growth pattern; armed with sharp, forked spines. Leaves are compound with just one pair of oval leaflets; greyish-green, hairy when young. Inconspicuous flowers appear on unarmed branches (Sep–Oct). Fruit is date-like and contains combustible oil.
Best viewing: Phinda, Thembe, Mkhuze, Kruger-Lowveld

Duncan Butchart

BIG NUM-NUM *Carissa macrocarpa*

Habitat: coastal bush, sand dunes **Height:** up to 4 m **Status:** common; often cultivated as a hedge; near-endemic

Small, evergreen shrub or tree with tangled, spiny branches; contains sticky, white latex. Bark is grey with longitudinal ridges. Rigid, Y-forked spines appear at the leaf axils, affording good protection against browsing animals. Leaves are simple, oval, leathery; dark glossy green above, duller below. Flowers are white, star-shaped and sweetly scented (Jul–Nov). Fruit is a grape-sized berry, ripening to red; relished by monkeys and humans.
Best viewing: widespread in suitable habitat

Duncan Butchart

KEI-APPLE *Dovyalis caffra*

Habitat: coastal scrub, thickets, open woodland, termite mounds **Height:** 3–5 m **Status:** common; cultivated as a hedge; near endemic

Dense, evergreen, spiny shrub or small tree with angular branches. Bark is grey and smooth, darker and rough with age. Stems are armed with stiff spines, up to 6 cm long. Leaves are simple, oval, borne in tight clusters on dwarf branchlets; dark glossy green above, paler below. Inconspicuous creamy-green flowers in clusters (Nov–Jan). Fruit is a fleshy, apricot-like berry; excellent for making jelly or jam.
Best viewing: widespread in suitable habitat

Duncan Butchart

COMMON SPIKETHORN *Gymnosporia buxifolia*

Habitat: most habitats **Height:** 2–3 m (rarely up to 8 m)
Status: common

Small, evergreen shrub or gnarled tree with sparse, stiff foliage;
often grows as a pioneer on disturbed soils. Bark is reddish-brown,
becoming dark, almost black, and corky with age. Young branches
are sparsely covered in sharp spines. Leaves are simple, dull grey-
green, arranged in clusters on branchlets. Strongly scented white
flowers appear in clusters (Sep–Apr), but not as showy as the
Confetti Spikethorn *G. senegalensis.*
Best viewing: widespread in suitable habitat

Duncan Butchart

BLACK MONKEY-ORANGE *Strychnos madagascariensis*

Habitat: sandy soils **Height:** up to 6 m
Status: common

Small, spineless tree with crooked branches and dense crown. Bark
is light grey with white patches and dark, knobbly ridges. Simple
leaves are clustered at stem tips; oval, bright green with 5 bold
veins, 3 originating at the base. Large, tennis-ball-sized fruits are
blue-green at first, turn orange when ripe (Feb–Nov). Monkeys and
baboons break the hard outer shell to eat the sweet pulp. Spiny
Monkey-orange *S. spinosa* has paired spines at leaf axils; unripe
fruit is glossy apple-green.
Best viewing: widespread in suitable habitat

Duncan Butchart

JACKAL-BERRY *Diospyros mespiliformis*

Habitat: alluvial soils of river valleys, drainage
lines and termite mounds **Height:** up to 20 m
Status: common

Large, almost-evergreen tree that reaches greatest size along
watercourses; may lose leaves briefly at the end of winter. Bark is
dark, peeling off in square sections. Leaves are simple, alternate,
oval and usually with wavy margins; turn yellow-orange in autumn.
Flowers are tiny, pale yellow bells (Sep–Dec). Round berries ripen
to yellow and are relished by birds, antelope, baboons and, it is
said, by jackals.
Best viewing: Kruger-Lowveld, Mapungubwe

Duncan Butchart

BLADDER-NUT *Diospyros whyteana*

Habitat: forest fringe, bush clumps **Height:** up to 8 m
Status: common

Bushy, evergreen shrub or small, slender tree with drooping shape.
Bark is dark grey and smooth. Leaves are simple, oval, alternate; dark
shiny green, with soft hairs on the margins; bright orange or red
leaves remain on the tree for some time before dropping. Flowers
are small, creamy-white bells (Aug–Nov). Fruits are held in a papery
capsule, which turns reddish when ripe.
Best viewing: widespread in suitable habitat

Duncan Butchart

Duncan Butchart

CROSS-BERRY *Grewia occidentalis*

Habitat: tolerant of many habitats **Height:** up to 6 m
Status: common

Small, evergreen shrub or multi-stemmed tree with slender, drooping branches. Bark is pale grey, smooth. Leaves are simple, oval, with three distinct veins originating a the base (a trait shared by most *Grewia* species); margin is scalloped, pale green above, hairy on both surfaces. Star-shaped flowers are showy, pink petals with tight mass of yellow stamens (Oct–Jan). Distinctive fruit consists of 4 lobes in a square, cross shape.
Best viewing: widespread in suitable habitat

Duncan Butchart

KAREE *Searsia (Rhus) lancea*

Habitat: streambanks, open woodland, termite mounds **Height:** up to 6 m **Status:** common to abundant

Willowy, evergreen tree with contorted trunk and branches. Branches usually close to the base. Bark is dark and rough. Trifoliate leaves are glossy; dark green with no serrations. Flowers are inconspicuous, male and female on separate trees (Apr–Sep). Small, round berries hang in dense terminal bunches. Fire and drought resistant. *Rhus* is a complex genus with many similar species that are hard to distinguish.
Best viewing: widespread in suitable habitat

Braam van Wyk

RESIN-TREE *Ozoroa paniculosa*

Habitat: rocky hillsides **Height:** up to 6 m
Status: fairly common

Small, deciduous shrub or tree with gnarled trunk and branches. Bark is grey; rough on older specimens; contains a milky, resinous latex. Leaves are simple, narrowly elliptic with distinctive parallel veins; greyish-green above, paler and velvety below. Flowers are small, creamy, in terminal clusters; sweetly scented (Aug–Feb). Berries are greyish, becoming wrinkled and black when ripe.
Best viewing: Pilanesberg, Magaliesberg, Marakele, Ithala, KwaZulu-Natal Midlands

SHINY-LEAF *Rhamnus prinoides*

Habitat: forest margins, watercourses, rocky ridges and termite mounds **Height:** up to 6 m
Status: common

Small, evergreen, leafy shrub or small tree with glossy foliage that shimmers in sunlight. Bark is grey-brown; rough on older trees. Leaves are simple, elliptic, shiny green above, paler below; margin is finely toothed or scalloped. Small, greenish flowers appear in clusters (Oct–Dec). Berries are small, red, ripening to shiny black; relished by birds, monkeys and humans.
Best viewing: widespread in suitable habitat

Duncan Butchart

TREE-FUCHSIA *Halleria lucida*

Habitat: montane forest fringe, streambanks
Height: up to 10 m **Status:** common

Scrambling, evergreen shrub or small, multi-stemmed tree. Bark is pale brown, longitudinally fissured. Simple leaves are dull green, oval, leathery, opposite, with margins toothed. Tubular flowers are orange, borne in clusters on old wood, sometimes from leaf axils; rich in nectar and highly attractive to sunbirds (May–Feb). Fruit is a small, fleshy berry; black when ripe and relished by bulbuls, mousebirds, barbets and other birds.
Best viewing: widespread in suitable habitat

Duncan Butchart

CAPE-HONEYSUCKLE *Tecomaria capensis*

Habitat: hillsides and riverbanks **Height:** up to 2 m
(may scramble higher into tall trees) **Status:** common,
extensively cultivated

Scrambling, semi-deciduous shrub or climber. Bark becomes dark and rough with age. Compound leaves are emerald-green, arranged in opposite pairs; leaflet margins scalloped. Brilliant orange, trumpet-shaped flowers appear in profusion on terminal sprays (Jun–Nov); rich in nectar and attractive to sunbirds. Seedpods are papery, splitting to release seeds. Popular garden plant; yellow and coral-pink cultivars are available.
Best viewing: widespread in suitable habitat

Duncan Butchart

PRIDE-OF-DE-KAAP *Bauhinia galpinii*

Habitat: streambanks, wooded hillsides
Height: up to 4 m (able to scramble higher in tall trees)
Status: common to abundant

Scrambling, evergreen shrub that may form tangled thickets. Bark is medium brown, smooth. Leaves are compound, two-lobed and notched, becoming yellow before dropping. Large, coral-red flowers appear in profusion throughout summer (Sep–Mar). Long, woody pods have pointed tips, splitting and twisting to release hard seeds.
Best viewing: Kruger-Lowveld, Ithala, Hluhluwe-iMfolozi

Duncan Butchart

FLAME CLIMBING-BUSHWILLOW *Combretum microphyllum*

Habitat: alluvial soils of river valleys, riverbanks
Height: up to 4 m (may scramble higher into tall trees)
Status: common

Vigorous climber or tangled shrub; deciduous. Trailing stems reach upwards, encircling branches of supporting trees. Bark is pale brown; stringy with age. Leaves are simple, oval, apple-green, with wavy margin. Tiny, scarlet flowers with conspicuous stamens are produced in great abundance along trailing stems; sunbirds relish the nectar, canaries and manikins eat the buds (Aug–Sep). Pale, papery-winged pods contain a single seed.
Best viewing: Kruger-Lowveld, Mapungubwe, Ndumo, Mkhuze

Duncan Butchart

Duncan Butchart

SAGEWOOD *Buddleja salviifolia*

Habitat: streambanks, rocky hillsides **Height:** up to 3 m
Status: abundant

Scrambling, evergreen shrub or small tree, usually multi-stemmed. Trailing branches arch downwards. Simple leaves lance-shaped, opposite; dark green above, white below; margins finely scalloped, upper surface is quilt-like. Tiny lilac flowers are bell-shaped with orange throat; borne in showy spikes or rounded heads, sweetly scented (Jun–Oct). Highly attractive to butterflies. Related False Olive *B. saligna* has smooth leaves; occurs on dry hillsides and in coastal thicket.
Best viewing: Drakensberg, Blyde Canyon, Magaliesberg

GINGER-BUSH *Tetradenia riparia*

Habitat: rocky hillsides, streambanks
Height: up to 2 m (may scramble higher into tall trees)
Status: common

Multi-stemmed, deciduous shrub with semi-succulent branches. Simple leaves are large, heart-shaped, opposite, coarsely-toothed; pale green, densely-hairy and sticky to the touch. Crushed leaves have strong ginger scent. Tiny mauve or lilac flowers are borne in spikes: male up to 8 cm, female up to 3 cm (Jul–Sep); dense flower clusters resemble mist from a distance.
Best viewing: Kruger-Lowveld

Duncan Butchart

COASTAL SILVER-OAK *Brachylaena discolor*

Habitat: dune and coastal forest, invariably on fringes
Height: 3–10 m **Status:** common to abundant

Small to medium-sized, evergreen tree with bushy, pendulous branches. Highly conspicuous in breezy or windy conditions when silvery-white underside to leaves are obvious. Usually multi-stemmed with pale brown bark grooved vertically. Simple leaves are alternate; glossy dark green above, white below. Small, creamy-yellow, thistle-like flowers appear in terminal clusters (Jul–Sep). Fruit is a small, hairy nutlet. Mountain Silver-oak *B. rotundata* has broad leaves; occurs inland on dry hillsides.
Best viewing: KwaZulu-Natal coast, Wild Coast

Duncan Butchart

CAMPHOR-BUSH *Tarchonanthus littoralis*

Habitat: coastal dunes **Height:** up to 8 m
Status: common to abundant

Small, evergreen tree or shrub with dense, drooping foliage. Main stem is gnarled and twisted. Bark is grey-brown, furrowed on older trees. Simple leaves are alternate; grey-green above, paler below. Female trees bear small, yellow flowers in branched terminal sprays (Jun–Sep). Seeds are contained in white, cotton-like balls; most showy in autumn and winter. This coastal species is a recent split from the widespread *T. camphoratus*.
Best viewing: Cape Peninsula, Drakensberg

Braam van Wyk

UMBRELLA PINE *Pinus pinea*

Habitat: invades mountain fynbos and grassland
Height: up to 30 m **Status:** locally common in south-western Cape; lower slopes of Table Mountain

Massive, open-branched coniferous tree. Bark is reddish, deeply furrowed. Needle-like leaves are in pairs. Female cones age to grey; seeds are eaten by Grey Squirrel and humans. Introduced to the Cape Peninsula by early settlers. Not aggressively invasive, but subject to controversial eradication programme on the Peninsula.
Origin: native to Mediterranean Europe

Duncan Butchart

CLUSTER PINE *Pinus pinaster*

Habitat: invades mountain and lowland fynbos
Height: up to 15 m **Status:** locally abundant

Large, coniferous tree with dense, conical crown. Bark has distinctive, dark furrows. Introduced to Cape Peninsula by early settlers. Needle-like leaves are in pairs. Initially planted in a misguided attempt to improve water flow from Table Mountain, now invasive. Related *P. radiata* and *P. halepensis* also invade winter-rainfall fynbos.
Origin: native to Mediterranean Europe and North Africa

Duncan Butchart

PATULA PINE *Pinus patula*

Habitat: invades moist grassland, forest margins and road cuttings **Height:** up to 20 m **Status:** abundant in grassland of eastern escarpment and foothills

Large, coniferous tree with dense, rounded crown when mature. Bark is dark and very rough. Needle-like leaves are in clusters of three; hang downwards in drooping form. Grown in extensive commercial plantations for structural timber and paper pulp. Related *P. elliottii* and *P. taeda* also invade grasslands in summer-rainfall region.
Origin: native to Mexico – Central America

Duncan Butchart

SILKY NEEDLEBUSH *Hakea sericea*

Habitat: invades mountain fynbos **Height:** up to 5 m
Status: locally abundant

Multi-branched, prickly shrub or small tree. Young stems are hairy, bark is smooth. Needle-shaped leaves are dark green. Small, cream flowers appear in leaf axils (Jun–Sep). Fruit is a wooden capsule with wrinkled surface. Cultivated for hedging and dune reclamation. Similar Rock Hakea *H. gibbosa* and Sweet Hakea *H. drupacea* are also invaders of mountain fynbos in the south-western Cape.
Origin: native to south-eastern Australia

Estate of Piet van Wyk

Duncan Butchart

SALIGNA GUM ('BLUE GUM')   *Eucalyptus grandis*

Habitat: invades watercourses, forest edge and grassland   **Height:** up to 55 m   **Status:** locally common to abundant

Large to massive tree with straight, shaft-like trunk and spreading crown. Rough bark peels off in long strips to reveal smooth, pale grey or white underbark. Simple leaves are dark green above, leathery, lance-shaped. Cream flowers with protruding stamens attractive to honey bees (Apr–Aug). Fruit is a small, pear-shaped capsule. Grown in commercial plantations for timber.
Origin: native to eastern Australia

Braam van Wyk

SPIDER GUM   *Eucalyptus lehmannii*

Habitat: invades coastal fynbos and dunes of eastern and south-western Cape   **Height:** up to 10 m   **Status:** locally common to abundant

Dense, evergreen, multi-stemmed tree or bush, with branches often trailing close to the ground. Simple leaves are pale green, oval, thick and leathery. Greenish-yellow flowers with protruding stamens attractive to honey bees (Jun–Jan). Red buds resemble plastic spiders. Fruit is a cluster of spiky woody capsules. Cultivated for sand binding, timber and honey source. Closely related Sugar Gum *E. cladocalyx*, Tuart Gum *E. gomphocephala*, Red River Gum *E. camaldulensis* and Karri *E. diversicolor* are also invasive in South Africa.
Origin: native to south-western Australia

Duncan Butchart

AUSTRALIAN SILKY OAK   *Grevillea robusta*

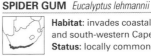

Habitat: invades streamsides and forest margins   **Height:** up to 30 m   **Status:** locally common

Slender, evergreen tree with straight trunk; often has bare branches and an untidy appearance. Leaves are compound, fern-like; grey-green above, silvery below. Most striking in early summer when the sprays of golden yellow flowers are produced (Sep–Nov). Fruit is a hard, woody capsule. Fast growing and cultivated in gardens and parks.
Origin: native to eastern Australia

Duncan Butchart

WEEPING WILLOW   *Salix babylonica*

Habitat: invades watercourses on Highveld plateau   **Height:** up to 18 m   **Status:** locally common

Large, deciduous tree with short trunk and broad crown. Outer branches are pendulous with drooping foliage. Simple leaves are narrow with finely serrated margin. Flowers are borne in catkins on separate male and female trees; male trees are unknown in South Africa, females reproduce from cuttings or fallen branches washed down streams. Soft wood is favoured by hole-nesting birds.
Origin: native to China; naturalized in England and western Europe

GREY POPLAR *Populus x canescens*

Habitat: invades riverbanks and marshes
Height: up to 20 m **Status:** locally abundant

Slender, deciduous tree with upright growth form; typically in
dense groves. Bark is white or grey with horizontal bands. Simple
leaves are round with entire margins on older trees; triangular and
toothed on saplings. Pale underside of the leaves is conspicuous in
windy conditions. Being a hybrid, it is sterile but coppices when
cut; colonies form from root suckers. Related White Poplar *P. alba*,
Cottonwood *P. deltoides* and Lombardy Poplar *P. nigra* are also
invasive in South Africa.
Origin: a hybrid of two or more Eurasian *Populus* species

Duncan Butchart

WHITE MULBERRY *Morus alba*

Habitat: invades streamsides and forest margins
Height: up to 15 m **Status:** locally abundant

Large, deciduous, bushy tree with pendulous outer branches. Leaves
are simple, oval, glossy, ending in sharp tip; strongly veined, shiny
bright green above, paler below. Small, greenish flowers appear in
spikes (Sep-Oct). Cylindrical fruits are white, red or purple; appear
in early summer; relished by birds, which disperse seeds.
Origin: native to China and Japan, where it sustained the
silk industry

Duncan Butchart

ENGLISH OAK *Quercus robur*

Habitat: invades forest margins, roadsides and
riverbanks in grassland and fynbos
Height: up to 30 m **Status:** locally common

Large to massive, deciduous tree with broad, rounded crown.
Bark is dark brown and rough. Simple leaves are oval, apple-green
with scalloped lobes. Small, yellowish flowers appear in catkins.
Fruit is a distinctive acorn, held in a scaly cup. Widely planted by
early colonists, some ancient specimens (over 200 years) are now
giant landmarks in towns. Other alien oaks include the Pin Oak
Q. palustris and Turkey Oak *Q. cerris*.
Origin: native to England and rest of Europe, western Asia

Duncan Butchart

BLACK WATTLE *Acacia mearnsii*

Habitat: invades grassland, roadsides, watercourses
and forest fringe **Height:** up to 15 m
Status: locally abundant

Medium-sized, thornless tree with drooping, fern-like foliage.
Bark is smooth, slightly hairy on young stems. Compound leaves
are bipinnate with tiny leaflets; dark green. Globular flowers
are pale yellow, sweet scented; appear in massed clusters
(Aug-Nov). Seedpod is flattened, with constrictions between seed
compartments. Cultivated for tanbark, shelter and firewood.
Origin: native to south-eastern Australia, including Tasmania

Duncan Butchart

Braam van Wyk

PEARL ACACIA *Acacia podalyriifolia*

Habitat: invades roadsides, urban areas, watercourses
Height: up to 8 m **Status:** locally abundant

Medium-sized, thornless tree with silvery-grey foliage. Bark is smooth, pale grey. Simple leaves are oval or elliptic; velvety. All new growth is covered in powdery hairs. Globular flowers are golden yellow; appear in long, showy sprays (Jun–Aug). Seedpod has wavy margin. Cultivated as an ornamental. Similar Bailey's Wattle *A. baileyana* has compound leaves.
Origin: native to east and south-eastern Australia

Duncan Butchart

RED-EYE WATTLE *Acacia cyclops*

Habitat: invades fynbos, dunes, watercourses, roadsides **Height:** up to 4 m **Status:** locally abundant

Medium-sized, evergreen, thornless shrub or small tree; often low and wind-shaped at coast. Bark is smooth, pale grey. Simple leaves are elliptic, bright green. Globular flowers are yellow, sparse in leaf axils (all year). Seedpod is flat, twisted; splits to reveal black seeds surrounded by scarlet aril; relished by birds. Cultivated for dune reclamation and firewood.
Origin: native to south-western Australia

Braam van Wyk

PORT JACKSON WATTLE *Acacia saligna*

Habitat: invades fynbos, coastal dunes, roadsides, watercourses, woodland **Height:** up to 7 m
Status: locally abundant

Medium-sized, evergreen, thornless shrub or small tree with willowy shape. Bark is smooth, pale grey. Stems are often deformed with large brown galls or swellings. Simple leaves are elliptic, bright green. Globular flowers are bright yellow, profuse in leaf axils (Aug–Nov). Seedpod is slightly constricted with hardened, pale margin. Cultivated for dune reclamation and tanbark.
Origin: native to south-western Australia

MAURITIUS THORN *Caesalpinia decapetala*

Habitat: invades riversides, forest margins and gaps, roadsides **Height:** 2–4 m (but climbs up into canopy of tall trees) **Status:** locally abundant

Dense, evergreen, *Acacia*-like shrub or scrambler with feathery foliage. Forms tangled thickets or scales tall trees. Branches covered with short thorns that may be hooked or straight. Compound leaves are darker above. Showy, pale yellow flowers appear in cone-shaped spikes (May–Nov). Fruit is a woody pod, sharply beaked at the tip. Relative of the ornamental Leopard Tree *C. ferrea*.
Origin: native to south-east Asia (not Mauritius)

Duncan Butchart

HONEY MESQUITE *Prosopis glandulosa*

Habitat: invades riverbeds and watercourses
Height: up to 4 m **Status:** locally abundant

Small, *Acacia*-like tree with feathery foliage. Bark is smooth, dark brown, becoming rough with age. Compound leaves have widely spaced leaflets. Small, yellow flowers appear in dense, elongated spikes (Jun–Nov). Straight spines appear in pairs at leaf axils. Slender seedpod is constricted between seeds. Hybridizes with related *P. velutina* and *P. chilensis*, which also invade in the dry west.
Origin: native to Arizona, Texas, Mexico

Braam van Wyk

JACARANDA *Jacaranda mimosifolia*

Habitat: invades savanna, watercourses, rocky hillsides, wooded gulleys **Height:** up to 25 m
Status: locally abundant

Large, deciduous tree with spreading crown and feathery foliage; most striking when in bloom. Bark is fissured on older specimens; dark brown or ochre. Compound leaves finely divided into tiny leaflets. Dense clusters of mauve or lilac trumpet-shaped flowers appear on bare stems before new leaves (Sep–Nov). Fruit is a flat, spherical pod, splitting open to release seeds after about a year.
Origin: native to Argentina, Bolivia and Brazil

Duncan Butchart

RED SESBANIA *Sesbania punicea*

Habitat: invades riverbanks, wetlands and roadsides
Height: up to 4 m **Status:** locally abundant

Small, deciduous shrub or tree with slender, pendulous branches. Compound leaves are dark green, drooping. Showy sprays of pea-shaped flowers are brilliant orange or red; pollinated by bees and sunbirds (Sep–Mar). Distinctive, oblong pods have 4 wings; dispersed by water down streams. Originally cultivated as an ornamental garden plant.
Origin: native to southern Brazil, Uruguay and north-eastern Argentina

Braam van Wyk

YELLOW BELLS *Tecoma stans*

Habitat: invades savanna, watercourses and roadsides
Height: 2–4 m **Status:** locally abundant

Evergreen shrub or small tree with slender outer branches. Compound leaves bright green above, paler below; leaflet margins are sharply toothed. Showy, bright yellow, trumpet-shaped flowers appear in terminal sprays (Oct–May). Elongated seedpods contain many papery-winged seeds. Similar Golden Trumpet Tree *Tabebuia chrysotricha* flowers when leafless and has long, hairy seedpods. Yellow Oleander *Thevetia peruviana* has simple, lance-shaped leaves.
Origin: native to southern USA and Mexico

Duncan Butchart

Duncan Butchart

SERINGA *Melia azedarach*

Habitat: invades riverbanks, watercourses, savanna, disturbed soils, grassland **Height:** up to 20 m
Status: locally abundant

Small to large, deciduous tree with spreading branches and rounded crown. Bark is reddish-brown and smooth. Compound leaves are fern-like with sizeable oval leaflets strongly serrated; glossy green above turning yellow in autumn. Pale lilac flowers in dense terminal heads; sweetly fragrant (Sep–Oct). Pea-sized berries brown when ripe; relished by turacos and other birds.
Origin: native to Southeast Asia to Australia (South African form is an Indian cultivar)

TRIFFID WEED *Chromolaena odorata*

Habitat: invades savanna, watercourses, roadsides and forest margins **Height:** up to 4 m
Status: locally abundant

Dense, thicket-forming shrub with opposite, spreading branches. Simple leaves are pale green, oval to triangular in shape; smell of turpentine or paraffin when crushed. May be evergreen, but foliage turns pale during dry winter months. Small, white or pale blue, cylindrical flowers appear in terminal heads (Jun–Dec). Fine, wind-blown seeds appear in bristly clusters.
Origin: native to Central America to Argentina

Geoff Nichols

LANTANA *Lantana camara*

Habitat: invades savanna, roadsides, forest margins
Height: up to 2–3 m **Status:** locally abundant

Dense shrub or untidy scrambler that forms thickets. Stems are four-angled and covered with curved prickles. Simple leaves are heart-shaped, darker above with margin finely toothed; strong but pleasant verbena scent when crushed. Small, multi-coloured flowers appear in dense, spherical heads; pink, purple, orange, red, yellow or white (Sep–Apr). Raspberry-like berries relished by birds.
Origin: native to Central and South America

Duncan Butchart

GUAVA *Psidium guajava*

Habitat: invades savanna, watercourses, forest margins and roadsides **Height:** 2–5 m
Status: locally abundant

Small, evergreen tree or shrub with single stem and spreading branches. Pale bark is silky smooth, flaking off in patches to create an attractive pattern. Simple leaves broadly oval; thick, stiff and hairy below with conspicuous veins. Small, white flowers appear singly or in clusters (Oct–Dec). Large fruit is yellow when ripe; sweet, pink flesh contains many seeds, has pungent scent.
Origin: native to southern Mexico to Peru

Duncan Butchart

BUGWEED *Solanum mauritianum*

Habitat: invades forest margins, watercourses, roadsides **Height:** 2–4 m **Status:** locally abundant

Slender, open-branched shrub or small tree with velvety foliage and stems. Simple leaves, grey-green above, whitish below; furry felt-like texture with unpleasant odour when bruised or crushed. Small, purple flowers appear in terminal clusters (all year). Globular berries yellow when ripe; relished by Olive Pigeon, mousebirds and bulbuls, which spread seeds.
Origin: native to southern Brazil, Uruguay and Argentina

Duncan Butchart

CASTOR OIL PLANT *Ricinus communis*

Habitat: invades riverbanks, wetland fringes and roadsides **Height:** up to 4 m **Status:** common but heavily utilized for palm wine in northern KwaZulu-Natal

Slender shrub or small tree with distinctive foliage and clear sap (castor oil) in stems and leaves. Branches smooth with pale grey, powdery bloom. Simple leaves are large, star-shaped; shiny dark green above, paler below. Small, reddish flowers appear in terminal spikes (all year). Fruit is a three-lobed capsule covered with soft spines.
Origin: native to Equatorial Africa

Duncan Butchart

SWEET PRICKLY-PEAR *Opuntia ficus-indica*

Habitat: invades most habitats, especially semi-arid Karoo and savanna **Height:** up to 3 m **Status:** locally abundant

Succulent cactus with broad, flattened branches (cladodes) pinched together at joints. Leaves are tiny or non-existent; grey-green cladodes perform photosynthesis. May be heavily spined or virtually spineless. Yellow-orange flowers appear on cone-shaped cups (Oct–Dec) that ripen to form fleshy 'prickly pears'. Nine other *Opuntia* cacti are invasive weeds in South Africa.
Origin: native to Mexico

Duncan Butchart

QUEEN OF THE NIGHT *Cereus jamacaru*

Habitat: invades rocky ridges in semi-arid Karoo and savanna **Height:** 3–12 m **Status:** locally abundant

Succulent cactus with thick branches (cladodes) emerging from short trunk. Leaves are absent; blue-green cladodes perform photosynthesis. Sharp spines are in groups of 5–10 on branch ribs. Showy, white flowers open at night (Nov–Jan); pollinated by moths or bats. Fruit is a pink berry. Resembles native Naboom *Euphorbia ingens*, but that species exudes milky latex and does not bear showy flowers.
Origin: native to north-eastern Brazil

Duncan Butchart

BIBLIOGRAPHY AND FURTHER READING

The following list includes books that have been used in compiling this guide (including some out-of-print titles) as well as useful and interesting publications on the subjects.

MAMMALS

Estes, R. 1991. *Behaviour Guide to African Mammals*. University of California Press, California.

Friedman, Y. 2004. *Red Data Book of the Mammals of South Africa: a conservation assessment*. Endangered Wildlife Trust, Johannesburg.

Kingdon, J. 1997. *Kingdon Field Guide to African Mammals*. Academic Press, London.

Skinner, J. & Chimimba, C.T. 2005. *The Mammals of the Southern Africa Subregion*. 3rd edition. Cambridge University Press, Cape Town.

Stuart, C. & Stuart T. 2000. *Field Guide to the Tracks and Signs of Southern and East African Wildlife*. 3rd edition. Struik Publishers, Cape Town.

Stuart, C. & Stuart, T. 2006. *Field Guide to the Larger Mammals of Africa*. 3rd edition. Struik Publishers, Cape Town.

Stuart, C. & Stuart, T. 2007. *Field Guide to Mammals of Southern Africa*. Struik Publishers, Cape Town.

Walker, C. 1996. *Signs of the Wild*. 5th edition. Struik Publishers, Cape Town.

BIRDS

Barnes, K.N. 2000. *The Eskom Red Data Book of Birds of South Africa, Lesotho and Swaziland*. BirdLife South Africa, Randburg.

Cohen, C., Spottiswoode, C. & Rossouw, J. 2006. *Southern African Birdfinder*. Struik Publishers, Cape Town.

Hockey, P.A.R., Dean, W.R.J. & Ryan, P.G. (eds). 2005. *Roberts Birds of Southern Africa*. 7th edition. John Voelcker Bird Book Fund, Cape Town.

Loon, R. & Loon, H. 2005. *Birds: the Inside Story*. Struik Publishers, Cape Town.

Mundy, P.J., Butchart, D., Piper, S.E. & Ledger, J.A. 1992. *The Vultures of Africa*. Acorn Books, Johannesburg.

Newman, D. 2008. *Bird Calls for Beginners*. Struik Publishers, Cape Town.

Newman, K. (ed.). 1979. *Birdlife in Southern Africa*. Macmillan, Johannesburg.

Newman, K. 2002. *Newman's Birds of Southern Africa*. 8th edition. Struik Publishers, Cape Town.

Peacock, F. 2006. *Pipits of Southern Africa: The complete guide to Africa's ultimate LBJ's*. Published by the author, Pretoria.

Ryan. P. 2006. *Birdwatching in Southern Africa* . Struik Publishers, Cape Town.

Sinclair, I. & Hockey, P. 2005. *Larger Illustrated Guide to Birds of Southern Africa*. 2nd edition. Struik Publishers, Cape Town.

Steyn, P. 1982. *Birds of Prey of Southern Africa*. David Philip, Cape Town.

Steyn, P. 1996. *Nesting Birds: the breeding habits of southern African birds*. Fernwood Press, Cape Town.

Tarboton, W. 2001. *A Guide to the Nests & Eggs of Southern African Birds*. Struik Publishers, Cape Town.

REPTILES AND FROGS

Alexander, G. & Marais, J. 2007. *A Guide to the Reptiles of Southern Africa*. Struik Publishers, Cape Town.

Boycott, R. & Bourquin, O. 2000. *The Southern African Tortoise Book*. O. Borquin, Hilton.

Branch, B. 1998. *Field Guide to the Snakes and other Reptiles of Southern Africa*. 3rd edition. Struik Publishers, Cape Town.

Carruthers, V. 2001. *Frogs and Frogging in Southern Africa*. Struik Publishers, Cape Town

Marais, J. 2006. *A Complete Guide to the Snakes of Southern Africa*. Struik Publishers, Cape Town.

Carruthers, V. & Du Preez, L. 2009. *Complete Guide to Frogs of Southern Africa*. Random House Struik, Cape Town.

Tolley, K. & Burger, M. 2007. *Chameleons of Southern Africa*. Struik Publishers, Cape Town.

TREES AND SHRUBS

Burrows, J. & Burrows, S. 2003. *Figs of Southern & South-Central Africa*. Umdaus, Pretoria.

Coates Palgrave, M. 2002. *Trees of Southern Africa*. 3rd edition. Struik Publishers, Cape Town.

Esterhuyse, N., von Breitenbach, J. & Sohnge, H. 2001. *Remarkable Trees of South Africa*. Briza, Pretoria.

Henderson, L. 2001. *Alien Weeds and Invasive Plants*. Agricultural Research Council, Pretoria.

Manning, J. 2007. *Field Guide to Fynbos*. Struik Publishers, Cape Town.

Pooley, E. 1993. *Complete Field Guide to Trees of Natal, Zululand & Transkei*. Natal Flora Publications Trust, Durban.

Schmidt, E., Lotter, M. & McCleland, W. 2002. *Trees and Shrubs of Mpumalanga and Kruger National Park*. Jacana, Johannesburg.

Van Wyk, B. & van Wyk, P. 1997. *Field Guide to Trees of Southern Africa*. Struik Publishers, Cape Town.

Van Wyk, B. & van Wyk, P. 2005. *How to Identify Trees in Southern Africa*. Struik Publishers, Cape Town.

Van Wyk, B-E. & Smith, G. 1996. *Guide to the Aloes of South Africa*. Briza, Pretoria.

GLOSSARY

Alluvial soil – soil deposited by a river.

Alternate (of leaves) – arranged alternately along the stem, one above the other.

Aril – a brightly coloured, fleshy covering on part of a seed.

Axil – the angle between a leaf and the stem which supports it.

Biodiversity – the totality of species and ecosystems within a region.

Biome – a major geographical area of ecologically similar communities of plants, animals and soil organisms.

Bipinnately compound (of leaves) – a compound leaf that is twice-divided.

Browser – a herbivorous animal that feeds on leaves and shoots of trees, shrubs and forbs.

Buttressed (of tree trunks) – wide and spreading at its base.

Carapace – the upper half of a turtle or tortoise shell.

Catkin – flower spike; a linear inflorescence.

Cere – the fleshy upper part of a bird's bill.

Colonial – living in close proximity while roosting or nesting.

Compound (of leaves) – divided into leaflets.

Conifer – evergreen tree or shrub with compressed, waxy leaves that bears cones rather than flowers or fruits.

Crepuscular – active at dusk and dawn.

Critically endangered – a specific level of threat to a species, defined by the IUCN as 'facing an extremely high risk of extinction in the wild'.

Cytotoxic (of venom) – affecting the body tissue.

Digitate (of leaves) – compound, with 3 to 9 leaflets radiating from a central point.

Diurnal – active during daylight hours.

Drupe – fleshy fruit with a single hard seed or 'stone'.

Elliptic (of leaves) – narrow, tapering at both ends.

Endangered – a specific level of threat to a species, defined by the IUCN as 'facing a very high risk of extinction in the wild'.

Endemic – a species whose breeding and non-breeding ranges are confined to a particular region (most often applied to a country's boundaries).

Eye-stripe – a line through a bird's eye.

Fissured (of bark) – deeply grooved.

Flight feathers – longest feathers on a bird's wings.

Inflorescence – a flowering shoot bearing more than one flower.

Mantle – the area between the back and neck (on a bird).

Margin – the edge of a leaf.

Midrib – the central vein of a leaf.

Moustachial stripe – a line from the base of a bird's bill to the side of the throat.

Near-endemic – a species whose range is largely restricted to a particular region.

Neurotoxic (of venom) – affecting the nervous system.

Opposite (of leaves) – arranged opposite one another on a stem or rachis.

Palearctic – region of the northern hemisphere from the Arctic circle to Europe, Africa north of the Sahara, and Asia north of the Himalayas.

Pelagic – ocean dwelling.

Petiole – stalk of a leaf.

Pinnate (of leaves) – once-divided with leaflets arranged in two ranks on opposite sides of the rachis.

Primary feathers – longest/outer wing feathers.

Quartzite – very hard sedimentary rock.

Rachis – a central axis or stalk to which leaflets are attached on a compound leaf.

Receptacle – enlarged end of a stalk containing reproductive parts.

Recurved – bent or curved backwards.

Resident – a species not prone to migration; present all year.

Scalloped (of leaf margin) – having blunt, rounded teeth'.

Secondary feathers – the smaller wing feathers, close to the body of the bird.

Sedimentary rocks – rock composed of sediments deposited by water or wind.

Sexual dimorphism – distinct differences between males and females.

Simple (of leaves) – undivided.

Spike – an inflorescence with a single, unbranched axis.

Stamen – male part of a flower, topped by the pollen-bearing anther.

Stipule – a leaf-like appendage to the petiole of a leaf.

Terminal leaf – a leaflet at the end point of a compound leaf.

Termitarium – the earthen nest of a termite colony.

Trifoliate (of leaves) – divided into three leaflets emerging from a central point.

Venation – the veins of a leaf.

Vent – the group of feathers between the belly and tail of a bird.

Vulnerable – a specific level of threat to a species, defined by the IUCN as 'facing a high risk of extinction in the wild'.

Wattle – fleshy growth around a bird's eyes or at the base of its bill.

Whorl – three or more leaves emerging at the same level on a stem.

INDEX